Math and Science Workout for the

ACT®

3rd Edition

The Staff of The Princeton Review

PrincetonReview.com

Penguin
Random
House

The Princeton Review
24 Prime Parkway, Suite 201
Natick, MA 01760
Email: editorialsupport@review.com

Published in the United States by Penguin Random
House LLC, New York, and in Canada by Random House
of Canada, a division of Penguin Random House Ltd.,
Toronto.

ISBN: 978-1-101-88167-5
ISSN: 2157-6017

Editor: Colleen Day
Production Editor: Liz Rutzel
Production Artist: Deborah A. Silvestrini

Printed in the United States of America on partially
recycled paper.

10 9 8 7 6 5 4 3 2 1

3rd Edition

Editorial
Rob Franek, Senior VP, Publisher
Casey Cornelius, VP Content Development
Mary Beth Garrick, Director of Production
Selena Coppock, Managing Editor
Meave Shelton, Senior Editor
Colleen Day, Editor
Sarah Litt, Editor
Aaron Riccio, Editor
Orion McBean, Editorial Assistant

Random House Publishing Team
Tom Russell, Publisher
Alison Stoltzfus, Publishing Manager
Melinda Ackell, Associate Managing Editor
Ellen Reed, Production Manager
Kristin Lindner, Production Supervisor
Andrea Lau, Designer

Acknowledgments

A special thanks to Jonathan Chiu, the National Content Director of High School Programs at The Princeton Review.

The Princeton Review would also like to thank Melissa Hendrix for her thorough and extensive overhaul of this title, and Kathryn Menefee, Jonathan Edwards, Erik Kolb, Eliz Markowitz, and Steve Voigt for their work in updating this edition.

Special thanks to Adam Robinson, who conceived of and perfected the Joe Bloggs approach to standardized tests, and many of the other successful techniques used by The Princeton Review.

Contents

Register Your

1 Go to **PrincetonReview.com/cracking**

2 You'll see a welcome page where you can register your book using the following ISBN: 9781101881675.

3 After placing this free order, you'll either be asked to log in or to answer a few simple questions in order to set up a new Princeton Review account.

4 Finally, click on the "Student Tools" tab located at the top of the screen. It may take an hour or two for your registration to go through, but after that, you're good to go.

If you are experiencing book problems (potential content errors), please contact EditorialSupport@review.com with the full title of the book, its ISBN number (located above), and the page number of the error. Experiencing technical issues? Please e-mail TPRStudentTech@review.com with the following information:

- your full name
- e-mail address used to register the book
- full book title and ISBN
- your computer OS (Mac or PC) and Internet browser (Firefox, Safari, Chrome, etc.)
- description of technical issue

Book Online!

Once you've registered, you can...

- Find any late-breaking information released about the ACT

- Get valuable advice about the college application process, including tips for writing a great essay and where to apply for financial aid

- Sort colleges by whatever you're looking for (such as Best Theater, Best Dorm, or Top Notch Professors), learn more about your top choices, and see how they all rank according to *The Best 380 Colleges*

- Check to see if there have been any corrections or updates to this edition

Look For These Icons Throughout The Book

 Online Articles

 Applied Strategies

 Proven Techniques

 More Great Books

The Princeton Review®
Your Goals. Our Expertise.™

Part I
Orientation

Chapter 1
All About the ACT

WELCOME

The ACT is an important part of college admissions. While many schools do not require applicants to submit either ACT or SAT scores, most require one of them. For a long time, different schools would accept only one or the other. If you wanted to apply to schools in the Midwest, you took the ACT; if you wanted to apply to schools on the East or West Coast, you took the SAT.

The good news is that these rules are obsolete. All schools that require a standardized test will take either the ACT or SAT.

This is good news indeed for test takers. While there are many similarities between the two tests, many students find they do better on one than the other. The expert advice of The Princeton Review is to take whichever test whose practice version you do better on. While you can certainly take both, you should focus your efforts on one for substantive score improvement. True improvement takes hard work, and it can be tough to become an expert in both. And because schools will take either one, you won't win any brownie points for punishing yourself.

Because you bought this book, we assume you've already made the decision to boost your ACT score. This book provides a strategic and efficient way to improve your scores, specifically on the Math and Science sections. For a more thorough review of content and exhaustive practice, we recommend purchasing the latest editions of *Cracking the ACT* and *1,460 ACT Practice Questions*.

For more on admissions, see The Princeton Review's *The Best 380 Colleges* or visit our website, PrincetonReview.com.

FUN FACTS ABOUT THE ACT

The ACT is nothing like the math and science tests you take in school. All of the content review and strategies we teach in the following lessons are based on the specific structure and format of the ACT. Before you can beat a test, you have to know how it's built.

If you feel like you need help with the English and Reading sections, please see our companion book, *English and Reading Workout for the ACT*.

Structure

The ACT is made up of four multiple-choice tests and an optional Writing test.

The five tests are always given in the same order.

English	Math	Reading	Science	Writing
45 minutes	60 minutes	35 minutes	35 minutes	Current ACT: 30 minutes Future ACT: ?
75 questions	60 questions	40 questions	40 questions	1 Essay

Scoring

When students and schools talk about ACT scores, they mean the composite score, a range of 1–36. The composite is an average of the four multiple-choice tests, each scored on the same 1–36 scale. Neither the Writing test score nor the combined English plus Writing score affects the composite.

As of 2015 exam administrations, students will now receive subscores in addition to their traditional (1–36) ACT score. These indicators are designed to measure student performance and predict career readiness, as well as competency in STEM (Science, Technology, Engineering, Mathematics) and English language arts. ACT believes that these additional scores will give students better insight into their strengths and how those strengths can be harnessed for success in college and beyond. In addition to the 1–36 score for each of the tests and their composite score, students will now see score breakdowns in the following categories:

- STEM score
- Progress Toward Career Readiness indicator
- English Language Arts score
- Text Complexity Progress indicator

These categories are described in more detail beginning on page 7. In addition, ACT plans to add new reporting categories in 2016 that align with federal academic standards. For further information and updates about test changes, visit **PrincetonReview.com/ACTChanges**.

It's All About the Composite

Whether you look at your score online or wait to get it in the mail, the biggest number on the page is always the composite. While admissions offices will certainly see the individual scores of all five tests (and their subscores), schools will use the composite to evaluate your application, and that's why, in the end, it's the only one that matters.

The composite is an average: Let the full weight of that sink in. Do you need to bring up all four scores equally to raise your composite? Do you need to be a superstar in all four tests? Should you focus more on your weaknesses than your strengths? No, no, and absolutely not. The best way to improve your composite is to shore up your weaknesses but exploit your strengths as much as possible.

> To improve your ACT score, use your strengths to lift the composite score as high as possible.

You don't need to be a rock star on all four tests. Identify two, maybe three tests, and focus on raising those scores as much as you can to raise your composite. Work on your weakest scores to keep them from pulling you down. Think of it this way: If you had only one hour to devote to practice the week before the ACT, spend that hour on your best subjects.

Math and Science Scores

These two subjects make a good pair. Every student is different, but many students begin with Math as one of their higher scores and Science as one of the lower. There are good reasons for this. The Math test, perhaps deceptively so, resembles school tests more than the other three. Science feels the most different, and many students are intimidated by both the content and format.

When it comes to improving scores, many students find Math scores the easiest to bring up. A strategic review of the rules and formulas, coupled with rigorous practice, can add several points. Science, on the other hand, can be the most difficult. The Science test is designed to test your reasoning skills using passage-based information, not tap specific outside knowledge. There are no rules or content you can review. Who knows what specific topics will appear on the next ACT? On the goods-news front, however, The Princeton Review can teach you a smart, effective approach designed to maximize your performance every time, regardless of content. It can be tough to change your ways, but dedicated practice with a strategic method can prevent the Science score from pulling down that composite.

Time

How often do you take a final exam in school that gives you *at most* a minute per question? Probably never. The ACT isn't a school test, and you can't approach it as if it is. While speed and accuracy depend on individual skills and grasp of content, almost all students struggle to finish the Math and Science tests on time. The more you treat these tests the same way you would a school final, the less likely you are to finish, much less finish with the greatest accuracy. The Princeton Review's strategies are all based on this time crunch: There's a difference between knowing *how* to do a question under the best of circumstance and getting it *right* with a ticking clock and glowering proctor in the room.

IS THE ACT CHANGING?

Starting in late 2015, the ACT will be changing. Many of the changes to the test won't impact how students test or the types of questions they'll need to answer, but rather how their scores are reported and the kind of information they'll be able to gather from their results. (See the Scoring section on page 5.)

One section that will be affected by the changes is the Writing test. As of the publication of this book, we know that the ACT Writing test will be changing at some point during "fall 2015" (that's a pretty big window). Here is what we do know about this revised Writing test.

Watch for Updates!
Visit **PrincetonReview. com/ACTchanges** for late-breaking news and updates.

Writing Test

The ACT Writing test will have one essay prompt, and you'll have time to craft a response (As of this writing, ACT, Inc. has not yet revealed how much time you will have). The prompt will define an issue and present three points of view on the issue; you will be asked to respond to a question by analyzing the three positions, coming up with your own view on the issue, and explaining how your position relates to the other three. While the topics in the past have related directly to high school life, the present topics cover a diverse range of issues. One prompt asked students to assess the growing presence of technology in our lives. Does our reliance on machines take away part of our humanity? Are automatons a good solution for tackling mindless, repetitive jobs? Do intelligent machines force us to broaden what we consider human? What is your position on the rising sub-class of increasingly intelligent robots? The strange thing about the Writing test is that it isn't a mandatory part of the ACT. When you register for the test, you'll have to decide whether you need to take this part of the exam. We'll talk more about that later.

Scoring Changes

As we mentioned in the Scoring section, starting in fall 2015 you'll also be receiving readiness scores and indicators. These include:

- **STEM score.** This score will show you how well you did on the Math and Science portions of the test.
- **Progress Toward Career Readiness indicator.** The ACT would have you believe this indicator measures how prepared you are for a career, but really it just measures how prepared you are to take yet another test: the ACT National Career Readiness Certificate™.
- **English Language Arts score.** If you take the Writing test, this score will give you a combined score for the English, Reading, and Writing section.
- **Text Complexity Progress indicator**—This score will tell you how well you fared on those hard passages throughout the test.

Crack It Open

For more comprehensive review and practice for the ACT, pick up a copy of *Cracking the ACT Premium,* which includes sample questions and guidance for all sections of the exam.

So as we said before, these changes to the test won't impact how students test or the types of questions they'll need to answer, but rather how their scores are reported and the kind of information they'll be able to gather from their results.

If you do take the Writing test, you will receive an additional score: your Writing subscore, which will range from 2–12. This score is not factored into the composite, so taking the Writing test will not have a direct impact on your composite score. Be sure to check ACT's website to determine whether your target schools want you to take the ACT Writing test.

Chapter 2
Strategies

ACT TEST-TAKING STRATEGIES

You will raise your ACT score by working smarter, not harder, and a smart test taker is a strategic test taker. You will target specific content to review, you will apply an effective and efficient approach, and you will employ the common sense that frequently deserts many of us when we pick up a number 2 pencil.

Each test on the ACT demands a different approach, and even the most universal strategies vary in their applications. In the chapters that follow, we'll discuss these terms in greater detail customized to Math and Science.

Personal Order of Difficulty (POOD)

If time is going to run out, would you rather it run out on the most difficult questions or on the easiest questions? Of course you want it to run out on the points you are less likely to get right. The trick is to find all of the easiest questions and get them done first.

The Best Way to Bubble In

Work one page at a time, circling your answers right on the booklet. Transfer a page's worth of answers to the answer sheet. It's better to stay focused on working questions rather than disrupt your concentration to find where you left off on the answer sheet. You'll be more accurate at both tasks. Do not wait to the end, however, to transfer all the answers of that test on your answer sheet. Go one page at a time.

Now

Does a question look okay? Do you know how to do it? Do it *Now*.

Later

Does a question make you go, "hmm"? If you can't find a way to get your pencil moving right away, consider leaving it and coming back *Later*. Circle the question number for easy reference to return.

Never

Test taker, know thyself. Know the topics that are most difficult for you, and learn the signs that flash danger. Don't waste time on questions you should *Never* do. Instead, use more time to answer the Now and Later questions accurately.

Letter of the Day (LOTD) Just because you don't *work* a question doesn't mean you don't *answer* it. There is no penalty for wrong answers on the ACT, so you should never leave any blanks on your answer sheet. When you guess on Never questions, pick your favorite two-letter combo of answers and stick with it. For example, always choose A/F or C/H. If you're consistent, you're statistically more likely to pick up more points.

Process of Elimination (POE)

In a perfect world, you'll know how to work all of your Now and Later questions, quickly and accurately, circling the correct answer among the choices. The ACT is *not* a perfect world. But even with a ticking clock and a number 2 pencil in your sweaty hand, wrong answers can be obvious. POE can be a great Plan B on Math when you're stuck, or it may be the best way to find the correct answer on Science. But even when you can't narrow the answers to only one, using POE to get rid of at least one or two wrong answers will substantially increase your odds of getting a question right.

Pacing

The ACT may be designed for you to run out of time, but you can't rush through it as quickly as possible. All you'll do is make careless errors on easy questions you should get right and spend way too much time on difficult ones you're unlikely to get right.

To hit your target score, you have to know how many raw points you need. Use the entire time allotted where it will do the most good: Go slowly enough to avoid careless errors on Now questions, but go quickly enough to get to as many Later questions as you need to hit your goal.

On each test of the ACT, the number of correct answers converts to a scaled score of 1–36. ACT works hard to adjust the scale of each test at each administration as necessary to make all scaled scores comparable, smoothing out any differences in level of difficulty across test dates. Thus, there is no truth to any one test date being "easier" than the others, but you can expect to see slight variations in the scale from test to test.

This is the scale from the free test ACT makes available on its website, **ACT.org**. We're going to use it to explain how to pick a target score and pace yourself.

Math Pacing

Scale Score	Raw Score	Scale Score	Raw Score	Scale Score	Raw Score
36	60	27	45–47	18	24–25
35	59	26	42–44	17	21–23
34	58	25	40–41	16	17–20
33	56–57	24	37–39	15	14–16
32	55	23	35–36	14	11–13
31	54	22	33–34	13	9–10
30	52–53	21	31–32	12	7–8
29	50–51	20	29–30	11	6
28	48–49	19	26–28	10	5

Our advice is to add 5 questions to your targeted raw score. You have a cushion to get a few wrong—nobody's perfect—and you're likely to pick up at least a few points from your LOTDs. Track your progress on practice tests to pinpoint your target score.

Let's say your goal on Math is a 24. Find 24 under the scaled score column, and you'll see that you need 37–39 raw points. Take all 60 minutes and work 45 questions, using your Letter of the Day on 15 Never questions. With 60 minutes to work on just 45 questions, you'll raise your accuracy on the Now and Later questions. You may get a few wrong, but you're also likely to pick up a few points in your LOTDs, and you should hit your target score of 24. Spend more time to do fewer questions, and you'll raise your accuracy.

Here's another way to think about pacing. Let's say your goal is to move from a 24 to a 27. How many more raw points do you need? As few as six. Do you think you could find six careless errors on your last practice test that you *should* have gotten right?

Science Pacing

Scale Score	Raw Score	Scale Score	Raw Score	Scale Score	Raw Score
36	40	27	32	18	16–17
35	39	26	30–31	17	15
34	--	25	28–29	16	14
33	38	24	26–27	15	13
32	37	23	25	14	12
31	--	22	23–24	13	11
30	36	21	21–22	12	10
29	35	20	19–20	11	9
28	33–34	19	18	10	7–8

For Science, pacing is less scientific, no pun intended, than it is for Math. In the lesson that follows, we'll teach you how to pick the best passages to do first. But even the easiest passages will have some tough questions.

Our advice is to be aggressive. Spend the time needed on the easiest passages first, but keep moving to get to your targeted raw score. Use the chart on the next page to figure out approximately how many passages to work.

Target Score	# of Passages to Attempt
< 20	5 passages
20–23	5–6 passages
24–27	6–7 passages
> 27	7 passages

Be Ruthless

The worst mistake a test taker can make is to throw good time after bad. You read a question and don't understand it, so you read it again. And again. If you stare at it really hard, you know you're going to just *see* it. And you can't move on, because really, after spending all that time, it would be a waste not to keep at it, right? Actually, that way of thinking couldn't be more wrong.

You can't let one tough question drag you down. Instead, the best way to improve your ACT score is to follow our advice.

1. Use the techniques and strategies in the lessons to work efficiently and accurately through all your Now and Later questions.
2. Know your Never questions, and use your LOTD.
3. Know when to move on. Use POE, and guess from what's left.

Now move on to the lessons, and learn the best way to approach the content.

Part II
Science

Chapter 3
All About the Science Test

THE ACT SCIENCE TEST

For many students, the Science test is the most difficult. Whether the subject matter alone intimidates or the time crunch stresses, the Science test can be difficult to finish. In this chapter, you'll learn how to order the passages and apply a basic approach that makes the most of the time you have.

FUN FACTS ABOUT THE SCIENCE TEST

The Science test consists of 7 passages and 40 questions that you must answer in 35 minutes.

This is not a test of science content, but of science reasoning. ACT describes the necessary skills required for the natural sciences as "interpretation, analysis, evaluation, reasoning, and problem solving."

Trends and Relationships

We think all those skills are best understood as identifying trends and relationships. Whether you are asked to look up a value or synthesize information, it all comes down to the patterns and connections shown by variables, figures, experiments, and scientists. Look for trends *within* a figure, and look for relationships *between* figures.

Outside Knowledge

For the topics of the passages, ACT will pull from biology, chemistry, physics, and the Earth/space sciences, such as geology, astronomy, and meteorology. Most of the questions are answered by the passages and figures provided, but you should also expect two to three questions on outside knowledge.

The Passages

On each ACT, the order of the passages will vary, but the distribution of passage types is always the same.

Charts and Graphs

ACT calls these "Data Representations." We call them "Charts and Graphs" because that's what they're all about. They *always* come with figures. There are three Charts and Graphs passages, each with five questions.

Experiments

ACT calls these "Research Summaries." They look a lot like the Charts and Graphs passages because they *usually* come with figures. However, they come with more reading because they include the descriptions of the experiment set up. There are three Experiments passages, each with six questions.

Fighting Scientists

ACT calls these "Conflicting Viewpoints," but admit it: Our name is way more fun. There is only one Fighting Scientists passage, featuring seven questions, on each ACT. It is inherently different from the other six, even if it *sometimes* comes with figures. The fundamental task of the Fighting Scientists passage is to compare and contrast opposing views of an issue.

PERSONAL ORDER OF DIFFICULTY (POOD)

There are many factors about the structure of this test that make it difficult. It's last, which doesn't help at all. But even if it were first, many would find it the most challenging. Science phobes are intimidated by the subject matter. Science geeks are thwarted by the time crunch. Pick your poison; no one benefits from following ACT's order. On every ACT, you need to work the passages in an order that makes sense for you.

NOW PASSAGES

Every time you take the ACT, for practice and for real, pick the order of the passages that makes sense for you. The best passages to do Now are those with the most transparent relationships. When you pick your Now passages, choose exclusively among the Charts and Graphs and Experiments passages. By nature, the Fighting Scientists passage is different, and even superior readers find it takes longer to work than the best of the Now passages. So what makes a good Now passage? There are five signs to abide by.

1. Small Tables and Graphs

A good Now passage can have only tables, only graphs, or both. Tables should be no more than 3–4 rows or columns, and graphs should have no more than 3–4 curves.

2. Easy-to-Spot Consistent Trends

Look for graphs with all the curves heading in the same direction: all up, all down, or all flat. Look for tables with numbers in a consistent direction: up, down, or flat.

3. Numbers, not Words or Symbols

To show a consistent trend, the figure has to feature numbers, not words or symbols.

4. Short Answers

Look for as many questions as possible with short answers, specifically answers with values and short relationship words like "increase" or "decrease."

5. Your Science POOD

Don't forget to factor in your familiarity and comfort with the topic when spotting good Now passages. For example, if you've just studied DNA, a passage on DNA will strike you as easier, regardless of how the figures look.

Now Versus Easy

We are deliberately calling these Now passages rather than Easy passages. Even a passage with great figures will have one or two tough questions, but even the toughest questions are easier to crack when you get the central trends and relationships. On passages with incomprehensible figures, even the easiest questions will take you longer because you will keep asking yourself, "What is this saying again?" You'll always work good Now passages more quickly, and good time management is what the ACT is all about.

PACING

With just 35 minutes to do 7 passages and 40 questions, you have an average of five minutes for every passage. But should you spend 5 minutes on every passage? Of course not. If you make smart choices of good Now passages, you should be able to work them in less time, leaving yourself more time for the tougher passages. Think about the pacing chart we discussed in Chapter 1. Think about how many points you need to hit your goal.

Be Ruthless and Flexible

Every Now passage will have one or two tough questions, just as every Later passage will have at least one or two easy questions. Use Chapters 3 and 4 to practice, but even on the Now passages, know when to guess on a tough question and move onto the next passage. Don't let one tough question drag you down.

Need More Practice?
1,460 ACT Practice Questions provides 6 tests' worth of Science passages. That's 42 passages and 240 questions.

POE

The most direct Science questions will ask you to look up a value or a relationship. But the most complex will ask you to synthesize information or draw a conclusion. The more difficult the question, the less it will help to just stare at the figure waiting for divine guidance to help you magically *see* the answer. As is often the case on the ACT, spotting the wrong answers can be much easier than magically divining the right answers. In our 3-step Basic Approach, we'll discuss in greater detail how to use POE.

THE BASIC APPROACH

The most efficient way to boost your Science score is to pick your order and apply our 3-step Basic Approach to passages with figures. Follow our smart, effective strategy to earn as many points as you can.

Fighting Scientists
The Fighting Scientists passage is fundamentally different from the Charts and Graphs and Experiments passages and requires a different approach.

Step 1: Work the Figures

Take 10–30 seconds to review your figures. What are the variables? What are the units? In what direction do the variables move?

Graphs present trends visually. For tables, you need to make it visual. Mark the trends for each variable with an arrow. Here are three tables from a good Now passage with the trends marked.

Passage II

Table 1	
Angle between axis of first and second filters (degrees)	Intensity of emerging beam (W/m^2)
0	4.00
15	3.73
30	2.99
45	2.01
60	1.00
75	0.27
90	0.00

↑   ↓

Table 2	
Angle between axis of first and second filters (degrees)	Intensity of emerging beam (W/m^2)
0	8.00
15	7.46
30	6.01
45	3.99
60	2.00
75	0.54
90	0.00

↑   ↓

Table 3	
Angle between axis of first and second filters (degrees)	Intensity of emerging beam (W/m²)
0	6.01
15	5.60
30	4.49
45	2.99
60	1.50
75	0.41
90	0.00

↑ ↓

Step 2: Work the Questions

For each question, look up the value or relationship on the figures as directed. Use your POOD to leave for Later tougher questions. Read if and only when you can't answer a question from the figures.

Try an example.

12. According to Table 3, if the angle between the axes of polarization increases by 15°, the intensity of the resulting beam:

    F. halves.
    G. doubles.
    H. increases, but not by any constant factor.
    J. decreases, but not by any constant factor.

Here's How to Crack It

Because you've already marked the trends, you know that as the angle increases, the intensity decreases. Eliminate (G) and (H). Look closely at the trend, and choose (J).

Both the Charts and Graphs and Experiments passages will include actual text. Read the passage intros and experiment descriptions *only* when you can't answer a question from a figure.

Try another example.

———————————○———————————

10. How does the setup of Experiment 1 differ from that of Experiment 2 ?

    F. In Experiment 1, the original beam was polarized, but in Experiment 2, it was unpolarized.

    G. In Experiment 1, the original beam was unpolarized, but in Experiment 2, it was polarized.

    H. In Experiment 1, the scientists tested a wider range of angles than they did in Experiment 2.

    J. In Experiment 1, the original beam of light was more intense than the one in Experiment 2.

Here's How to Crack It

The variables are the same in Tables 1 and 2. To answer this question, you have to read the experiment descriptions.

Experiment 1

The scientists used a laser emitting unpolarized light. The light was directed toward a polarization filter with an axis of polarization pointing straight up, and then through another whose axis of polarization varied. The scientists chose to describe the axis of the second filter by examining the angle between its axis and the axis of the first filter. The intensity of the original beam was 8 W/m^2 (watts per square meter). Their results are shown in Table 1.

Experiment 2

The scientists repeated the experimental setup of Experiment 1 but used a laser emitting polarized light with an axis of polarization pointing straight up. The intensity of the original beam was still 8 W/m^2. The results are shown in Table 2.

The light in Experiment 1 was unpolarized, while the light in Experiment 2 was polarized. Choice (G) provides this information correctly.

———————————○———————————

Step 3: Work the Answers

In question 12, the central task involved looking up a relationship you've already marked. You used POE to eliminate two answers, but from the beginning you were in command of the question. On question 10, the difference between the two experiments was addressed in the first line of the experiment descriptions. However, if you didn't spot that, good POE would have eliminated (F), and you'd have been able to eliminate (H) and (J) as well.

On more difficult questions, POE will always be the best bet. You'll be asked to synthesize information from several figures, evaluate a hypothesis, or draw a conclusion, and it will always be easier to eliminate what the figures and passage disprove.

Try another example.

> **11.** The scientists hypothesize that the color of the original beam of light will affect the intensity of the emerging beam. The frequency of a beam of light determines its color. Which of the following would be the best way to test this hypothesis?
>
> **A.** Repeating the experiments using more than two polarizing filters
> **B.** Repeating the experiments on different planets
> **C.** Repeating the experiments using beams of both high and low frequencies
> **D.** Repeating the experiments using different intensities for the original beam

Here's How to Crack It

Use POE. Whenever a question asks about how to test something, eliminate answers that have nothing to do with the goal. The question identifies color as an important variable on intensity and identifies frequency as the determinant of color. Eliminate any choice that doesn't address color or frequency. Only (C) is left standing.

Repeat

Steps 3 and 4 repeat: Make your way through the rest of the questions. Look up your answers on the figures, and read only when you can't answer a question from the figures. The less the questions involve a value or relationship, the more you should rely on POE to find the answers.

LATER PASSAGES

The Basic Approach works on all passages with figures, not just the Now passages featuring consistent trends in tables and graphs.

Step 1: Work the Figures

Some ACT passages will feature an illustration, a diagram, or tables and graphs with no consistent trends. Take 10–15 seconds to review the figure. When there are no consistent trends, a figure doesn't reveal the main point as readily. You'll learn the main point as you work the questions and answers. Spend the limited time devoted to Step 1 looking for any patterns or terms.

Step 2: Work the Questions

Even on Later passages, several questions will ask you to look something up on the figure. The more confusing the figure, however, the more likely you are to waste valuable time trying to figure everything out from staring at the figure, waiting for a flash of inspiration to hit. Use your POOD to seek out the most straightforward questions in a passage to tackle first. As we wrote above, most questions will ask you to look something up on the figure. For more complicated questions, move to Step 3 and use POE.

Step 3: Work the Answers

The wordier the answers, the more you should use POE. Read each answer, then review the figure and ask yourself: does the answer choice accurately describe the figure?

FIGHTING SCIENTISTS

Fighting Scientists passages sometimes come with figures, but Fighting Scientists utilizes different skills and thus requires a different basic approach.

Step 1: Preview

Go straight to the questions and identify which theory you'll need to read in order to answer the question. For example, if the passage features "Hypothesis 1" and "Hypothesis 2," then label any question that just covers the first "1" and any passage that just covers the second "2." Label questions on both with "1 & 2." For passages with multiple theories, label the questions as needed.

Step 2: One Side at a Time

Read Hypothesis 1 and do all the questions labeled "1." Reading and working the questions for one scientist at a time will give you the firm grasp of each theory you need.

Step 3: The Other Side

Read Hypothesis 2 and do all the questions labeled "2." On passages with multiple hypotheses, read each theory one at a time and work its stand-alone questions before moving on to the next theory.

Step 4: Compare and Contrast

Save for last all the questions on multiple theories. You'll have a much easier time keeping track of who said what, how they agree, how they disagree, and so on. Use POE as much as possible.

PRACTICE

Try the Basic Approach on your own. Start with the Now passages in Chapter 4 before moving on to the Later Passages in Chapter 5. Then try a complete Science practice test in Chapter 6.

Summary

o The Science test is not a test of science content but of science reasoning skills.

o Pick your order of the passages.

o Now passages feature small tables and graphs with easy-to-spot consistent trends made up of numbers, not words or symbols, and feature short answers.

o Use the 3-step Basic Approach.
   1. Work the Figures. Note the variables and mark the trends.
   2. Work the Questions. Look up answers on your figures. Read if and only when you can't answer a question from a figure.
   3. Work the Answers. On tougher questions, lean heavily on POE to eliminate wrong answers.

Chapter 4
Now Passages

Passage I

Reduction by carbon process, thermite process, and reduction by heating alone are different ways of converting a metal oxide to pure metal. Reactions 1–3 are examples of these processes using zinc oxide, manganese dioxide, and mercuric oxide, respectively.

Reaction 1: $ZnO + C \rightarrow Zn + CO$

Reaction 2: $3MnO_2 + 4Al \rightarrow 3Mn + 2Al_2O_3$

Reaction 3: $2HgO \xrightarrow{\text{heating}} 2Hg + O_2$

In each case, the resulting sample is composed of the metal and another product, which is filtered out to leave only the pure metal.

Figures 1–3 below show how *percent pure metal* (% PM) varied as a function of time in each of the reactions in the presence of a magnetic field and without a magnetic field.

$$\% \text{ PM} = \frac{\text{mass of pure metal}}{\text{mass of metal oxide} + \text{mass of pure metal}} \times 100$$

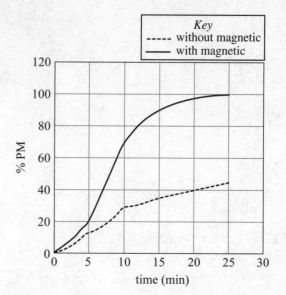

Figure 2

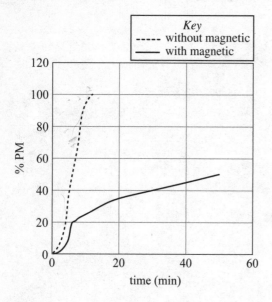

Figure 1

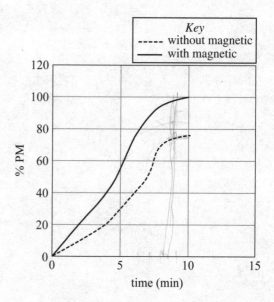

Figure 3

Redox equations

1. According to Figure 1, during Reaction 1 with a magnetic field, the % PM observed at 20 mins was approximately:

   A. 40%.
   B. 35%.
   C. 25%.
   D. 20%.

2. Suppose that during Reaction 3 with a magnetic field, the magnetic field had been removed at time = 5 min. Three minutes later, at time = 8 min, the % PM would most likely have been:

    F. greater than 60%.
    G. between 40% and 60%.
    H. between 20% and 40%.
    J. less than 20%.

dang

3. According to Figure 2, in Reaction 2, how did the removal of the magnetic field affect the yield of pure metal at time = 20 min? The yield obtained without a magnetic field was about:

    A. $\frac{2}{5}$ the yield obtained with a magnetic field.

    B. $\frac{4}{5}$ the yield obtained with a magnetic field.

    C. $2\frac{1}{2}$ times that of the yield obtained with a magnetic field.

    D. 3 times the yield obtained with a magnetic field.

4. A chemist claimed that separating pure metal using a magnetic field is always faster than without a magnetic field. Do Figures 1–3 support this claim?

    F. No; in Reaction 1 the % PM reached 0% sooner without a magnetic field than with a magnetic field.
    G. No; in Reaction 1 the % PM reached 100% sooner without a magnetic field than with a magnetic field.
    H. Yes; the % PM consistently reached 0% sooner with a magnetic field for all three reactions than without.
    J. Yes; the % PM consistently reached 100% sooner with a magnetic field for all three reactions than without.

5. If Reaction 3 had been graphed as *percent of metal oxide* (% MO) as time increases instead of % PM:

$$\% \text{ MO} = \frac{\text{mass of metal oxide}}{\text{mass of metal oxide } + \text{ mass of pure metal}} \times 100$$

Which of the following graphs best represents how Figure 3 would have appeared?

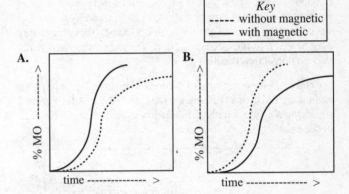

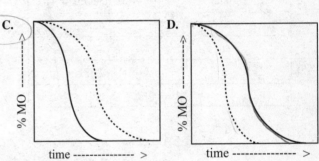

Passage II

When light strikes a metal surface, the energy of the photons is transferred to the metal surface and frees electrons from the metal in a process called the *photoelectric effect*. The energy required to free an electron differs depending on the type of metal and is called the *work function* of the metal. The energy contained within a photon can be determined by that photon's frequency. The *threshold frequency* for a metal, or f_T, is the minimum frequency at which the photon energy will be sufficient to free an electron. This is the frequency at which photon energy is equal to work function. If the frequency is higher than f_T, the extra energy may be given to the ejected electron. The maximum energy that may be transferred is called K_{max}.

Table 1 shows the work functions in electron volts (eV) for aluminum, (Al), zinc (Zn), nickel (Ni), and silver (Ag). Figure 1 shows the K_{max} of each metal in relation to the frequency for each of the metals.

Table 1	
Metal	Work function (eV)
Al	4.08
Zn	4.30
Ag	4.73
Ni	5.01

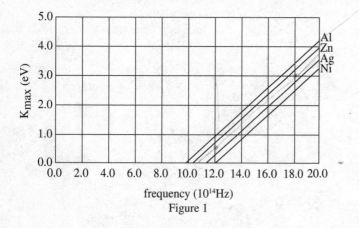

frequency (10^{14}Hz)

Figure 1

1. For a photon to free an electron from Zn, the photon's work function must be at least:

    A. 4.23 eV.
    B. 4.30 eV.
    C. 4.61 eV.
    D. 5.31 eV.

2. Based on Figure 1, which of the following correctly ranks Al, Ni, and Ag in order of increasing K_{max} at 15.0×10^{14} Hz ?

    F. Al, Ag, Ni
    G. Al, Ni, Ag
    H. Ni, Ag, Al
    J. Ni, Al, Ag

3. Based on Table 1 and Figure 1, as frequency increases, K_{max}

    A. decreases.
    B. increases.
    C. increases, then decreases.
    D. decreases, then increases.

4. Based on Figure 1, for electrons ejected from Al by photons with frequency = 26.0×10^{14} Hz, K_{max} would be:

    F. greater than 5.0 eV.
    G. between 4.5 eV and 5.0 eV.
    H. between 4.0 eV and 4.5 eV.
    J. less than 4.0 eV.

5. Photons having frequencies of 12.0×10^{14} Hz and 18.0×10^{14} Hz strike a new metal, Metal Q, resulting in freed electrons with the following K_{max}:

Photon frequency (10^{14} Hz)	K_{max} (eV)
12.0	0.5 eV
18.0	3.0 eV

Based on Table 1 and Figure 1, the work function of Metal Q is most likely closest to which of the following?

    A. 4.01 eV
    B. 4.20 eV
    C. 4.28 eV
    D. 4.51 eV

Passage III

Scientists studied the effects of Drug X on various strains of bacteria in the *Staphylococcus* genus. Table 1 shows the bacteria that were tested and the ED_{50} (the dosage necessary to achieve a therapeutic effect for 50% of the population that is given the medication) of each bacterial strain.

Table 1		
Bacterium	Species	ED_{50} of Drug X (mg/L)
A	*Staphylococcus aureus*	15.3
B	*Staphylococcus carnosus*	30.6
C	*Staphylococcus gallinarum*	22.7
D	*Staphylococcus vitulinus*	91.3
E	*Staphylococcus warneri*	62.6

Six flasks containing 500 mL of nutrient broth were prepared, each with 10,000 cells of *Staphylococcus aureus*. Drug X was then added to five of the flasks in different concentrations, and all six flasks were incubated at 37°C for 24 hours. This procedure was then repeated for the four other bacterial strains. Figure 1 shows the percentage of cells killed for each bacterial strain at each concentration of Drug X.

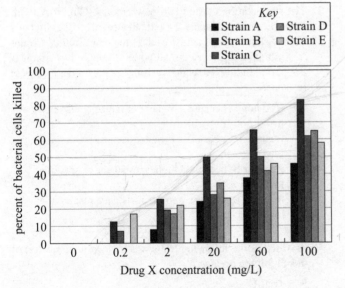

Figure 1

1. According to Figure 1, as the concentration of Drug X increased, the percent of bacterial cells killed from Strain C:

   A. increased, then remained the same.
   B. decreased, then remained the same.
   C. increased only.
   D. decreased only.

2. Based on Table 1, which strain of bacterium requires the highest concentration of Drug X to achieve a therapeutic effect for 50% of the population that is given the medication?

   F. Strain A
   G. Strain B
   H. Strain D
   J. Strain E

3. Based on Figure 1, if cells from Strain B had been treated with Drug X at a concentration of 200 mg/L, the percent of bacterial cells killed would most likely have been:

   A. less than 75%.
   B. between 75% and 80%.
   C. between 80% and 85%.
   D. greater than 85%.

4. According to Table 1, the concentration of Drug X necessary to achieve a therapeutic effect for 50% of the population from Strain E was approximately 4 times the concentration of Drug X necessary to achieve a therapeutic effect for 50% of the population from:

   F. Strain A.
   G. Strain B.
   H. Strain C.
   J. Strain D.

5. Between which of the following concentrations did Drug X most increase in effectiveness in killing bacterial cells of Strain E?

   A. Between 0 mg/L and 0.2 mg/L
   B. Between 2 mg/L and 20 mg/L
   C. Between 20 mg/L and 60 mg/L
   D. Between 60 mg/L and 100 mg/L

Passage IV

A *resistor* is an object that creates electrical resistance in a circuit.

R is the electrical resistance, in *ohms* (Ω), which describes the tendency of a resistor to oppose electric conduction. Conductance, G, in siemens (S), is the inverse of R: it describes the tendency of a resistor to allow electric conduction. When a voltage V, in volts (V), is run across a circuit, R will affect the resulting current I, measured in amperes (A).

Students tested several different resistors. For each trial, the students applied a series of voltages across a circuit that contained a resistor and measured the resulting current. The students then calculated the power, P, in watts (W), delivered through the circuit. P is a measure of the rate at which current flows across a circuit.

Study 1

In Trials 1–5, the circuit contained a blue resistor with $R = 0.005\ \Omega$. The results are shown in Table 1. Each Trial had a different voltage (V) across the circuit.

Table 1			
Trial	V (V)	I (A)	P (W)
1	0.02	4	0.08
2	0.04	8	0.32
3	0.06	12	0.72
4	0.08	16	1.28
5	0.09	18	1.62

Study 2

In Trials 6–10, the circuit contained a red resistor with $R = 0.015$. As in Study 1, each trial had a different voltage (V) across the circuit.

Table 2			
Trial	V (V)	I (A)	P (W)
6	0.02	1.3	0.03
7	0.04	2.7	0.11
8	0.06	4	0.24
9	0.08	5.3	0.43
10	0.09	6	0.54

Study 3

In Trials 11–15, the circuit contained a green resistor with $R = 0.04\ \Omega$. As in the prior studies, each trial had a different voltage (V) across the circuit.

Table 3			
Trial	V (V)	I (A)	P (W)
11	0.02	0.5	0.01
12	0.04	1	0.04
13	0.06	1.5	0.09
14	0.08	2	0.16
15	0.09	2.2	0.20

1. If an additional trial had been conducted in Study 1 with $V = 0.03$ V, the value of P for this additional trial would most likely have been:

   A. less than 0.08 watts.
   B. between 0.08 watts and 0.32 watts.
   C. between 0.32 watts and 0.72 watts.
   D. greater than 1.62 watts.

2. In each study, as the voltage across each circuit increased, the electrical power:

   F. remained the same.
   G. varied, but with no general trend.
   H. decreased only.
   J. increased only.

3. The students then tested two new circuits, Circuit A (with Resistor A) and Circuit B (with Resistor B). The students ran the same voltage across each of the new circuits. Circuit A exhibited a higher electrical power compared to circuit B. Based on Studies 1–3, which resistor has the higher electrical resistance?

   A. Resistor A, because a higher resistance results in a lower power.
   B. Resistor A, because a lower resistance results in a lower power.
   C. Resistor B, because a higher resistance results in a lower power.
   D. Resistor B, because a lower resistance results in a lower power.

4. In which of the following trials was the *conductance* (G) of the circuit the greatest?

   F. Trial 1
   G. Trial 6
   H. Trial 11
   J. Trials 1, 6, and 11 all have the same conductance.

5. Prior to the studies, 4 students made predictions about which of the 3 resistors, if any, would have the lowest P for a given V. Student L predicted that it would be the blue resistor. Student M predicted that it would be the red resistor. Student N predicted that it would be the green resistor, and Student O predicted that all three resistors would have the same P for a given V. Which prediction is correct?

A. Student L
B. Student M
C. Student N
D. Student O

6. A student concluded that, for a constant resistance, increasing the value of V by a factor of 3 increases the value of P by a factor of 9. Which pair of trials best supports this conclusion?

F. 1 and 8
G. 2 and 4
H. 6 and 13
J. 11 and 13

Passage V

In 3 studies, students investigated the thermal expansion of rectangular metal rods various lengths and materials (see Figure 1).

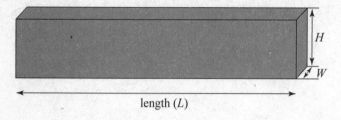

length (*L*)

Figure 1

Using the water bath shown in Figure 2, the students heated the rods to different temperatures.

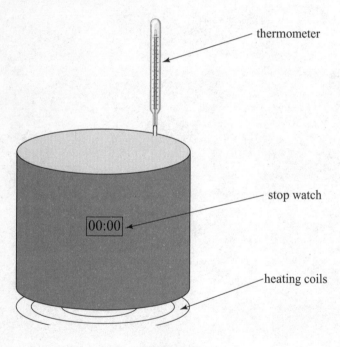

Figure 2

In each trial, the rod was transferred to a water bath preheated to a particular temperature and then allowed to incubate for a set amount of time. During the incubation process, water temperature was kept constant while the metal rods underwent thermal expansion.

After completion of the incubation, the metal rod was removed, and the length, width, and height of the metal rod were promptly measured. After being measured, the metal rod returned to room temperature and reverted to its original dimensions.

The intrinsic thermal expansion of the metal rod was represented by the *volumetric expansion constant*, *β*.

Study 1

In Trials 1–4, students determined the change in volume, ΔV, for rods of different lengths, *L* (see Table 1). In every trial, the time of incubation was 30 minutes and the temperature was 80°C.

Table 1		
Trial	*L* (mm)	ΔV (mm³)
1	50	1.5
2	100	3.1
3	150	4.5
4	200	5.9

Study 2

In Trials 5–8, students determined ΔV for rods of the same *L* composed of Metals W–Z, respectively. Each metal had a different value of *β* (see Table 2). In every trial, *L* = 100mm, the time of incubation was 30 minutes, and the temperature was 80°C.

Table 2			
Trial	Metal	β (°C⁻¹)	ΔV (mm³)
5	W	0.8	1.7
6	X	1.4	3.1
7	Y	2.2	4.9
8	Z	4.6	10.2

Study 3

In Trials 9–12, students determined ΔV for rods at different temperatures (see Table 3). In every trial, *L* = 100 mm, and the incubation time was 30 minutes.

Table 3		
Trial	Temperature (C°)	ΔV (mm³)
9	40	5.1
10	60	7.7
11	80	10.2
12	100	12.8

1. If density is defined as mass divided by volume, which of the following is true concerning the change in density of the metal beam after incubation in the water bath?

   A. Density increases because the volume increases.
   B. Density decreases because the volume decreases.
   C. Density increases because the mass increases.
   D. Density decreases because the volume increases.

2. If, in Study 3, a trial had been conducted in which the incubation temperature was 70°C, ΔV would most likely have been closest to which of the following?

   F. 6.5 mm³
   G. 7.2 mm³
   H. 8.9 mm³
   J. 10.4 mm³

3. If the thermal energy contained within the metal rod is proportional to the product of the incubation time and the initial length, in which of the following trials does the rod contain the greatest amount of thermal energy following incubation?

   A. Trial 2
   B. Trial 4
   C. Trial 10
   D. Trial 12

4. The results of Study 1 are best represented by which of the following graphs?

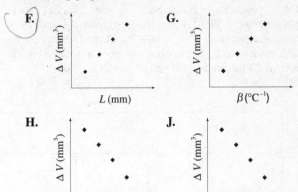

5. The beam tested in Study 3 was most likely composed of which of the metals tested in Study 2 ?

   A. Metal Z
   B. Metal Y
   C. Metal X
   D. Metal W

6. Based on the results of Studies 1 and 2, for a given temperature, which of the following combinations of L and β would yield the greatest thermal expansion?

	L (mm)	β (°C^{-1})
F.	100	4.6
G.	100	2.2
H.	200	4.6
J.	200	2.2

Passage VI

The pesticides *propargyl bromide* (PBr) and *1,3-dichloropropene* (1,3-D) are removed from the soil by a variety of factors, including uptake by plants, adsorption by soil, and breakdown by microorganisms, such as those found in manure. Also, PBr can degrade into *propargyl alcohol*.

Three pairs of pesticide-free soil samples were collected for a study: heavily manure-amended (H1, H2), slightly manure-amended (S1, S2), and unamended (U1, U2), as described in Table 1. On day 1, PBr was added to H1, S1, and U1 and 1,3-D was added to H2, S2, and U2 to produce an initial pesticide concentration of 500 mg/L in each soil sample. PBr, propargyl alcohol, and 1,3-D concentrations in the soil were measured at intervals over the next 12 weeks (see Figures 1–3).

Table 1	
Soil	Description of soil
Heavily manure-amended (H1, H2)	Abundant composted steer manure throughout the soil
Slightly manure-amended (S1, S2)	Moderate composted steer manure throughout the soil
Unamended (U1, U2)	Small amount of composted steer manure throughout the soil

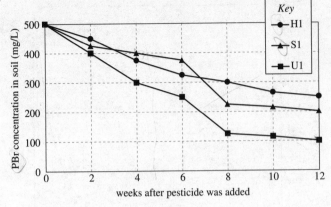

Figure 1

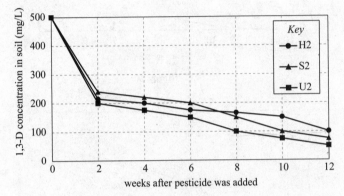

Figure 2

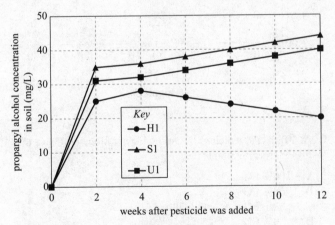

Figure 3

1. Assume that the environmental factors (ultraviolet radiation, wind drift, temperature, and moisture) for each soil sample remained constant over the 12 weeks of the study. According to Figure 2, 12 weeks after 1,3-D was added, what percent of the original 1,3-D concentration remained in the water in H2 ?

  A. Less than 10%
  B. Between 10% and 30%
  C. Between 30% and 50%
  D. Greater than 50%

2. According to Figure 1, 5 weeks after PBr was added, the concentration in the soil in S1 compared to its concentration in H1 was about:

  F. 112 mg/L lower.
  G. 112 mg/L higher.
  H. 275 mg/L lower.
  J. 275 mg/L higher.

3. According to Figures 1 and 3, as the PBr concentration in S1 decreased, the propargyl alcohol concentration:

  A. decreased only.
  B. decreased, then increased.
  C. increased only.
  D. increased, then decreased.

4. Is the statement "Over the 12 weeks of the study, PBr concentration was most reduced in the water in the unamended soil sample" supported by the data in Figure 1 ?

  F. Yes; 12 days after PBr was added, its concentration was least in the water in U1.
  G. Yes; 12 days after PBr was added, its concentration was least in the water in H1.
  H. No; 12 days after PBr was added, its concentration was least in the water in U1.
  J. No; 12 days after PBr was added, its concentration was least in the water in H1.

5. As shown in Figure 2, every time the 1,3-D concentrations in the soil in H2, S2, and U2 were measured during the study, the concentrations in S2 and H2 were found to be very similar to the concentration in U2. The most likely explanation for this is that in S2 and H2:

  A. adsorption onto soil particles and plant uptake played a more significant role in removing 1,3-D than did breakdown to form PBr.
  B. adsorption onto soil particles and plant uptake played a less significant role in removing 1,3-D than did breakdown to form PBr.
  C. bacterial decomposition played a more significant role in removing 1,3-D than did adsorption onto soil particles and plant uptake.
  D. bacterial decomposition played a less significant role in removing 1,3-D than did adsorption onto soil particles and plant uptake.

Passage VII

Ethylene glycol is the main ingredient in antifreeze and has the chemical structure shown below:

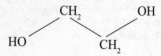

Figures 1–3 show how solutions of antifreeze vary as the concentration of ethylene glycol changes. Concentration is given as the percent ethylene glycol by volume in water (% EG) at atmospheric pressure (101.3 kPa). Figure 1 shows how the melting point (the temperature at which solid antifreeze would begin melting) of antifreeze varies with % EG. Figure 2 shows how the boiling point of antifreeze varies with % EG. Figure 3 shows how the density at 25°C varies with % EG.

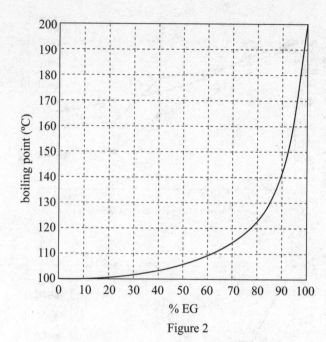

Figure 2

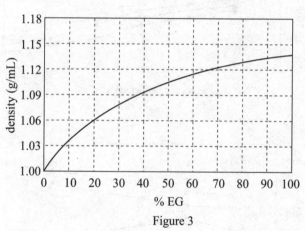

Figure 3

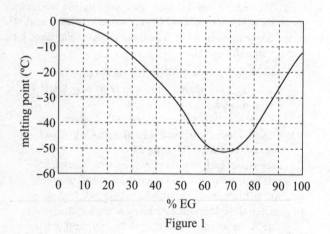

Figure 1

1. At 101.3 kPa, which of the following solutions will have the *lowest* freezing point?

   A. 100% EG
   B.   68% EG
   C.   50% EG
   D.   0% EG

2. According to Figure 1, the temperature at which solid anti-freeze begins to melt in a 60% EG solution at 101.3 kPa is closest to which of the following?

   F.   0°C
   G. −12°C
   H. −48°C
   J. −60°C

3. Based on Figure 2, which of the following solutions has a boiling point equal to pure water at 101.3 kPa?

   A.   0% EG
   B.   13% EG
   C.   68% EG
   D. 100% EG

4. At 25°C, as the % EG increases from 0% to 100%, the mass per unit volume:

   F. increases only.
   G. decreases only.
   H. increases, then decreases.
   J. decreases, then increases.

5. According to Figures 2 and 3, a solution of antifreeze that has a density of 1.09 g/mL at 25°C will have a boiling point closest to which of the following?

   A. 100°C
   B. 104°C
   C. 111°C
   D. 122°C

Passage VIII

A series of studies have been conducted to determine the level of harmful radiation at nuclear-waste clean-up facilities. One method of determining the level of radiation in an area is to measure the growth of certain crystals such as $Bi_4Ge_3O_{12}$ (BGO). BGO crystals come in two basic configurations that grow in environments exposed to high levels of gamma radiation. BGO (I) has a hexagonal crystalline structure and typically grows in environments that are continuously exposed to 100–200 rads of gamma radiation per day, while BGO (II) has an octagonal crystalline structure and typically grows in environments that are continuously exposed to 500–800 rads of gamma radiation per day. Scientists conducted two studies to determine which configuration of BGO crystal would be more useful in determining the amount of exposure to gamma radiation around a nuclear-waste clean-up site.

Study 1

BGO (I) and BGO (II) crystals of 4 cm³ to 8 cm³ were collected from a nuclear waste clean-up site west of Phoenix, AZ. Crystals of both types were placed into individually sealed clear-plastic containers. Ten crystals of each type were then exposed to 3 different levels of gamma radiation—150 rads per day, 450 rads per day, and 750 rads per day—for a period of 7 days. The average volume for each type of crystal and each of the 3 levels of radiation was then determined. The results are shown in Figure 1.

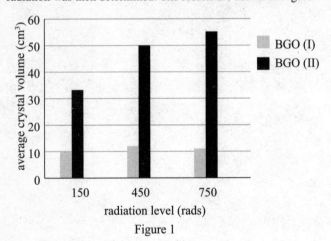

Figure 1

Study 2

The BGO (I) and BGO (II) crystals were removed from the radiation sources and weighed. The average mass of the BGO (I) was determined to be about 13 gm. The average mass of the BGO (II) crystals at each of the three levels of radiation is shown in Figure 2.

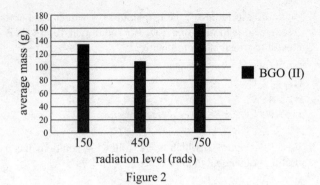

Figure 2

For each radiation level, the volume and mass of the BGO (II) crystals were plotted. The best-fit curve for each is shown in Figure 3.

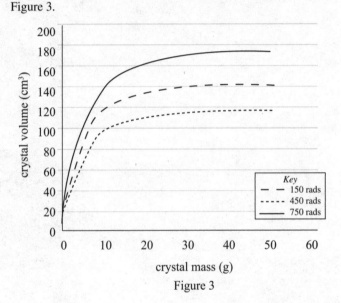

Figure 3

1. Based on Figure 3, for a radiation level of 450 rads, the size and mass of how many BGO (II) crystals were plotted?

   A. 10
   B. 12
   C. 32
   D. Cannot be determined from the given information

2. Suppose that a fourth group of BGO (II) had been exposed to radiation at a level of 300 rads. After 7 days, the average volume of each of these crystals would have been:

   F. less than 35 cm³.
   G. between 35 cm³ and 50 cm³.
   H. between 50 cm³ and 60 cm³.
   J. greater than 60 cm³.

3. Which of the following sets of data points most likely yielded the best-fit curve for BGO (II) crystals exposed to 150 rads of radiation?

F.

G.
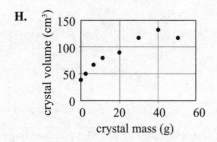

H.
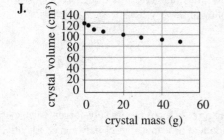

J.
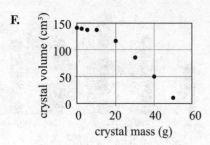

4. At the end of Study 2, a crystal of BGO (II) was found to have a mass of 10 g and a volume of 100 cm³. Based on Figure 3, this crystal most likely had been exposed to radiations of which of the following levels?

  A. 150 rads
  B. 300 rads
  C. 450 rads
  D. 750 rads

5. According to the results of Studies 1 and 2, for a given level of radiation, how did the crystals of BGO (I) compare to the crystals of BGO (II)? On average BGO (I) had:

  A. larger volume and greater mass.
  B. larger volume but lesser mass.
  C. smaller volume and lesser mass.
  D. smaller volume but greater mass.

6. Of the 10 crystals of BGO (I) that were exposed to 450 rads of radiation, 2 cracked and 8 remained whole. The total mass of all of the crystals combined can be calculated using which of the following expressions?

  F. 13 gm × 10
  G. 13 gm + 10
  H. 13 gm × 8
  J. 13 gm + 8

Passage IX

In 1789, Mt. Mantu erupted off the coast of Brunei releasing a cloud of ash that lowered global temperatures for 15 years. When a volcano erupts, it releases a cloud of ash, dust, and debris into the atmosphere thousands of times the volume of the volcano. In addition, at the time of the eruption, the volcano produces a mud and ash flow along the sides of the volcano. The ash flow around Mt. Mantu covered an area 30 times larger than the original size of the volcano. Figure 1 shows the volume of the ash clouds released by volcanoes of differing diameters during the last 200 million years.

Figure 2 shows the average amount of time elapsed between consecutive major eruptions of various volcanoes of similar sizes, for a range of volcano sizes. Figure 3 represents the percentage of land area covered by volcanic ash flows in three different mountain ranges—the Cascades, the Appalachians, and the Himalayas—for various volcanic ash flow diameters.

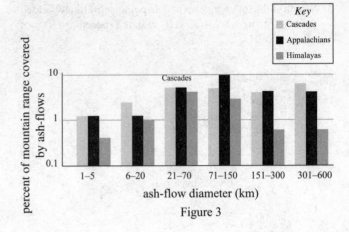

Figure 3

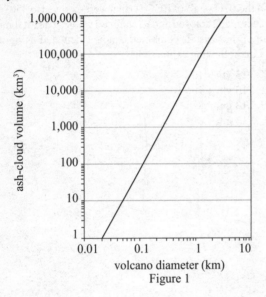

Figure 1

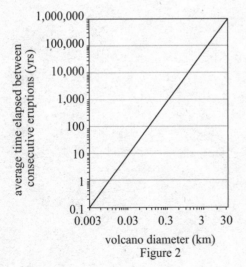

Figure 2

1. If 100 km³ of ash was released by Mt. Mantu, according to Figure 1, Mt. Mantu's diameter was most likely closest to which of the following?

   A. 0.02 km
   B. 0.01 km
   C. 0.1 km
   D. 1 km

2. According to Figure 2, for progressively larger volcanoes, the average amount of time that elapses between consecutive eruptions with the same diameter:

   F. increases only.
   G. decreases only.
   H. varies, but with no general trend.
   J. remains the same.

3. According to Figure 3, for any given range of volcanic ash flows, the percent of area covered in the Himalayas by ash flows is:

   A. less than the Cascades and the Appalachians.
   B. less than the Cascades but greater than the Appalachians.
   C. greater than the Cascades or than the Appalachians.
   D. greater than the Cascades but less than the Appalachians.

4. Suppose a volcano similar to Mt. Mantu created an ash flow that was 30 km in diameter. Based on Figure 1 and other information provided, that volcano would have released a volume of ash closest to which of the following?

F.   5,000 km^3
G.   10,000 km^3
H.   50,000 km^3
J.   100,000 km^3

5. Assume that a volcano with a diameter of 30 km erupted 500,000 years ago. If the time that elapses between eruptions is equal to the average amount of time given in Figure 2, the volcano should erupt approximately:

A.   250,000 years from now.
B.   500,000 years from now.
C.   1,000,000 years from now.
D.   1,500,000 years from now.

Passage X

Electromagnets are used in a variety of industrial processes and often consist of a large *solenoid*, a helical coil of wire, that produces a uniform *magnetic field strength* when a current passes through it (see Figure 1).

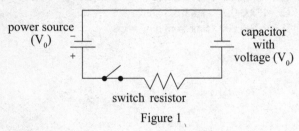

Figure 1

The magnetic field of a solenoid is a factor of its resistance to changes in current, a property called *inductance* (L). The *relative permeability*, μ, is a property of the material within the solenoid coils which may magnify the magnetic field strength.

Figure 2 shows at 25°C, for specific values of μ and L (the length of the solenoid), how the magnetic field strength varies with the current and with the number of coils (N).

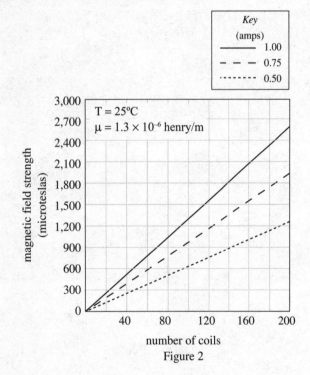

Figure 2

Figure 3 shows, for specific values of A (cross-sectional area of the solenoid) and N, how L varies with solenoid length at 25°C.

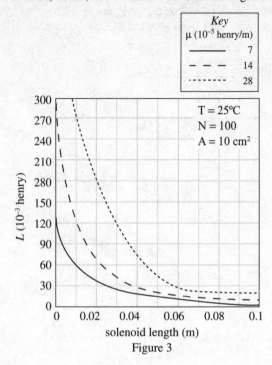

Figure 3

1. For the conditions specified in Figure 2 and I = 0.75 Amps, the solenoid will attract iron metal particles most strongly when the number of coils is closest to which of the following?

   A.   0 coils
   B.   40 coils
   C.   120 coils
   D.   200 coils

2. According to Figure 2, does magnetic field strength vary with current?

   F.   Yes; as magnetic field strength increases, the current decreases.
   G.   Yes; as magnetic field strength increases, the current increases.
   H.   No; as magnetic field strength increases, the current decreases.
   J.   Yes; as magnetic field strength increases, the current remains the same.

3. According to Figure 3, for $\mu = 14 \times 10^{-5}$ henry/m, as the length of the solenoid increases, L:

   A.   increases only.
   B.   decreases only.
   C.   varies, but with no consistent trend.
   D.   remains the same.

4. For a given solenoid length, what is the correct ranking of the values of μ in Figure 3, from the μ associated with the highest L to the μ associated with the lowest L ?

F. 7×10^{-5} henry/m, 14×10^{-5} henry/m, 28×10^{-5} henry/m
G. 14×10^{-5} henry/m, 28×10^{-5} henry/m, 7×10^{-5} henry/m
H. 7×10^{-5} henry/m, 28×10^{-5} henry/m, 14×10^{-5} henry/m
J. 28×10^{-5} henry/m, 14×10^{-5} henry/m, 7×10^{-5} henry/m

5. Based on Figure 2, a solenoid containing 100 coils with a magnetic field strength of 300 would most likely have been produced by a current:

A. greater than 1.00 amps.
B. between 1.00 and 0.75 amps.
C. between 0.75 and .50 amps.
D. less than 0.50 amps.

NOW PASSAGES: ANSWERS AND EXPLANATIONS

Passage I

1. **B** Look at Figure 1. At time = 20 min, the % PM is between 20% and 40%. Therefore (A) and (D) can be eliminated. Since the point lies closer to 40 than 20, (B) is the correct answer.

2. **F** The question asks you to determine what the % PM will be for Reaction 3 at time = 8 min. Eight minutes is a little more than halfway between 5 minutes and 10 minutes. At time = 8 min, the graph lies somewhere above 60%, making (F) the correct answer.

3. **A** Compare the % PM at time = 20 min for the reaction with a magnetic field and the reaction without a magnetic field. At time = 20 min, % PM with a magnetic field was almost 100% and % PM without a magnetic field was 40%. That means that % PM without a magnetic field was 40%, or $\frac{2}{5}$ of the % PM with a magnetic field.

4. **G** Figures 1–3 do not all express the same relationship between % PM with a magnetic field and % PM without a magnetic field. Eliminate (H) and (J). Both (F) and (G) refer to Figure 1, and since the % PM increases as time increases, eliminate (F).

5. **C** The question asks about % MO as opposed to % PM. If % PM increases in Reaction 3, then the metal oxide is being used up as the pure metal forms. Therefore, the graphs for % MO should decrease as time increases, eliminating (A) and (B). For Reaction 3, % PM reaches 100% faster with a magnetic field than without. Therefore, the metal oxide will get used up faster for the reaction with a magnetic field, eliminating (D) and making (C) the correct answer.

Passage II

1. **B** From Table 1, the work function for Zn is listed as 4.30 eV. Therefore, (B) is the correct answer.

2. **H** Examine Figure 1 closely. At a frequency of 15×10^{14} Hz, Ni has the lowest K_{max} (1.25 eV), and Al has the highest K_{max} (2.1 eV). Thus, (H) is the correct answer.

3. **B** As frequency increases, the K_{max} value increases.

4. **F** Look closely at the line plot of Al in Figure 1. At a frequency of 10.0×10^{14} Hz, the K_{max} is 0.1 eV, and at a frequency of 20.0×10^{14} Hz, the K_{max} is 4.2 eV. If this trend continues, as frequency increases by 2.0×10^{14} Hz, K_{max} increases by approximately 0.8 eV. Thus, the correct answer is (F) since at a frequency of 26×10^{14} Hz, K_{max} for Al will be considerably greater than 5.0 eV.

5. **D** We can use the given data for Metal Q and apply it to Figure 1. If Metal Q's K_{max} is 0.5 eV and 3.0 eV at frequencies of 12.0×10^{14} Hz and 18.0×10^{14} Hz, respectively, we can see that these points lie between zinc and silver. Table 1 shows the work functions of Zn and Ag as 4.30 eV and 4.73 eV, respectively. Therefore, Metal Q's work function should be between 4.30 eV and 4.73 eV, as in (D).

Passage III

1. **C** Look at Figure 1. As the concentration of Drug X increases, the percent of bacterial cells of Strain C also increases. Therefore, (C) is the correct answer.

2. **H** From Table 1, compare the values of ED_{50}. Strain D has the maximum value, so (H) is the correct answer.

3. **D** In Figure 1, the percent of bacterial cells killed increases as the concentration of Drug X increases. Thus, according to the data, a concentration of 200 mg/L would result in a greater percentage of bacterial cells killed. Since the percentage killed at a concentration of 100 mg/L is approximately 83%, the correct answer is (D).

4. **F** From the data in Table 1, Strain E has an ED_{50} of 62.6. Look for a strain with an ED_{50} that when multiplied by 4 is about 62.6. Strain A has an ED_{50} of 15.3, which when multiplied by 4 is approximately 60. Four times the ED_{50} for Strains B, C, and D are about 120, 90, and 360, respectively. Thus, the correct answer is (F).

5. **C** Examine the bars for Strain E in Figure 1. The percentages for 2 mg/L and 20 mg/L are similar, so (B) is incorrect. The greatest difference between two concentrations is an increase from approximately 25% to 45% from a concentration of 20 mg/L to 60 mg/L.

Passage IV

1. **B** Table 1 shows that as voltage increases, power increases. For $V = 0.03$ V, the voltage is between the values for Trials 1 and 2, so the expected value for P should lie between the results for Trial 1 (0.08 W) and Trial 2 (0.32W). Therefore, (B) is the correct answer.

2. **J** Tables 1, 2, and 3 all show that P increases when V increases. Choice (J) reflects this trend.

3. **C** Look at Tables 1–3 to compare trials with different resistances and the same voltage. Take trials 2, 7, and 12, for example, which all have the same voltage. Trial 12 has the highest resistance, and Trial 2 has the lowest. Trial 12, however, has the lowest power, and Trial 2 has the highest. Therefore, as resistance increases, power decreases, and so (C) is the correct answer.

4. **F** Conductance (G) is defined in the passage as the inverse of resistance (R). The passage states that Study 1 has the lowest resistance and therefore the greatest conductance. Since the resistance differs between the three studies, eliminate (J). Choice (F) is correct because it is the only answer choice in Study 1.

5. **C** Since the different circuits had different power outputs at a given voltage, (D) is incorrect. Compare three trials, one from each study, that have the same voltage. Trials 1, 6, and 11 show that the power output is lowest for a given voltage in Study 3.

6. **J** Inspect each pair of trials to determine which has the same resistance, 3 times the value of V, and 9 times the value of P. Eliminate (F) and (H) because the trials are in different studies, so the value of R is not constant. Choice (G) is incorrect because the value of V in Trial 4 is double that in Trial 2, and the value of P is 4 times greater. Choice (J) shows the correct relationship.

Passage V

1. **D** During thermal expansion of the metal rod, the only variable that changes according to the passage is the volume. Since density is defined as mass divided by volume, when the thermal expansion causes an increase in volume, the density decreases.

2. **H** The data in Table 3 shows that ΔV for 60°C is 7.7 mm³ and ΔV for 80°C is 10.2 mm³. Since 70°C is between these two values, the corresponding value of ΔV should be between 7.7 mm³ and 10.2 mm³, so the answer is (H).

3. **B** The question states that thermal energy is proportional to the product of incubation time and initial length. In each Study, incubation time is held constant. Use POE, and look for the Trial with the greatest initial length, as in (B).

4. **F** According to Table 1, the two variables are the length of the metal rod (L) and the change in volume of the metal rod (ΔV). Notice that as L increases, ΔV increases. Choices (G) and (H) display a relationship between β and ΔV, which is part of Study 2, not Study 1. Choice (J) incorrectly displays an inverse relationship between L and ΔV.

5. **A** The incubation temperature in Study 2 was held constant at 80°C. Compare the value of ΔV in Table 3 at 80°C to the values in Table 2. In Study 3, ΔV was 10.2 mm³ at 80°C, which corresponds to Metal Z in Table 2.

6. **H**   Refer to Tables 1 and 2. The greatest thermal expansion, ΔV, occurs when L is 200 mm and when β is 4.6 °C^{-1}, (H).

Passage VI

1. **B**   Examine Figure 2. At the end of 12 weeks, the PBr concentration for H2 has decreased from 500 mg/L to 100 mg/L. 100 out of 500 is 20%, as in (B).

2. **G**   In Figure 1, find the difference in PBr concentration between S1 and U1 after 5 weeks. Choices (H) and (J) do not reflect the actual amount of U1 after 5 weeks instead of the difference. Choice (F) reverses the relationship between U1 and S1.

3. **C**   According to Figure 1, as number of weeks increases, the concentration of PBr decreases for all three soil samples. In Figure 3, as number of weeks increases, the propargyl alcohol concentration in S1 also increases. Choice (D) expresses the relationship in H1 instead of S1.

4. **F**   Look at Figure 1. The unamended soil sample refers to U1, which has the lowest concentration. The statement is therefore supported, so eliminate (H) and (J). You can also safely eliminate (G) because the explanation does not match the information in Figure 1. Choice (F) is the correct answer.

5. **D**   This question is asking you to explain the similarity in concentration between H2, S2, and U2 in Figure 2. Since all three soil samples differed greatly in steer manure content, according to the passage, the bacterial count should also vary. This means that bacterial decomposition does not play a significant role in the PBr concentration in the soil, which is (D). Choice (C) is the opposite of (D), and (A) and (B) incorrectly mention propargyl alcohol.

Passage VII

1. **B**   "Freezing point" does not appear on any of the figures, so you'll need a bit of outside knowledge here. Think about it this way: The freezing point is the point at which a substance turns from a liquid into a solid. The melting point is the point at which a substance turns from a solid into a liquid. Therefore, freezing point and melting point are one and the same. Use Figure 1. According to the passage, all readings are taken at atmospheric pressure 101.3 kPa, so you can disregard that part of the question. The melting point of the solution seems to be lowest around 70% EG. The closest of the answers is (B), 68%.

2. **H**   Use Figure 1. According to the passage, all readings are taking at atmospheric pressure 101.3 kPa, so you can disregard that part of the question. According to Figure 1, at 60% EG, the melting point is roughly −48°C, as in (H).

3. **A** The substance that will behave most like pure water and boil at the same temperature would be pure water itself. Choice (A), 0% EG, would mean a solution of no ethylene glycol and all water. Increasing the % EG, as in (B), (C), and (D), and therefore decreasing the percentage of water, would make the solution behave less like water.

4. **F** This question requires a bit of outside knowledge: "density" and "mass per unit length" are one in the same. Therefore, you can use Figure 3 to answer this question even though the word "density" does not appear explicitly in this question. According to the passage, all density readings are taken at a temperature of 25°C, so you can disregard that temperature and just look at the graph. According to this graph, as % EG increases, the density steadily increases as well. The best answer, therefore, comes from (F).

5. **B** According to Figure 2, a substance with a density of 1.09 g/mL has 40% EG. Use this EG value on Figure 3. According to Figure 3, a substance with 40% EG has a boiling point of approximately 104°C. Only (B) works.

Passage VIII

1. **D** The axes given in Figure 3 are "crystal mass (g)" and "crystal volume (cm³)." According to the key, different levels of radiation were measured. Nowhere in any of these axes or curves do we have any indication of the *number of crystals* measured. Without this information, and without any relevant information in the introduction, we can't determine how many crystals were measured, making (D) the only possible answer.

2. **G** Although this question does not mention one specific figure, look at the variables to be compared. We'll need to make a prediction about volume based on radiation level. The only one of the three figures that compares these two variables is Figure 1. According to the information in Study 1, these readings were taken after *a period of 7 days*, so we can disregard that bit of information from the question. Now, the question asks about BGO (II), which is represented on Figure 1 by the darker of the two bars. According to the figure, as radiation level increases, crystal volume increases. Therefore, it is reasonable to assume that the volume of a crystal with a radiation level of 300 rads will be greater than that of a crystal with a radiation level of 150 rads and lesser than that of a crystal with a radiation level of 450 rads. According to Figure 1, a BGO (II) crystal with a radiation level of 150 rads has a volume of about 35 cm³, and a BGO (II) crystal with a radiation level of 450 rads has a volume of 50 cm³. Only (G) gives the appropriate range of values between these two volumes.

3. **G** Figure 3 gives the curve for 150 rads, so find the plot in the answer choices that matches up most closely with the curve for 150 rads in Figure 3. Use POE. The curve starts at 0 cm³, heads in an upward direction, and maxes out around 140 cm³. Eliminate (F) and (J) because these curves decrease. Eliminate (H) because this curve does not start at 0 cm³. Only (G) meets all the requirements and is therefore the best answer.

4. **C**   Plot the information from the problem onto Figure 3. A crystal with a mass of 10 g and a volume of 100 cm³ matches most closely the curve appearing lowest on the figure. According to the key, this is the curve for 450 rads, as in (C).

5. **C**   Use POE. Figure 1 contains a side-by-side comparison of the volumes of the crystals at different radiation levels. The BGO (I) crystals are represented by the lighter bar, and the BGO (II) crystals are represented by the darker bar. In all cases, the BGO (I) crystals had a smaller volume, so eliminate (A) and (B). Figure 2 contains the masses of BGO (II) but not BGO (I). According to the passage, though, *The average mass of the BGO (I) crystals was determined to be about 13 gm.* Therefore, since the masses shown in Figure 2 are all well above this value, it can also be inferred that BGO (I)'s mass was smaller, eliminating (D).

6. **H**   According to the passage, *The average mass of the BGO (I) was determined to be about 13 gm.* Therefore, since there are 8 *whole* crystals left at the end of the experiment, their total mass can be found by multiplying the number of crystals by the mass of each: 13 gm × 8, as in (H).

Passage IX

1. **C**   According to Figure 1, when the volcano releases 100 km³ of ash, its diameter is approximately 0.1 km, which is (C). If you had trouble with this problem, you may have been looking at the wrong axis.

2. **F**   Figure 2 shows a direct relationship. As "average time elapsed" increases, "volcano diameter" also increases. Only (F) represents this trend.

3. **A**   Use POE. Pick any point on the graph: For 1–5% covered, for example, the bar showing the ash-flow of the Himalayas is lower than both the bars for the Cascades and the Appalachians. This same trend holds true for the other percentages as well. Only (A) accurately describes this trend.

4. **H**   The passage states that Figure 1 *shows the volume of the ash clouds released by volcanoes of differing diameters.* It also states that the *ash flow around Mt. Mantu covered an area 30 times larger than the original size of the volcano.* Therefore, if the ash flow in the question is 30 km, the original size of the volcano must be 30 times smaller, or 1 km. According to Figure 1, a volcano with a diameter of 1 km will have an ash-cloud volume of approximately 54,000 km³. Choice (H) gives the best approximation of this value.

5. **B**   According to Figure 2, a volcano with a diameter of 30 km should have approximately 1,000,000 years between eruptions. Therefore, since this volcano erupted 500,000 years ago, it will not erupt for another 1,000,000 − 500,000 = 500,000 years, as in (B).

Passage X

1. **D**   The words *magnetic field strength* don't appear explicitly in the question, but they are suggested by the word *attract*. Therefore, use Figure 2 to figure out the relationship between the number of coils and the magnetic field strength. According to this Figure, the magnetic field strength increases with increasing number of coils for all three curves shown. Therefore, in order to get the strongest possible magnetic field, we will need the maximum number of coils, or 200, as in (D).

2. **G**   Review the trends in Figure 2. As the number of coils increases, magnetic field strength increases, which is why all curves show a positive slope. But the key identifies the difference between each curve: The greater the current, the greater the magnetic field strength. Choice (G) provides the correct relationship.

3. **B**   Find $\mu = 14 \times 10^{-5}$ in the key for Figure 3. Notice, though, that all three of these curves follow the same trend: As solenoid length increases, L decreases and then levels off at the end. Only (B) is consistent with this information.

4. **J**   According to Figure 3, as solenoid length increases, L decreases. The μ curves don't follow quite so consistent a relationship. Pick a point and see how these μ values relate to one another. At a solenoid length of 0.02 m, the μ value associated with the largest L value is $\mu = 28 \times 10^{-5}$. The μ value associated with the smallest L value is $\mu = 7 \times 10^{-5}$. Therefore, the correct answer should have 28×10^{-5} as its first value and 7×10^{-5} as its last. Only (J) works.

5. **D**   Find the point on Figure 2 that corresponds to 100 coils and a magnetic field strength of 300 microteslas. This point lies below all three curves. Since the magnetic field strength increases as current increases, the current should be less than 0.50 amps, as in (D).

Chapter 5
Later Passages

Passage I

In an experimental device known as a cloud chamber, energetic protons and neutrons pass through a vapor of condensed alcohol, causing the ionization (acquired charge) of some of the alcohol molecules. The ionized alcohol molecules begin as condensation nuclei around which the alcohol vapor continues to condense until a high-energy mist is formed. When the mist has acquired enough charge, energetic particles passing through the vapor form tracks visible to the naked eye. These tracks can be accelerated by the application of a magnetic force, under which positively and negatively charged ions will travel in opposite directions.

Two studies using cloud chambers were done at a research center in a temperate climate, using supercooled gaseous ethanol as a medium. The cloud chamber temperature ranged from 0°C to –150°C.

Study 1

Four types of anions (A–D) were used. Anions of each type, when released into the cloud chamber, emit groups of electrons into the chamber with a specific distribution of charges (see Table 1).

Table 1				
Anion type	Percent of groups of electrons having charges (coulombs):			
	0.1–0.5	0.6–1.0	1.1–1.5	1.6–2.0
A	70	20	8	2
B	75	10	8	7
C	80	8	7	5
D	85	7	5	3
Note: 1 coulomb is the charge of 6.24×10^{18} electrons.				

A device containing all 4 types of anions was placed next to the cloud chamber. A computer in the device determined whether or not to immediately release at least 1 anion, emitting electrons into the chamber. The computer also selected which type of anion to release, and how many anions to release to generate 10, 100, 1,000, or 10,000 condensation nuclei per cm^3 within the chamber. The average number of tracks produced by each type of anion and at each concentration of condensation nuclei is shown in Figure 1.

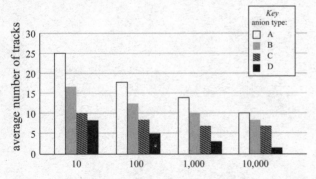

concentration of condensation nuclei
(nuclei/cubic centimeter)

Figure 1

Study 2

The magnetic force required to make each track to accelerate away from a straight line was recorded over an hour following the release of the four types of anions into two types of cloud chambers: one with ethanol vapor and one with water vapor. The averaged results for both types of cloud chambers are shown in Figure 2.

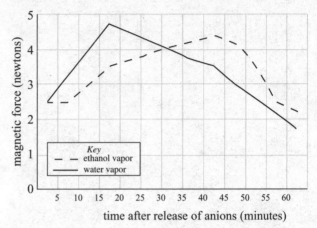

time after release of anions (minutes)

Figure 2

1. According to the results of Study 1, as the condensation nuclei concentration increased, the average number of tracks generated:

   A. increased for all 4 types of anions.
   B. increased for anion types A and B but decreased for anion types C and D.
   C. decreased for all 4 types of anions.
   D. decreased for anion types A and B but increased for anion types C and D.

2. Based on the passage, what is the correct order of tracks, high-energy mist, and condensation nuclei, according to the stage of development, from earliest to latest?

   F. High-energy mist, track, condensation nucleus
   G. High-energy mist, condensation nucleus, track
   H. Track, high-energy mist, condensation nucleus
   J. Track, condensation nucleus, high-energy mist

3. According to the results of Study 2, how did the magnetic force required in the cloud chamber with ethanol vapor differ from the magnetic force required in the cloud chamber with water vapor, with respect to their maximum strength?

A. It took more time for the magnetic force in the ethanol vapor to reach a maximum strength, and it reached a greater maximum strength.
B. It took less time for the magnetic force in the ethanol vapor to reach a maximum strength, and it reached a greater maximum strength.
C. It took more time for the magnetic force in the ethanol vapor to reach a maximum strength, and it reached a lesser maximum strength.
D. It took less time for the magnetic force in the ethanol vapor to reach a maximum strength, and it reached a lesser maximum strength.

4. The design of Study 1 differed from the design of Study 2 in that Study 1, the:

F. tracks of condensation nuclei were analyzed, whereas in Study 2, the concentration of condensation nuclei was analyzed.
G. strength of magnetic fields was measured, whereas in Study 2, the concentration of condensation nuclei was analyzed.
H. tracks of condensation nuclei were analyzed, whereas in Study 2, the strength of magnetic fields was analyzed.
J. strength of magnetic fields was analyzed, whereas in Study 2, tracks of condensation nuclei were analyzed.

5. Which of the following statements gives the most likely reason that data from the cloud chamber was not recorded below a temperature of –150°C? Below –150°C, there would be present:

A. only water vapor.
B. only alcohol vapor.
C. ice crystals but little water vapor.
D. solidified alcohol but little alcohol vapor.

6. Which of the following statements about the concentration of condensation nuclei in the 4 types of anions is supported by Table 1 ?

F. For all 4 types of anions, the majority of particles belonged to the largest charge category.
G. For all 4 types of anions, the majority of particles belong to the smallest charge category.
H. For anion types A and B, most anions belong to the largest charge category, whereas for anion types C and D, most anions belong to the smallest charge category.
J. For anion types A and B, most anions belong to the smallest charge category, whereas for anion types C and D, most anions belong to the largest charge category.

Passage II

Escherichia coli (E. coli) are commonly used in laboratories for the expression, replication, and purification of introduced circular pieces of DNA called *plasmids*. Engineered plasmids encode a gene of interest and often genes that confer resistances to select antibiotics. Antibiotic resistance may be analyzed using the *disk diffusion method*. During the disk diffusion method, bacteria from a single *colony*, or a cluster of genetically identical cells, are incubated in liquid growth media and spread on agar plates (see Figure 1). Small paper disks containing a known concentration of antibiotic are set on the agar plates, and the bacteria are allowed to grow at optimal temperatures. Laboratory strains of *E. coli* lacking plasmids containing genes of resistance to select antibiotics will be unable to grow near the disk containing that antibiotic. Only bacteria that have received the introduced plasmid containing an antibiotic resistance gene should be able to grow in the presence of the antibiotic-containing disk.

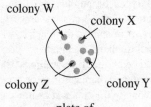

colony W
colony X
colony Z
colony Y

plate of
transformed colonies

Figure 1

Experiment 1

A biotech company has engineered new laboratory strains (A–E) of *E. coli* and is testing whether each strain could grow in the presence of a variety of common antibiotics—ampicillin (Amp), kanamycin (Kan), penicillin (Pen), and tetracycline (Tet). Each of the strains was incubated in a clear nutrient media containing either extra sugar (glucose) or an antibiotic at 37°C for 24 hours. After 24 hours, the growth media was examined for *turbidity* or cloudiness, a signal of bacterial growth (see Table 1).

Strain	Nutrient Media				
	Glu	Amp	Kan	Pen	Tet
A	+		+		
B	+			+	
C	+			+	+
D	+	+	+		
E	+		+	+	

Table 1

Note: + indicates presence of turbidity; indicates no change in appearance

Experiment 2

The scientists at the biotech company tested strain A for growth after *transformation*, a process of introducing engineered plasmids with antibiotic-resistance containing plasmids. Four different transformed colonies (W, X, Y, and Z) and untransformed strain A were incubated in liquid growth media and spread on agar plates. To identify which colonies had received which resistance genes, disks containing one of each of the common antibiotics were then placed on the agar plate, and the bacteria were permitted to grow at 37°C (see Figure 2).

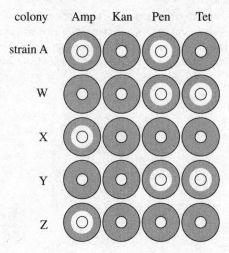

colony   Amp   Kan   Pen   Tet

strain A

W

X

Y

Z

Figure 2

1. Suppose *E. coli* Strain D had been incubated on plates containing kanamycin and tetracycline (Kan⁺Tet⁺) disks and growth near both disks was observed. Do the data in Table 1 support this observation?

   A. Yes; the results shown in Table 1 indicate that Strain D can grow in the presence of both Kan and Tet.
   B. Yes; the results shown in Table 1 indicate that Strain D cannot grow in the presence of Kan.
   C. No; the results shown in Table 1 indicate that Strain D can grow in the presence of both Kan and Tet.
   D. No; the results shown in Table 1 indicate that Strain D cannot grow in the presence of Tet.

2. Which of the labeled colonies shown in Figure 2 is most likely to have received a plasmid conferring resistance to tetracycline?

   F. Colonies W and X
   G. Colonies X and Z
   H. Colonies Y and Z
   J. Colonies X and Z

3. According to Table 1, how many strains tested in Experiment 1 were able to grow in nutrient media containing penicillin?

   A. 0
   B. 1
   C. 2
   D. 3

4. Based on Table 1 and Figure 2, which colonies, if any, likely received a plasmid with resistance genes to penicillin and tetracycline?

   F. Colony W only
   G. Colony X only
   H. Colonies X and Z
   J. Colonies W and Y

5. Before beginning the experiments, the scientists sprayed the lab area down with a disinfectant. The most likely reason that the disinfectant was used was to avoid contaminating:

   A. the nutrient growth media with strains that were lab generated.
   B. the agar plates with strains that were lab generated.
   C. both the nutrient growth media and agar plates with strains that were lab generated.
   D. both the nutrient growth media and agar plates with strains that were not lab generated.

6. Which of the colonies shown in Figure 2 did NOT grow in the presence of ampicillin?

   F. Colony W
   G. Colony X
   H. Colony Y
   J. None of the strains

Passage III

A group of students added 100 mg of Salt A to an Erlenmeyer flask containing 100 mL of water at 20°C. The mixture was heated over a Bunsen burner, and a thermometer was placed in the flask to acquire temperature readings (Figure 1).

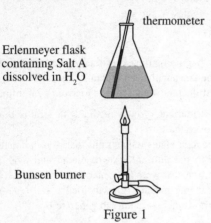

Figure 1

The mixture was heated, and temperature readings were acquired every 30 sec until the solution reached a full boil and the solid had completely dissolved. The boiling temperature for the solution was measured to be 104°C. The procedure was repeated with Salt B, which resulted in a boiling temperature of 110°C.

The teacher asked 3 of the students in the group to explain why the solutions had different boiling temperatures.

Student 1

The solution containing Salt B had a higher boiling point because Salt B produces more ions in solution than Salt A. As the solid dissolves, the salt ionizes and interacts with water molecules. This causes more interactions between the ions and water thus requiring more energy for water molecules to break these interactions and become a gas (boiling). Since salts become ions in solution, salts that produce more ions will have more interactions with water than salts producing fewer ions. Thus, if two salts of equal amounts are added to water, the solution containing the salt that produces more ions will boil at the higher temperature.

Student 2

The solution containing Salt B had a higher boiling point because it had a lower *molar mass* (the mass of 6.02×10^{23} particles). Consider equal amounts of two salts with different molar masses. More mass is required of the salt with the greater molar mass to result in the same number of particles. Since more heat energy is required to boil water with more interactions, the solution with more salt particles will boil at a higher temperature. Thus, if equal amounts of two salts with different molar masses are added, the salt with the lower molar mass will result in more particles and a greater solution boiling point than a salt with a greater molar mass.

Student 3

The solution containing Salt B had a higher boiling point because Salt B releases more heat upon dissolving than Salt A. The *enthalpy change of dissolution* ($\Delta H°_{diss}$) is a measure of the net amount of heat energy absorbed in the process of dissolving a salt. Salts that absorb more energy to dissolve will have more positive $\Delta H°_{diss}$ values and will make the solution cooler. Salts that absorb less energy than they release will have more negative $\Delta H°_{diss}$ values and will make the solution warmer. If equal amounts of two salts with different $\Delta H°_{diss}$ values are dissolved in solution, the solution containing the salt with the more negative $\Delta H°_{diss}$ value will release more heat and thus result in a greater boiling point.

The number of ions produced, molar mass, and enthalpy change dissolution ($\Delta H°_{diss}$) of some common salts are shown in Table 1.

Table 1			
Salt	Ions produced	Molar mass (g/mol)	$\Delta H°_{diss}$ (kJ/mol)
Sodium chloride	2	58.4	+ 3.9
Calcium chloride	3	111.0	– 81.2
Ammonium nitrate	2	80.1	+ 25.7
Potassium hydroxide	2	56.11	– 57.6
Magnesium sulfate	2	120.38	– 91.0

1. Suppose that Salt A had been potassium hydroxide and Salt B had been magnesium sulfate. The results of the experiment would have supported the explanation(s) provided by which student(s)?

   A. Student 2 only
   B. Student 3 only
   C. Students 1 and 3 only
   D. Students 2 and 3 only

2. Suppose that the students also tested ammonium nitrate in the experiment and found it to have resulted in a boiling temperature in solution of 107°C. Student 2 would claim that ammonium nitrate:

   F. has a greater molar mass than Salt A, but a smaller molar mass than Salt B.
   G. has a greater molar mass than Salt B, but a smaller molar mass than Salt A.
   H. has a greater enthalpy change of dissolution than Salt A, but a smaller enthalpy change of dissolution than Salt B.
   J. has a greater enthalpy change of dissolution than Salt B, but a smaller enthalpy change of dissolution than Salt A.

3. Which of the following graphs of the relative number of particles produced is most consistent with Student 2's explanation?

A.

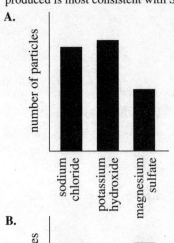

B.

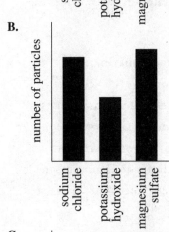

C.

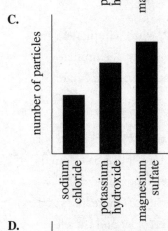

D.

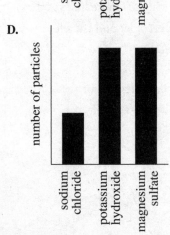

4. During the experiment, the temperature reading in the thermometer as readings were taken every 30 sec:

F. increased only.
G. decreased only.
H. increased, then decreased.
J. decreased, then increased.

5. Based on Student 3's explanation, which of the salts in Table 1 would result in the greatest solution boiling temperature?

A. Calcium chloride
B. Ammonium nitrate
C. Potassium hydroxide
D. Magnesium sulfate

6. Consider the data for cesium hydroxide shown in the table below:

Ions produced	Molar mass (g/mol)	ΔH°_{diss} (kJ/mol)
2	149.91	−71.6

Which student(s), if any, would predict that cesium hydroxide would produce a solution with a lower boiling temperature than calcium chloride?

F. Student 1 only
G. Students 2 and 3 only
H. Students 1, 2, and 3
J. None of the students

7. Is the claim "If equal amounts of salt are dissolved, sodium chloride will result in a greater boiling point than ammonium nitrate" consistent with Student 2's explanation?

A. No, because sodium chloride has a smaller molar mass than ammonium nitrate.
B. No, because sodium chloride has a more negative enthalpy change of dissolution.
C. Yes, because sodium chloride has a smaller molar mass than ammonium nitrate.
D. Yes, because sodium chloride has a more negative enthalpy change of dissolution.

LATER PASSAGES: ANSWERS AND EXPLANATIONS

Passage I

1. **C**   In Figure 1, all four anions follow the same trend, so eliminate (B) and (D) immediately. From left to right in the graph, the concentration of condensation nuclei is increasing for all four anions, and as this value increases, the average number of tracks decreases for all four anions. Only (C) accurately reflects this trend.

2. **G**   Read if and only when a question can't be answered from the figures. The introduction provides the order of development, correctly described in (G).

3. **C**   Notice from the answer choices that this question has two components: time to maximum magnetic force and maximum magnetic force itself. Notice also that all the answer choices focus on the *ethanol vapor*. According to Figure 2, the ethanol vapor took about 40 minutes to reach its maximum magnetic force, whereas the water vapor took only about 15 minutes. Therefore, the ethanol vapor took more time, eliminating (B) and (D). The ethanol vapor reached a maximum magnetic force of approximately 4.25 Newtons, while the water vapor reached a maximum magnetic force of approximately 4.75 Newtons. Therefore, the ethanol vapor's magnetic force reached a lesser maximum strength, eliminating (A) and making (C) the correct answer.

4. **H**   Note the axes on each of the graphs. *Magnetic force* appears only in Study 2, which eliminates (G) and (J) immediately. Then, since magnetic force is the primary focus of Study 2, eliminate (F) because it contains no mention of magnetic force. Only (H) remains and contains accurate information regarding both studies.

5. **D**   This requires a bit of logical thinking and some outside knowledge. Only Study 2 is concerned with *water vapor*, whereas the general introduction discusses *alcohol vapor*. Therefore, it can be inferred that the entire experiment deals with *alcohol vapor*, making changes in water vapor only partially relevant, eliminating (A) and (C). Then, between the two answer choices, which is more likely to be the case at temperatures *below* –150°C? Alcohol in this temperature range is colder and therefore more likely to be solid than vapor. Only (D) reflects this information correctly.

6. **G**   According to Table 1, 75–80% of all four types of anions fit in to the 0.1–0.5 category, or the *smallest charge category*. There are no exceptions in Table 1, so the only answer choice that can work is (G).

Passage II

1. **D** Use POE. If you're not sure whether to answer "yes" or "no," check the reasons. According to Table 1, Strain D can grow in the presence of Glu, Amp, and Kan. Eliminate (B), which states that Strain D cannot grow in the presence of Kan. Also according to Table 1, Strain D cannot grow in the presence of Pen or Tet. Eliminate (A) and (C), which suggest that Strain D can grow in the presence of Tet. Only (D) remains.

2. **J** The question refers to Figure 2, but the presence of Strain A at the top of the figure links back to Figure 1. According to Figure 1, Strain A can grow only when cultured in the antibiotic-free control medium (Glu) or in the presence of Kan. It cannot grow in the presence of Amp, Pen, or Tet. It can be inferred that if growth occurred in a culture, it will be pictured in Figure 2 with a smaller white region than in those colonies where growth did not occur. Therefore, the colonies that have received a *plasmid conferring resistance to tetracycline* should show a smaller white region in the Tet column. Colonies X and Z have this small white region, making (J) the best answer.

3. **D** According to Table 1, Strains B, C, and E were able to grow in the presence of penicillin, or +Pen. Choice (D) gives the correct number.

4. **H** According to Table 1, Strain A can grow in Glu and Kan media. It cannot grow in the presence of Amp, Pen, or Tet. It can be inferred that if growth occurred in a culture, it will be pictured in Figure 2 with a smaller white region than in those colonies where growth did not occur. Therefore, the colonies that have received a *plasmid with resistance genes to penicillin and tetracycline* should show a smaller white region in the Pen and Tet columns. Colonies X and Z have this small white region, making (H) the best answer.

5. **D** This question requires a bit of outside knowledge about why scientists do what they do when setting up experiments. Use POE and common sense. Notice (A), (B), and (C) all contain mention of substances that are *lab generated*. Only (D) contains mention of strains that are *not lab generated*. Think about it this way: Scientists are trying to control the environment of their experiment, so they don't want things from outside (things that are *not lab generated*) to contaminate the things in the experiment. Also, notice that (C) and (D) are direct opposites, a good indication that one of them will be correct.

6. **G** According to Table 1, Strain A can grow in Glu and Kan media. It cannot grow in the presence of Amp, Pen, or Tet. It can be inferred that if growth occurred in a culture, it will be pictured in Figure 2 with a smaller white region than in those colonies where growth did not occur. Therefore, a colony that did NOT grow in the presence of ampicillin should show a larger white region in the Amp column. Of the choices given, only colony X has a larger white region, making (G) the best answer.

Passage III

1. **B**   According to Table 1, potassium hydroxide produced 2 ions, had a molar mass of 56.11 g/mol, and had a $\Delta H°_{diss}$ of –57.6 kJ/mol. Magnesium sulfate produced 2 ions, had a molar mass of 120.38 g/mol, and had a $\Delta H°_{diss}$ of –91.0 kJ/mol. Use POE. Student 1 writes, *The solution containing Salt B had a higher boiling point because Salt B produces more ions in solution than Salt A.* These findings do not agree with Table 1 for the given substances, which produced the same number of ions. Eliminate (C). Student 2 writes, *The solution containing Salt B had a higher boiling point because it had a lower molar mass (the mass of 6.02×10^{23} particles).* Salt B in this question is magnesium sulfate, which does not have a lower molar mass than potassium hydroxide, so you can eliminate (A) and (D). This leaves only (B), and the findings in the table do agree with Student 3's hypothesis.

2. **G**   The passage gives the following information: *The boiling temperature for the solution of Salt A was measured to be 104°C.* The procedure was repeated with Salt B, which resulted in a boiling temperature of 110°C. According to this question, ammonium nitrate has a boiling point of 107°C, right between Salts A and B. According to Student 2, the solution containing Salt B had a higher boiling point because it had a lower molar mass. Therefore, because ammonium nitrate has a higher boiling point than Salt A, it must have a lower molar mass. Only (G) can work. Choices (H) and (J) can be eliminated because Student 2 does not discuss enthalpy change.

3. **A**   According to Student 2, *the salt with the lower molar mass will result in more particles.* In other words, the lower the molar mass of a substance, the more particles it will produce. According to Table 1, sodium chloride has a molar mass of 58.4 g/mol, potassium hydroxide has a molar mass of 56.11 g/mol, and magnesium sulfate has a molar mass of 120.38 g/mol. Since potassium hydroxide has the lowest molar mass, it should produce the *most* particles. With this information alone, you can eliminate (B), (C), and (D). Only (A) remains and puts the substances in the correct relation to one another.

4. **F**   The passage states, *the mixture was heated and temperature readings acquired every 30 sec until the solution reached a full boil and the solid had completely dissolved.* Since the mixture is only heated, it can be inferred that its temperature increases only. There's no indication that the substance is ever cooled, so (F) is the only answer supported by information from the passage.

5. **D**   Student 3 offers the following hypothesis: *The solution containing the salt with the more negative $\Delta H°_{diss}$ value will release more heat and thus result in a greater boiling point.* According to Table 1, magnesium sulfate has the most negative $\Delta H°_{diss}$ value at –91.0 kJ/mol. Therefore, according to Student 3, this substance should have the greatest boiling point of the substances listed.

6. **H**   Compare the new values given in the question to those for calcium chloride given in Table 1. Cesium hydroxide produces 2 ions, while calcium chloride produces 3. Student 1 writes, *The solution containing Salt B had a higher boiling point because Salt B produces more ions in solution than Salt A.* According to this hypothesis, calcium chloride produces more ions, so it should have a higher boiling point. The findings therefore support the hypothesis of Student 1, eliminating (G) and (J). Cesium hydroxide has a molar mass 149.91 g/mol, while calcium chloride has a molar mass of 111.0 g/mol. Student 2 writes, *The solution containing Salt B had a higher boiling point because it had a lower* molar mass *(the mass of* 6.02×10^{23} *particles)*. According to this hypothesis, calcium chloride has a lower molar mass, so it should have a higher boiling point. The findings therefore support the hypothesis of Student 2, eliminating (F). There's no need to test the findings against Student 3's hypothesis: The only option left is (H).

7. **C**   According to Student 2, the salt with the lower molar mass will result in more particles and a greater solution boiling point than a salt with a greater molar mass. Student 2 is not concerned with "enthalpy change," so you can eliminate (B) and (D) immediately. According to Table 1, sodium chloride has a molar mass of 58.4 g/mol, and ammonium nitrate has a molar mass of 80.1 g/mol. Therefore, because sodium chloride has a smaller molar mass, it should have a greater boiling point, as suggested in (C).

Chapter 6
Science Practice
Test

SCIENCE TEST

35 Minutes—40 Questions

Directions: There are seven passages in this test. Each passage is followed by several questions. After reading a passage, choose the best answer to each question and fill in the corresponding oval on your answer document. You may refer to the passages as often as necessary.

You are NOT permitted to use a calculator on this test.

Passage I

Moth body coloration (see Figure 1) is a *hereditary* trait that can be passed from organisms to their offspring.

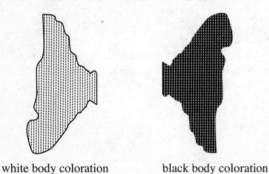

white body coloration   black body coloration

Figure 1

Scientists studied the body coloration of 2 subspecies of moths, *Biston betularia f. typica* and *Biston betularia f. carbonaria*. Both species live in City X. Only *B. betularia f. typica* lives in City Y, while only *B. betularia f. carbonaria* lives in City Z. Both subspecies live on trees found in temperate climates, such as birch. Moths with light body coloration are camouflaged from predators while living on light-colored trees but are not hidden in heavily polluted areas where the tree bark is darkened. Moths with dark body coloration are camouflaged from predators on trees that are darkened by pollution but not on light-colored trees.

Study 1

Scientists captured 100 *B. betularia f. typica* and 100 *B. betularia f. carbonaria* in City X. They labeled each one, recorded its color, and released it. Then they calculated the percent of birds having each of the body color intensities on a scale of 1 to 10, with 1 being completely black and 10 being completely white. The researchers followed the same methods with 100 *B. betularia f. typica* moths from City Y and 100 *B. betularia f. carbonaria* moths from City Z. The results of this study are shown in Figure 2.

Study 2

After the end of Study 1, the scientists returned to City Y over the course of 10 years, from 1983 to 1992. During each visit, they captured at least 50 *B. betularia f. typica* moths and measured their body color intensities. They then calculated the average *B. betularia f. typica* body color intensity from the 1–10 scale for each of the 10 years. The scientists noted that during the 10-year period, 2 years were particularly wet, while 3 years were especially dry (see Figure 3). During wet years, pollutants tend to be washed from the surfaces of tree bark. During dry years, pollutants are more likely to concentrate on tree bark, and the tree bark itself tends to become thicker.

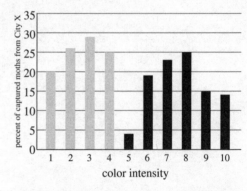

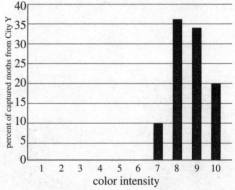

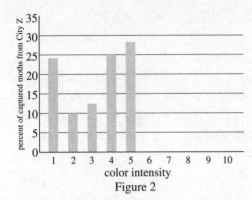

Figure 2

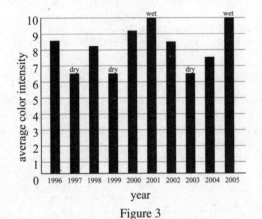

year

Figure 3

1. Based on the results from Study 1, the largest percentage of moths in City Y and City Z had a color intensity of:

	City Y	City Z
A.	8	1
B.	8	5
C.	9	4
D.	9	5

2. During which of the following years was birch bark most likely to be thickest in City Y ?

F. 2000
G. 2001
H. 2002
J. 2003

3. How was Study 1 different from Study 2 ?

A. *B. betularia f. carbonaria* moths were captured in Study 1 but not in Study 2.
B. *B. betularia f. typica* moths were captured in Study 1 but not in Study 2.
C. The moth body coloration was measured in Study 1 but not in Study 2.
D. The moth body coloration was measured in Study 2 but not in Study 1.

4. The scientists most likely labeled the moths in Study 1 to:

F. determine how body coloration was affected by pollution in City X.
G. determine the average wingspan of each population of moths.
H. make sure that the body coloration of each moth was measured only once.
J. make sure that the body coloration of each moth was measured multiple times.

5. Based on the results from Study 2, would a moth with a body color intensity measuring 6.5 or a moth with a body color intensity measuring 9.5 have had a greater chance of surviving in 2005 ?

A. A moth with a body color intensity of 6.5, because pollutants concentrate more on tree bark during dry years.
B. A moth with a body color intensity of 6.5, because pollutants are removed from tree bark during dry years.
C. A moth with a body color intensity of 9.5, because pollutants concentrate more on tree bark during dry years.
D. A moth with a body color intensity of 9.5, because pollutants are removed from tree bark during dry years.

6. A scientist hypothesized that there would be a greater range in body coloration in the *B. betularia f. typica* moths when they are forced to coexist with another subspecies of moths. Do the results from Study 1 support this hypothesis?

F. Yes; the range of body coloration for *B. betularia f. typica* moths was greater in City X than in City Y.
G. Yes; the range of body coloration for *B. betularia f. typica* moths was greater in City Y than in City X.
H. No; the range of body coloration for *B. betularia f. typica* moths was greater in City X than in City Y.
J. No; the range of body coloration for *B. betularia f. typica* moths was greater in City Y than in City X.

Passage II

Ions in seawater, such as Cl^-, SO_4^{2-}, Na^+, and Mg^{2+}, are carried down to the ocean floor through a process known as *marine deposition*. SO_4^{2-} and Mg^{2+} primarily come from the erosion of rocks, while Cl^- and Na^+ come from both mineral erosion and underwater volcanoes and hydrothermal vents.

Study 1

A fluid motion sensor was placed on a section of the seabed in the Atlantic Ocean, and data were collected over 12 months. At 6:00 a.m. every morning, the movement of water past the sensor was recorded, and a small amount of water was sequestered. Figure 1 shows the movement of water in millions of cubic meters (m^3) per second.

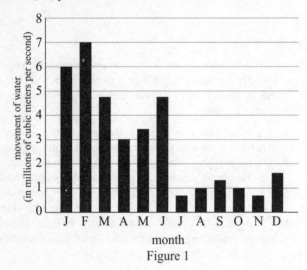

month
Figure 1

At the end of each month, the sequestered water was extracted by a science research crew, and a portion was analyzed for the concentrations of Cl^- and SO_4^{2-} ions. Using these data, the marine deposition was measured in kilograms (kg) per cubic meter (m^3) for each substance in each month (see Figure 2).

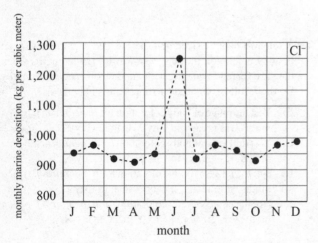

month

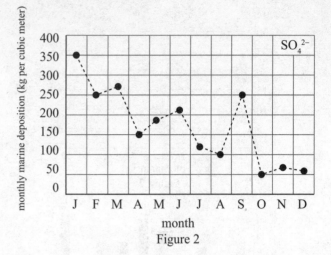

month
Figure 2

Study 2

Another portion of the monthly water sample was analyzed for concentrations of Na^+ and Mg^{2+} ions. The monthly marine deposition was calculated for each substance in equivalents (Eq) per m^3 (see Figure 3).

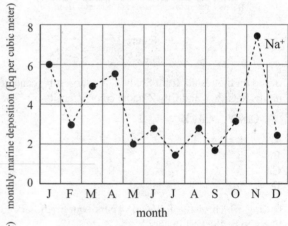

month

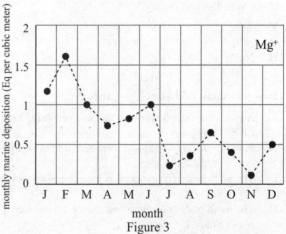

month
Figure 3

Study 3

The annual marine deposition of Cl^- and SO_4^{2-} ions over the 12-month period was calculated in kg/m^3 at the test site, and also at two sites in the Arctic Ocean, located 2,000 and 4,000 miles north, respectively (see Figure 4).

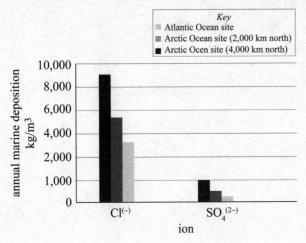

Figure 4

7. According to Figure 1, during the year over which data were collected, the movement of water was greatest in February and least in November. According to Figures 2 and 3, the marine deposition of which ion was also greatest in February and least in November?

   A. Cl^-
   B. Mg^{2+}
   C. Na^+
   D. SO_4^{2-}

8. Based on the results from Study 1, the mean monthly marine deposition for Cl^- over the year of the study was:

   F. less than $900 \ kg/m^3$.
   G. between $900 \ kg/m^3$ and $1,000 \ kg/m^3$.
   H. between $1,000 \ kg/m^3$ and $1,200 \ kg/m^3$.
   J. over $1,200 \ kg/m^3$.

9. A student states, "The marine deposition of Na^+ is highest in the winter and lowest in the summer, since the winter features greater activity of volcanoes and hydrothermal vents." Is this statement supported by the results of Study 2 ?

   A. No, because marine deposition of Na^+ was, on average, greater between November and January than it was between June and August.
   B. No, because marine deposition of Na^+ was, on average, less between November and January than it was between June and August.
   C. Yes, because marine deposition of Na^+ was, on average, greater between November and January than it was between June and August.
   D. Yes, because marine deposition of Na^+ was, on average, less between November and January than it was between June and August.

10. Suppose that the fluid motion sensor was placed in an underwater cave in the Atlantic Ocean where there is no net movement of water during one month of the 12-month study. The information provided indicates that during that month, there would have been:

   F. no marine deposition of any of the 4 substances.
   G. no marine deposition of Cl^- and SO_4^{2-}, but a high level of marine deposition of $Na+$ and Mg^{2+}.
   H. high marine deposition of Cl^- and SO_4^{2-}, but no marine deposition of $Na+$ and Mg^{2+}.
   J. high marine deposition of all 4 substances.

11. According to Study 3, as the distance from the fluid motion sensor in the Atlantic Ocean decreased, the annual marine deposition:

   A. decreased for both Cl^- and SO_4^{2-}.
   B. decreased for Cl^- but increased for SO_4^{2-}.
   C. increased for Cl^- but decreased for SO_4^{2-}.
   D. increased for both Cl^- and SO_4^{2-}.

12. Which of the following variables remained constant in Study 2 ?

   F. Marine deposition of SO_4^{2-}
   G. Marine deposition of Mg^{2+}
   H. Movement of water during the month
   J. Location of the study

Passage III

Leaf area index is a unitless measure of the percent of a rainforest floor that is covered by the leaves of tall trees. Leaf area index may increase because of an increase in *precipitation* (measured as millimeters of rainfall per km² per year). Table 1 shows how the leaf area index formed by the *canopy layer* (30 to 45 m above the rainforest floor) varies with precipitation in a 1000 km² section of the Amazon Rainforest. Figures 1–3 show the relative precipitation, RP (the percent below the rainfall measured on January 1, 1985), and the monthly average leaf area index of the *emergent layer* (45 to 55 m above the rainforest floor), *canopy layer*, and *understory layer* (0 to 30 m above the rainforest floor), respectively, from January 1990 to January 2005.

Table 1	
Precipitation (mm/km²/yr)	Leaf area index
1.80	5.2
1.85	5.4
1.90	5.6
1.95	5.8
2.00	6.0

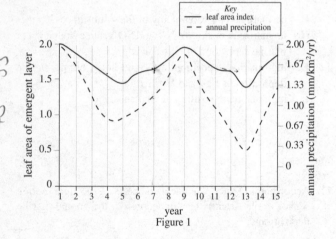

year
Figure 1

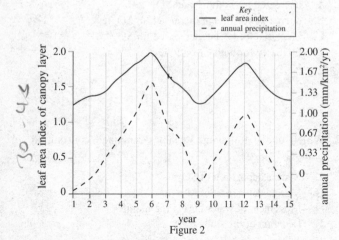

year
Figure 2

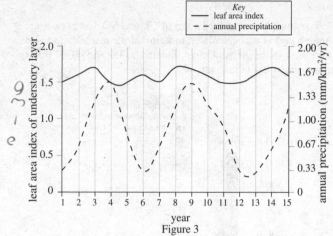

year
Figure 3

13. The leaf area index of the canopy layer covering the section of the rainforest in January of the 14th year studied was closest to which of the following?

 A. 1.0
 B. 1.3
 C. 1.7
 D. 2.0

14. Based on Table 1, a precipitation of 1.70 mm/km²/yr would correspond to a leaf area index that is closest to which of the following?

 F. 4.8
 G. 5.5
 H. 6.0
 J. 6.5

15. A botanist states, "The leaf area index of the understory layer is more directly correlated with annual precipitation than is the leaf area index of the canopy layer." Is this statement consistent with Figures 2 and 3 ?

 A. No, because the plot for the leaf area index of the canopy layer more closely resembles the plot for the annual precipitation.
 B. No, because the plot for the leaf area index of the understory layer more closely resembles the plot for the annual precipitation.
 C. Yes, because the plot for the leaf area index of the canopy layer more closely resembles the plot for the annual precipitation.
 D. Yes, because the plot for the leaf area index of the understory layer more closely resembles the plot for the annual precipitation.

16. Which of the following figures best represents the leaf area index measured in the 7th year of the study?

F.

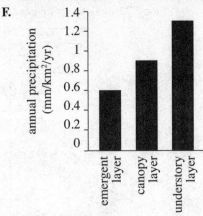

G.

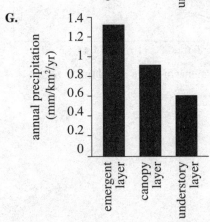

H.

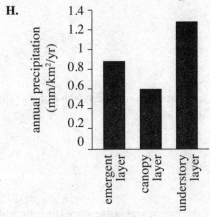

J.

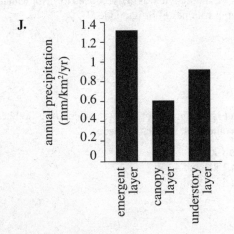

17. The emergent layer is primarily composed of small leaves that cover a wide area, while the understory layer is primarily composed of broad leaves that cover a small area. This difference is most likely because the average precipitation at heights of:

A. 0 to 30 m above the rainforest floor is above 2.00 mm/km^2/yr, whereas the average precipitation at heights of 30–45 m above the rainforest floor is below 0.33 mm/km^2/yr.

B. 0 to 30 m above the rainforest floor is above 2.00 mm/km^2/yr, whereas the average precipitation at heights of 45–55 m above the rainforest floor is below 0.33 mm/km^2/yr.

C. 0 to 30 m above the rainforest floor is below 0.33 mm/km^2/yr, whereas the average precipitation at heights of 30–45 m above the rainforest floor is above 2.00 mm/km^2/yr.

D. 0 to 30 m above the rainforest floor is below 2.00 mm/km^2/yr, whereas the average precipitation at heights of 45–55 m above the rainforest floor is above 1.33 mm/km^2/yr.

Passage IV

Oxidation-reduction titration is a method in which precise volumes of a *titrant* (an oxidizing or reducing agent) are added dropwise to a known volume of an *analyte* (a reducing or oxidizing agent, respectively). This process can be monitored by adding a *redox indicator* (a substance that changes color over a certain range of electrode potentials) to the analyte or by measuring the sample's *voltage* using a potentiometer. Voltage (measured in kilovolts, kV) is a measure of the force of an electrical current that could be transmitted by the solution.

Two titration experiments were performed at 298 K using a 0.10 M iodine (I_2) solution and either a 0.0010 M sulfur dioxide (SO_2) solution or a 0.0010 M sodium thiosulfate solution (where M is the number of moles of oxidizing or reducing agent per liter of solution). All solutions were aqueous. A redox indicator solution of *starch* was also used. Starch and I_2 form a complex with a deep blue color, but when I_2 is reduced to 2 iodide (I^-) ions, the complex dissipates and the solution becomes colorless.

Experiment 1

A drop of starch solution was added to an Erlenmeyer flask containing 100.0 mL of the SO_2 solution. A potentiometer, which acts as a control input for electronic circuits, was placed in the solution. The I_2 solution was incrementally added to the SO_2 solution. After each addition, the SO_2 solution was stirred and the solution's color and voltage were recorded (see Figure 1).

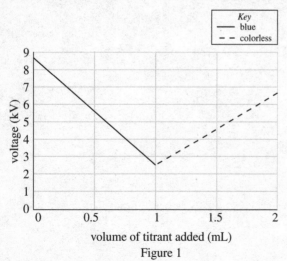

volume of titrant added (mL)
Figure 1

Experiment 2

Experiment 1 was repeated, except that the sodium thiosulfate solution was used instead of the SO_2 solution (see Figure 2).

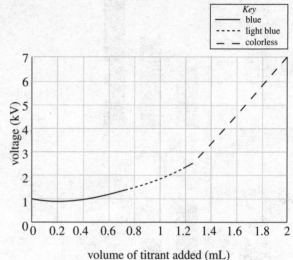

volume of titrant added (mL)
Figure 2

18. In Experiment 1, the analyte was blue at which of the following volumes of titrant added?

F. 0.7 mL
G. 1.1 mL
H. 1.5 mL
J. 1.9 mL

19. In Experiment 2, the analyte was in its reduced form for which of the following volumes of titrant added?

A. 0.3 mL
B. 0.6 mL
C. 0.9 mL
D. 1.2 mL

20. In Experiment 1, if 2.5 mL of titrant was added to the analyte, the voltage would most likely have been:

F. less than 1 kV.
G. between 1 kV and 4 kV.
H. between 4 kV and 7 kV.
J. more than 7 kV.

21. In Experiment 2, which solution was the analyte and which solution was the titrant?

titrant	sample solution
A. Sodium thiosulfate	I
B. SO_2	I_2
C. I_2	Sodium thiosulfate
D. I_2	SO_2

22. In Experiments 1 and 2, the potentiometer that was placed in the analyte most likely did which of the following?

F. Detected the concentration of starch in the solution

G. Conducted an electric current initiated by ions in the solution

H. Heated the solution to its boiling point

J. Cooled to solution to its freezing point

23. A chemist states that in Experiment 2, the analyte was fully reduced with 0.2 mL of titrant added, but not with 1.8 mL of titrant added. Do the results of Experiment 2 support this claim?

A. Yes; at a value of 0.2 mL of titrant added, the analyte was blue, while at a value of 1.8 mL of titrant added, the analyte was colorless.

B. Yes; at a value of 0.2 mL of titrant added, the analyte was colorless, while at a value of 1.8 mL of titrant added, the analyte was blue.

C. No; at a value of 0.2 mL of titrant added, the analyte was blue, while at a value of 1.8 mL of titrant added, the analyte was colorless.

D. No; at a value of 0.2 mL of titrant added, the analyte was colorless, while at a value of 1.8 mL of titrant added, the analyte was blue.

Passage V

An astrophysics class is given the following facts about the burning out of stars.

1. The burning out of a star can be divided into 3 stages: *helium fusion, planetary nebula formation*, and *white dwarf development*.

2. Mid-sized stars fuse hydrogen nuclei (composed of protons) into helium nuclei at their centers, in a process known as helium fusion. These include yellow dwarves, like our Sun, and the slightly smaller orange dwarves. Helium fusion releases a significant amount of kinetic energy.

3. As kinetic energy continues to be released, a planetary nebula may form, in which colorful, ionized gas spreads out from the star's center.

4. The remaining material at the center of the planetary nebula condenses into a white dwarf, which is relatively cool and small in size.

5. Red dwarves are smaller stars that can also carry out helium fusion. These stars can develop into white dwarves sooner than yellow and orange dwarves, and they do not form planetary nebulas.

Two students discuss the eventual fate of three stars in the Alpha Centauri system. Alpha Centauri A, a 1.10-solar-mass yellow dwarf star, where one *solar mass* unit is equivalent to the mass of the Sun; Alpha Centauri B, a 0.91-solar-mass orange dwarf star; and Alpha Centauri C, a 0.12-solar-mass red dwarf star. Alpha Centauri A and B comprise a binary star system that revolves around a common center of mass, while Alpha Centauri C revolves around a nearby center of mass.

Student 1

The 3 stars of the Alpha Centauri system all formed at the same time from the same collection of matter. Alpha Centauri C was initially the most massive of the three stars, and Alpha Centauri A and Alpha Centauri B had the same size. The large Alpha Centauri C had more helium fusion than the other two stars, so it quickly became the smallest of the stars. More of its matter flowed to Alpha Centauri A than to Alpha Centauri B, making Alpha Centauri A slightly larger than Alpha Centauri B.

Student 2

Alpha Centauri A and Alpha Centauri B formed at a different time than Alpha Centauri C. Alpha Centauri A and Alpha Centauri B formed at the same time from a common collection of matter, and Alpha Centauri A was initially more massive than Alpha Centauri B. Alpha Centauri C formed later from a different, smaller collection of matter and never became bigger than a red dwarf. At some point, the small Alpha Centauri C was attracted to the other two stars, resulting in a triple star system.

24. Based on Student 2's discussion, Alpha Centauri C is part of the Alpha Centauri system because of which of the following forces exerted on Alpha Centauri C by the original binary star system?

F. Electromagnetism
G. Gravitation
H. Strong nuclear interaction
J. Weak nuclear interaction

25. Based on Student 1's discussion and Fact 2, while matter flowed between Alpha Centauri C and Alpha Centauri A, Alpha Centauri C released most of its energy by fusing:

A. helium nuclei into hydrogen nuclei at its core.
B. hydrogen nuclei into helium nuclei at its core.
C. helium nuclei into hydrogen nuclei at its periphery.
D. hydrogen nuclei into helium nuclei at its periphery.

26. Suppose that stars that form from the same collection of matter have similar chemical composition, but stars that form from different collections of matter have different chemical compositions. Student 2 would most likely agree with which of the following statements comparing chemical compositions of the stars in the current Alpha Centauri system at the time that they were formed?

F. Alpha Centauri A and Alpha Centauri B had the most similar compositions.
G. Alpha Centauri A and Alpha Centauri C had the most similar compositions.
H. Alpha Centauri B and Alpha Centauri C had the most similar compositions.
J. Alpha Centauri A, Alpha Centauri B, and Alpha Centauri C all had the same compositions.

27. If the mass of the Sun is 2.0×10^{30} g, what is the mass of Alpha Centauri A ?

A. 1.8×10^{30} g
B. 2.0×10^{30} g
C. 2.2×10^{30} g
D. 2.4×10^{32} g

28. Which of the following statements best explains why the process described in Fact 2 requires a high initial temperature and pressure?

F. All electrons are negatively charged, and like charges attract each other.
G. All electrons are negatively charged, and like charges repel each other.
H. All protons are positively charged, and like charges attract each other.
J. All protons are positively charged, and like charges repel each other.

○ ○ ○ ○ ○ ○ ○ ○ ○

29. Based on Fact 5 and Student 1's discussion, which of the 3 stars in the Alpha Centauri system, if any, is most likely to develop into a white dwarf?

    A. Alpha Centauri A

    B. Alpha Centauri B

    C. Alpha Centauri C

    D. The three stars will likely develop into white dwarves at the same time.

30. Based on Fact 5, would Student 2 agree that by the time Alpha Centauri B develops into a white dwarf, it will have spent as much time as a mid-sized star as Alpha Centauri A ?

    F. Yes, because according to Student 2, Alpha Centauri A has always been less massive than Alpha Centauri B.

    G. Yes, because according to Student 2, Alpha Centauri A has always been more massive than Alpha Centauri B.

    H. No, because according to Student 2, Alpha Centauri A has always been less massive than Alpha Centauri B.

    J. No, because according to Student 2, Alpha Centauri A has always been more massive than Alpha Centauri B.

Passage VI

Three experiments were conducted using the gases nitrogen (N_2), nitrogen dioxide (NO_2), and xenon (Xe). For each gas:

1. A cap was placed on a 2 L metal chamber, containing sensors to measure temperature and pressure and a vale to allow gas to enter.

2. Air was pumped out of the chamber until the pressure inside was measured to be 0.00 mmHg.

3. The chamber was placed on an analytical balance, which was then reset to 0.00 g.

4. Some of the gas was added to the chamber.

5. When the gas in the vessel reached room temperature (298 K), the mass and pressure inside were recorded.

6. Steps 4 and 5 were repeated for different masses.

The experiments were repeated using a 4 L metal chamber (see Figures 1 and 2).

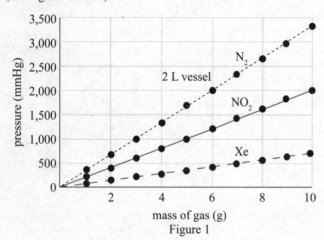

2 L vessel

N_2

NO_2

Xe

mass of gas (g)
Figure 1

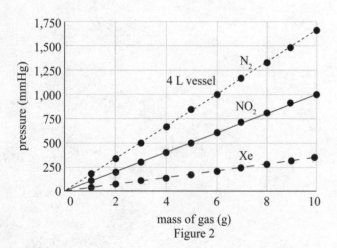

4 L vessel

N_2

NO_2

Xe

mass of gas (g)
Figure 2

31. Based on Figure 2, if 12 g of Xe had been added to the 4 L vessel, the pressure would have been:

A. less than 300 mmHg.
B. between 300 and 600 mmHg.
C. between 600 mmHg and 900 mmHg.
D. greater than 1,200 mmHg.

32. Suppose the experiments had been repeated, except with a 3 L vessel. Based on Figures 1 and 2, the pressure exerted by 10 g of NO_2 would most likely have been:

F. less than 1,000 mmHg.
G. between 1,000 and 2,000 mmHg.
H. between 2,000 and 2,500 mmHg.
J. greater than 2,500 mmHg.

33. Based on Figures 1 and 2, for a given mass of N_2 at 298 K, how does the pressure exerted by the N_2 in a 4 L vessel compare to the pressure exerted by the N_2 in a 2 L vessel? In the 4 L vessel, the N_2 pressure will be:

A. half as great as in the 2 L vessel.
B. the same as in the 2 L vessel.
C. twice as great as in the 2 L vessel.
D. 4 times as great as in the 2 L vessel.

34. Which of the following best explains why equal masses of N_2 and NO_2 at the same temperature and in vessels of similar sizes had different pressures? The pressure exerted by the N_2 was:

    F. greater, because there were fewer N_2 molecules per gram than there were NO_2 molecules per gram.

    G. greater, because there were more N_2 molecules per gram than there were NO_2 molecules per gram.

    H. less, because there were fewer N_2 molecules per gram than there were NO_2 molecules per gram.

    J. less, because there were more N_2 molecules per gram than there were NO_2 molecules per gram.

35. Suppose the experiment involving N_2 and the 4 L vessel had been repeated, except at a temperature of 287 K. For a given mass of N_2, compared to the pressure measured in the original experiment, the pressure measured at 287 K would have been:

    A. greater, because pressure is directly proportional to temperature.

    B. greater, because pressure is inversely proportional to temperature.

    C. less, because pressure is directly proportional to temperature.

    D. less, because pressure is inversely proportional to temperature.

Passage VII

The *absolute threshold pressure for hearing* is the minimum air pressure at each audio frequency that can produce a sound that is detectable by the human ear. The *pain threshold pressure for hearing* is the maximum air pressure at each frequency that the human ear can withstand without sensing pain.

Figure 1 below displays the absolute and pain threshold pressures for hearing in two media: air and water. The figure also shows *P*, the percentage increase in compression of the air or water with increasing sound pressure. Audio frequency is given in cycles per second (cyc/sec), and sound pressure level is given in decibels (db).

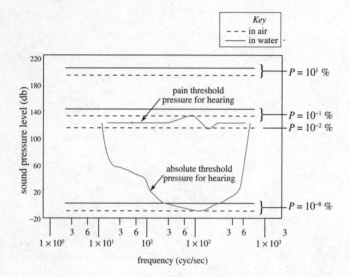

Figure 1

36. According to Figure 1, which of the following is the closest to the highest frequency that can be heard by a human being?

F. 1 cyc/sec
G. 10 cyc/sec
H. 100 cyc/sec
J. 1,000 cyc/sec

37. Based on Figure 1, a sound of a given frequency will have the highest sound level pressure for which of the following sets of conditions?

	Sound in	*P*
A.	Air	$10^{-8}\%$
B.	Air	$10^{-1}\%$
C.	Water	$10^{-8}\%$
D.	Water	$10^{-1}\%$

38. As humans grow older, there is often a loss in the ability to hear sounds at high frequencies. Which of the following figures best illustrates this?

F.

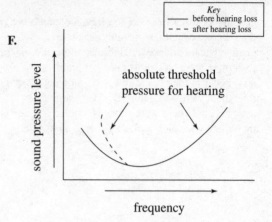

G.

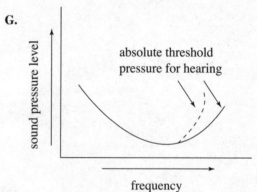

H.

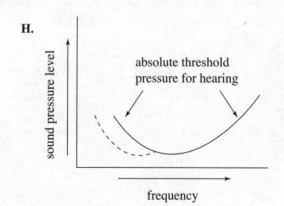

J.

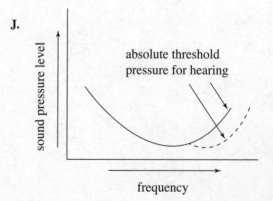

39. A scientist developed a hypothesis that sounds with any sound pressure level would be painful to humans if the frequency were 10^4 cyc/sec. Does the data from Figure 1 support this hypothesis?

   A. No, because humans are unable to hear sounds over 10^4 cyc/sec.
   B. No, because the absolute threshold of pain for hearing is relatively constant with changes in frequency.
   C. Yes, because the absolute threshold of pain for hearing is relatively constant with changes in frequency.
   D. Yes, because as frequency increases above 10^4 cyc/sec, the absolute threshold of pain for hearing also increases.

40. Based on Figure 1, does P depend on the frequency of sound at a given sound pressure level?

   F. No, because as frequency increases, P increases.
   G. No, because as frequency increases, P remains constant.
   H. Yes, because as frequency increases, P increases.
   J. Yes, because as frequency increases, P remains constant.

Chapter 7
Science Practice
Test: Answers and
Explanations

SCIENCE PRACTICE TEST ANSWER KEY

1. B	21. C
2. J	22. G
3. A	23. C
4. H	24. G
5. C	25. B
6. F	26. F
7. B	27. C
8. G	28. J
9. C	29. C
10. F	30. J
11. A	31. B
12. J	32. G
13. B	33. A
14. F	34. G
15. A	35. C
16. G	36. J
17. D	37. D
18. F	38. G
19. D	39. A
20. J	40. G

SCORE YOUR PRACTICE TEST

Step A
Count the number of correct answers: _____. This is your *raw score*.

Step B
Use the score conversion table below to look up your raw score. The number to the left is your *scale score*: _____.

Science Scale Conversion Table

Scale Score	Raw Score	Scale Score	Raw Score	Scale Score	Raw Score
36	40	27	32	18	16–17
35	39	26	30–31	17	15
34	--	25	28–29	16	14
33	38	24	26–27	15	13
32	37	23	25	14	12
31	--	22	23–24	13	11
30	36	21	21–22	12	10
29	35	20	19–20	11	9
28	33–34	19	18	10	7–8

SCIENCE PRACTICE TEST EXPLANATIONS

Passage I

1. **B**   This question asks about Study 1, so we'll need to look at Figure 2. The color intensity for the moths in City Y is shown on the right side of the second graph in black, and the highest percentage of these moths had a color intensity of 8. Eliminate (C) and (D). The color intensity for the moths in City X is shown on the left side of the third graph in gray, and the highest percentage of these moths had a color intensity of 5. Eliminate (A), and the only remaining answer is (B).

2. **J**   The blurb in Study 2 contains the following information: *During dry years, pollutants are more likely to concentrate on tree bark, and the tree bark itself tends to become thicker.* Therefore, bark is thickest during dry years, and of the years listed on Figure 3, only 2003 is listed as a "dry" year, so (J) is the best answer from the given choices.

3. **A**   Study 1 contains the following information: *Scientists captured 100 **B. betularia f. typica** and 100 **B. betularia f. carbonaria** in City X.* Study 2 contains the following information: *During each visit* [from 1983 to 1992], *they captured at least 50 **B. betularia f. typica** moths and measured their body color intensities.* Therefore, it can be assumed that they *did not* catch B. bethularia f. carbonaria in Study 2, making (A) the best answer. For color intensity, note the axes of each of the graphs. Color intensity is a variable plotted along the x-axis in Figure 2 and along the y-axis in Figure 3, meaning that it was measured in both studies.

4. **H**   Choices (H) and (J) are direct opposites, which means that one of them is likely to be true. You'll need to use a bit of science common sense here to choose between these two. In Study 1, the scientists are trying to count the number of moths in these various cities; therefore, in order to make this count accurate, they will need to make sure that each moth is only counted once, as in (H). Choice (F) is incorrect because *pollution* is measured in Study 2, and (G) is incorrect because *wingspan* is not measured in either study.

5. **C**   Figure 3 shows that 2005 was a wet year, and the average color intensity was 10. First, it is clear that moths with higher color intensities are more likely to survive in the wet years than the dry years, so the moth with a color intensity of 9.5 is more likely to survive than the moth with a color intensity of 6.5. Eliminate (A) and (B). Then, notice that Study 2 contains the following information: *During wet years, pollutants tend to be washed from the surfaces of tree bark.* This information agrees with (C).

6. **F**   This question is difficult to answer yes or "No" immediately, so work with the reasons given in each of the answer choices. In City X, the coloration of *B. betularia f. typica* ranges from 5 to 10. In City Y, the coloration of *B. betularia f. typica* ranges from only 7 to 10. Eliminate (G) and (J). The hypothesis that a greater range in body coloration is produced by a diversity in the subspecies is therefore

supported by this information because City X contains two subspecies and City Y contains only one. This question is tricky: You don't need to use the *y*-axis at all because nothing in the question asks about the percent of captured moths. The only variable at play is body coloration.

Passage II

7. **B**   According to Figure 3, the marine deposition of Mg^{2+} is highest in February and lowest in November, making (B) the correct answer. The marine deposition of Cl^- is highest in June and lowest in October, eliminating (A). The marine deposition of Na^+ is highest in November and lowest in July, eliminating (C). The marine deposition of SO_4^{2-} is highest in January and lowest in October, eliminating (D).

8. **G**   Look carefully at Figure 2. The marine deposition of Cl^- is around 950 kg/m^3 except in June, at which point it is much higher. Because it has only this single outlier, we can reasonably expect that the *mean*, or *average*, monthly deposition will be closer to 950, as (G) suggests.

9. **C**   This question is difficult to answer Yes or No immediately, so work with the reasons given in each of the answer choices. Use Figure 3 to check these reasons. According to Figure 3, the monthly deposition of Na^+ is highest in the winter months and lowest in the summer months. We can therefore eliminate (B) and (D), which give information that contradicts Figure 3. This information then *supports* the statement in the problem that the *marine deposition of Na+ is highest in the winter and lowest in the summer*, thus making (C) the correct answer.

10. **F**   The introduction to the passage gives the following information: *Ions in seawater, such as Cl⁻, SO₄²⁻, Na⁺, and Mg₂⁺, are carried down to the ocean floor through a process known as* marine deposition. Therefore, in order for there to be *marine deposition*, ions must be *carried down* somewhere. If the water does not move during an entire month, then the ions will not move and no marine deposition will occur during this month.

11. **A**   Make sure you pay careful attention to the key in Figure 4. According to Figure 4, the annual marine depositions of both ions were highest in the Arctic Ocean, the site farthest from the Atlantic Ocean. The annual marine depositions of both ions decrease as the sensor gets closer to the Atlantic Ocean site.

12. **J**   According to Figure 3, the marine deposition of SO_4^{2-} was not studied, eliminating (F). The marine deposition of Mg^{2+} changed during the study, eliminate (G). According to Figure 1, the movement of water during the month changed every month during the twelve-month period, eliminating (H). Only the location of the study, the Atlantic Ocean, was held constant, making (J) the correct answer. The location of the study was not changed until Study 3.

Passage III

13. **B**   We're dealing with Figure 2, which shows the data for the canopy layer. The question asks about the leaf area index, so we need the solid line and the y-axis shown on the left side of the figure. Once all those elements are in place, you find that the leaf area index in Year 14 was closest to 1.3. Make sure you are dealing with the correct figure and the correct axes given on that figure.

14. **F**   Table 1 shows a direct relationship: As precipitation goes up, leaf-area index goes up. Therefore, we can expect the leaf-area index at 1.70 mm/km²/yr of precipitation to be below the leaf-area index at 1.80 mm/km²/yr. The leaf-area index at 1.80 mm/km²/yr is 5.2, and the only answer choice that gives a value in between is (F).

15. **A**   This problem asks about the *canopy* layer and the *understory* layer, so we will need to use Figures 2 and 3. Take a look at these two graphs: The two curves in the *canopy*-layer graph seem to go up and down at roughly the same rate, whereas the two curves in the *understory*-layer graph don't seem to have a consistent relationship. Because the *canopy*-layer graph shows a more consistent relationship, we can eliminate (B) and (D). A more consistent *canopy*-layer graph also *disagrees* with the botanist's statement from the problem, eliminating (C). Only (A) contains the correct answer to the question and the correct reason for that answer.

16. **G**   Use Figures 1, 2, and 3 to determine each of the annual precipitation values in Year 7. This is the dotted curve, and the values are on the y-axis on the right side of each figure. For the *emergent* layer shown in Figure 1, the annual precipitation was roughly 1.33. For the *canopy* layer shown in Figure 2, the annual precipitation was roughly 1.0. For the *understory* layer shown in Figure 3, the annual precipitation was roughly 0.67. You don't need to worry about exact figures: *emergent* should be the largest and *understory* should be the smallest. Only (G) works.

17. **D**   Use POE. All the answers use values of meters above the rainforest, but meters is not a variable on any figure. A quick scan of the introduction for those values identifies "0–30" as the understory layer, "30–45" as the canopy layer, and "45–55" as the emergent layer. Eliminate (A) and (C) since each addresses the canopy layer and the question is about the other two. Choice (B) is disproven by Figure 3, and (D) is proven by Figures 1 and 3.

Passage IV

18. **F**   Use Figure 1. The key in the corner of the graph says that the anything graphed with a solid line is *blue,* and anything graphed with a dotted line is *colorless.* The curve shown in this graph changes from solid to dotted at 1 mL of titrant added, meaning that all the solution at all values less than 1 mL will be blue, and the solution at all values greater than 1 mL will be colorless. The only one of the answer choices that gives a value less than 1 mL is (F).

19. **D**   The blurb contains the following sentence: Starch and I_2 form a complex with a deep blue color, but when I_2 is reduced to 2 iodide (I^-) ions, the complex dissipates and the solution becomes colorless. In other words, when the solution is reduced, it becomes colorless. According to Figure 2, the solution is colorless (and therefore reduced) above 1 mL of titrant added. Only (D) gives a value greater than 1 mL.

20. **J**   Figure 2 does not show the voltage at 2.5 mL of titrant added, but the curve follows a clear trend. As the volume of titrant added increases, the voltage increases as well. At 2 mL of titrant added, the voltage is equivalent to 7 kV. Therefore, at 2.5 mL of titrant added, the voltage will most likely be greater than 7 kV, as in (J).

21. **C**   The experiment detailed in this passage is described in the first line as follows: *Oxidation-reduction titration is a method in which precise volumes of a titrant (an oxidizing or reducing agent) are added dropwise to a known volume of an analyte (a reducing or oxidizing agent, respectively)*. In other words, one substance (the titrant) is added gradually to a certain amount of another substance (the analyte). Therefore, when Experiment 1 says that the I_2 solution was incrementally added to the SO_2 solution, it can be inferred that the I_2 is the titrant, and the SO_2 is the analyte. In Experiment 2, the sodium thiosulfate solution was used instead of the SO_2 solution; therefore, in Experiment 2, the I_2 is still the titrant, and the sodium thiosulfate solution is the analyte, as in (C). If you picked (D), be careful—you may not have noticed the change from Experiment 1 to Experiment 2.

22. **G**   Use POE. Experiment 1 contains the following information: *A potentiometer, which acts as a control input for electronic circuits, was placed in the solution*. The key word here is *electric currents*. There's nothing to suggest that the potentiometer has anything to do with *concentration*, eliminating (F), or *freezing* or *boiling point*, eliminating (H) and (J). Only (G) contains any reference to *electric currents* and is therefore the best answer.

23. **C**   Use POE. If you're not sure how to answer "Yes" or "No", have a look at the reasons. According to the blurb, starch and I_2 form a complex with a deep blue color, but when I_2 is reduced to 2 iodide (I^-) ions, the complex dissipates and the solution becomes colorless. In other words, when the solution is reduced, it becomes colorless. At 0.2 mL of titrant added, the solution is blue, and at 1.8 mL of titrant added, the solution is colorless. Eliminate (B) and (D), whose reasons contradict this information. Then answer the question: Do these findings agree with the scientist's hypothesis? They don't because the titrant is not reduced at values below 1 mL, so the answer must be no, eliminating (A). Only (C) remains.

Passage V

24. **G**   This question requires a bit of outside knowledge. Student 2 concludes with the following sentence: *At some point, the small Alpha Centauri C was attracted to the other two stars, resulting in a triple star system*. Gravity is the attraction between two objects with mass, so attracted matches up most closely with (G), *gravitation*.

25. **B** Student 1's hypothesis contains the following sentence: *The large Alpha Centauri C had more helium fusion than the other two stars, so it quickly became the smallest of the stars. More of its matter flowed to Alpha Centauri A than to Alpha Centauri B.* In other words, Alpha Centauri C released most of its matter by helium fusion. According to Fact 2, mid-sized stars fuse hydrogen nuclei (composed of protons) into helium nuclei at their centers, in a process known as helium fusion. It can therefore be inferred that Alpha Centauri C, in undergoing this process of helium fusion, was fusing hydrogen nuclei into helium nuclei at its center. Only (B) contains information consistent with Student 1 and Fact 2.

26. **F** Student 2's hypothesis contains the following sentence: *Alpha Centauri A and Alpha Centauri B formed at the same time from a common collection of matter.* As the question suggests, stars that form from the same collection of matter have similar chemical compositions. Therefore, Student 2 would likely suggest that Alpha Centauri A and Alpha Centauri B have similar chemical compositions because they formed *from a common collection of matter.* Alpha Centauri C formed from a different collection of matter, eliminating (G), (H), and (J). Only (F) remains.

27. **C** The introduction to this passage contains the following information: *Alpha Centauri A, a 1.10-solar-mass yellow dwarf star, where one* solar mass *unit is equivalent to the mass of the Sun.* The question states that the mass of the Sun is 2.0×10^{30} g. Therefore, the mass of Alpha Centauri A must be 1.10 times this value, given the definition of solar mass. Don't worry about calculating the exact value: You know that this value must be slightly greater than the mass of the sun, and only (C) gives a value slightly greater than 2.0×10^{30} g.

28. **J** Use POE. This question requires a bit of outside knowledge, but it can be solved easily with a bit of common sense. First of all, Fact 2 states that the nuclei being fused are *composed of protons.* It is therefore not likely that the answer to this question will have anything to do with *electrons,* eliminating (F) and (G). *Helium fusion* describes the process by which these protons are *fused,* or put together. Think about it this way: If these protons are attracted to each other to begin with, do you think it would take a bunch of extra energy to put them together? Not likely! Eliminate (H), and only (J) remains.

29. **C** Fact 5 contains the following information: Red dwarves are smaller stars that can also carry out helium fusion. These stars can develop into white dwarves sooner than yellow and orange dwarves. Student 1 states, *The large Alpha Centauri C had more helium fusion than the other two stars, so it quickly became the smallest of the stars.* Therefore, according to this information, Alpha Centauri C is one of those smaller stars that can develop into white dwarves sooner. Choice (C) is our best answer. Also, Scientist 1 doesn't ever really talk about any differences between Alpha Centauri A and Alpha Centauri B, so it's unlikely that one would be correct and the other incorrect.

30. **J** Use POE. If you're not sure how to answer "Yes" or "No," look at the reasons. Student 2's hypothesis contains the following information: *Alpha Centauri A was initially more massive than Alpha Centauri B.* This eliminates (F) and (H) immediately. Fact 5 contains the following information: *Red dwarves*

are smaller stars that can also carry out helium fusion. These stars can develop into white dwarves sooner than yellow and orange dwarves. Therefore, since Alpha Centauri B is smaller, it is one of the smaller stars that can develop into white dwarves sooner. Therefore, it is not likely that it will spend the same amount of time as a white dwarf. Think about it this way: Fact 5 suggests that the main qualification for a white dwarf is its size. If Student 2 is correct about Alpha Centauri A and Alpha Centauri B having different sizes, their white dwarf qualifications can't be the same, so eliminate (G).

Passage VI

31. **B**   Figure 2 only gives the information up to 10 g of gas added, but fortunately, all these curves have a very consistent relationship: As mass of gas goes up, the pressure goes up. In the 4 L vessel, when 10 g of Xe is added, the pressure is approximately 300 mmHg. At 12 g of Xe, the pressure should be slightly higher, somewhere around 450 mmHg. Only (B) gives a range that contains this value.

32. **G**   As you compare Figures 1 and 2, notice how much higher the pressure values are in Figure 1. It can therefore be assumed that the 2 L vessel has higher pressure values than the 4 L vessel, shown in Figure 2. The pressure values in a 3 L vessel should therefore be greater than those of the 4 L vessel but less than those of the 2 L vessel. In the 2 L vessel, 10 g of NO_2 gives a pressure of approximately 2,000 mmHg. In the 4 L vessel, 10 g of NO_2 gives a pressure of approximately 1,000 mmHg. Therefore, in a 3 L vessel, 10 g of NO_2 should give a pressure between 1,000 and 2,000 mmHg, as in (G).

33. **A**   Temperature is not mentioned in either figure, but the passage indicates that the experiments were conducted at 298 K, so we can use Figures 1 and 2. Since we need to compare the N_2 values from Figures 1 and 2, it's best to find values as exact as possible. Notice that at mass 6 g, the 2 L vessel has a pressure of 2,000 mmHg, and the 4 L vessel has a pressure of 1,000 mmHg. Therefore, the pressure in the 4 L vessel is *half as great as* the pressure in the 2 L vessel. Only (A) works.

34. **G**   Use POE. In Figures 1 and 2, the pressure when N_2 is used is consistently greater than the pressure when the NO_2 is used. Eliminate (H) and (J). Then you'll need a bit of outside knowledge to complete the question. Simply stated, an N_2 molecule has fewer components than an NO_2 molecule, so it has a smaller mass. Therefore, in order to get the same mass of both molecules, we will need more N_2 molecules per gram, eliminating (F).

35. **C**   This question requires a bit of outside knowledge. You need to know the relationship between pressure and temperature: As pressure increases, so does temperature. This is a *direct* relationship, eliminating (B) and (D). Because of this relationship, as the temperature decreases from 298 K to 287 K, the pressure will decrease also, as in (C).

Passage VII

36. **J** The first line of the passage states the following: *The absolute threshold pressure for hearing is the minimum air pressure at each audio frequency that can produce a sound that is detectable by the human ear.* In other words, the absolute threshold pressure for hearing gives the highest pressure and frequency at which humans can hear. In order to answer this question, we'll need to use Figure 1 and the curve labeled *"Absolute pressure threshold for hearing,"* and we will need to find its maximum frequency, listed on the *x*-axis. According to Figure 1, this curve maxes out right around 1×10^3 cyc/sec, or 1,000 cyc/sec, as in (J). If you selected (H) be careful, this is the point of minimum sound pressure level, not the maximum frequency.

37. **D** Use POE. Note the key at the bottom of Figure 1. According to this key, *Water* is shown on the graph with a solid line, and *Air* is shown on the graph with a dotted line. The solid line is consistently higher than the dotted, suggesting that *Water* can withstand higher frequencies, eliminating (A) and (B). Then note the *P*-values on the right side of the graph. According to the graph, these *P*-values increase with increasing sound pressure level, so in order to increase the sound pressure level, we will want the highest possible *P*-value, which in the list of remaining answer choices is 10^{-1}%, as in (D).

38. **G** Use POE. According to this question, some change happens at high frequencies. Accordingly, whichever graph we choose will need to show a change at high frequency, rather than low frequency. Based on this information alone, we can eliminate (F) and (H). The dotted curve (*"after hearing loss"*) should indicate some kind of hearing loss at high frequencies, so it should show a curve that does not quite reach the highest frequencies, as only (G) does. If you selected (J), you may have reversed the two curves.

39. **A** The frequency of 10^4 cyc/sec doesn't appear on the graph, but according to Figure 1, the absolute threshold of hearing is around 10^3 cyc/sec. The pain threshold of hearing is within the absolute threshold, so if 10^4 cyc/sec isn't within the absolute threshold, it won't be within the pain threshold either. Think of it this way: In order for something to hurt when you hear it, you need to be able to hear it first. Therefore, only (A) can work because it is the only answer choice with a reason consistent with the information in Figure 1.

40. **G** Use POE. If you're unsure whether to answer yes or no, check the reasons. Use Figure 1. Frequency appears on the *x*-axis, and Pressure appears on the *y*-axis. According to the lines showing the pressure in *Air* and in *Water*, the increasing frequency has no effect on the pressure values. Eliminate (F) and (H). Therefore, the pressure does *not* depend on the frequency, making (G) the correct answer.

Part III
Math

ALL ABOUT THE MATH TEST

In some ways, the Math test of the ACT is the content-heaviest of all the tests: In other words, there are many problems on the Math that test concepts similar to those you've learned in your Math classes. In fact, ACT makes a big deal about how "curricular" the exam is, claiming that the Math test is "designed to assess the mathematical skills students have typically acquired in courses taken up to the beginning of grade 12." They even go so far as to offer a list of how the topics will break down in any given administration.

Topic	Number of Questions
Pre-algebra	14
Elementary Algebra	10
Intermediate Algebra	9
Plane Geometry	14
Coordinate Geometry	9
Trigonometry	4

But as with all things ACT, these distinctions may not mean a ton to you, the test taker. Nor should they. At best, this chart should help to drive home one main point:

> The Math test of the ACT is roughly half Algebra and half Geometry.

While there's really no substitute for a solid and complete knowledge of Math fundamentals (and not-so-fundamentals), there are a number of ways you can still get a really great Math score by being a smart test taker. You've already seen in the Introduction to this book (pages 4–6) some of the pacing strategies that can help you maximize your scores.

Test Tip
The ACT Math test is in Order of Difficulty. Keep an eye on the question numbers!

Let's have a look in the next two chapters at some of the specific ways you can improve your scores in Algebra and Geometry. As we move through the next two chapters in this book, keep an eye on the problem number. ACT Math is the one section that is in Order of Difficulty, so the problem numbers offer a nice gauge of how difficult ACT considers certain concepts and types of Word Problems.

Chapter 8
Algebra

So you've got roughly 33 algebra questions to tackle on any given Math test. It's probably a good idea to comb the test looking for those 14 pre-algebra questions first, and then to track down the 10 elementary-algebra questions, and then to go back and look for the intermediate-algebra questions, right? No way! That would be a tremendous waste of time, and even a nearly impossible task—what are the distinctions among these three categories anyway?

For our money, it's best to think of Algebra problems (and really all Math problems) as broken down into two categories: *Plug-and-Chug* and *Word Problems*. Plug and Chug questions are short, testing basic rules, formulas, or terms. Word problems are longer and place the math content in the context of a real-life setting. Many of the Math skills you use in these problems will be the same, but each will require a slightly different approach, for the obvious reason that Word Problems require that you deal with, well, words.

But let's start with a nice, straightforward, "Plug and Chug" problem:

MADSPM
(Multiply/Add, Divide/Subtract, Power/Multiply)

When you *multiply* two like bases, you *add* their exponents.

$$\text{e.g., } x^2 \times x^3 = x^5$$

When you *divide* two like bases, you *subtract* their exponents.

$$\text{e.g., } \frac{x^5}{x^3} = x^2$$

When you raise a base to a *power*, you *multiply* the exponents.

$$\text{e.g., } \left(x^2\right)^3 = x^6$$

25. The expression $-4y^2\left(9y^7 - 3y^5\right)$ is equivalent to:

   A. $-36y^9 + 12y^7$

   B. $-36y^9 - 12y^7$

   C. $-36y^{14} + 12y^{10}$

   D. $-36y^{14} - 12y^{10}$

   E. $-24y^4$

Here's How to Crack It
Sure, there are words in this problem, but all it's really asking you to do is to match up the expression in the question with one of the expressions in the answer choices. Remember to distribute and use MADSPM.

Let's see how this works with the equation given in question 25.

$$-4y^2(9y^7 - 3y^5) = y^2(-36y^7 + 12y^5)$$
$$= -36y^9 + 12y^7$$

This matches up with (A). If you worked through this problem and got one of the other answer choices, think about what you may have done wrong. If you chose (B), you may have forgotten to distribute the negative sign when you multiplied the −4. If you chose (C), you may have multiplied the exponents rather than adding them together. If you chose (D), you may have multiplied the exponents and forgotten to distribute the negative. If you chose (E), you may have forgotten that when you add or subtract like bases, do nothing to the exponents.

Whatever the case may be, don't sell these problems short. Even though they don't take as long, they're worth just as much as the "harder" problems. Recall from the introduction how few questions you really need to pull up your math score. Make sure you work carefully on all your Now and Later questions. There is no partial credit on the ACT, so a careless error leaves you with an answer just as wrong as a random guess.

> Fixing a few careless math errors can improve your ACT Math score significantly by ensuring that you get all the points on questions you know how to do.

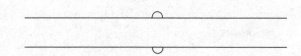

Let's take a look at the next question.

43. $4x^2 + 20x + 24$ is equivalent to:

    A. $(4x + 4)(x + 6)$
    B. $(4x − 4)(x − 6)$
    C. $(4x + 24)(x − 1)$
    D. $2(2x − 4)(x − 3)$
    E. $2(2x + 4)(x + 3)$

This one looks a lot like question 25, but the math is a good deal more difficult. In fact, even if you're pretty good at factoring quadratic equations, you might still find this one to be a bit of an issue. If you can do the factoring quickly and accurately, great, but if not, help is on the way!

PLUGGING IN

When you look at topic breakdown for the ACT, what is it about "Pre-algebra" that sounds so much easier than "Intermediate" or even "Elementary Algebra"? Well, for one thing, with Algebra inevitably come *variables*. You probably remember first hearing about these things in sixth or seventh grade and thinking to yourself how much easier life was when math was just plain numbers.

Here's the good news. Many of the algebra problems on the ACT, even the most complex, can be solved with what we like to call *Plugging In*. What Plugging In enables you to do is to solve difficult variable problems using basic arithmetic.

First, you'll need to identify whether you can Plug In.

Plug It In

A content-based approach to math questions isn't always necessary! Simply "Plug In" to find the correct answer.

Plug In when

- there are variables in the answer choices

- there are variables in the question

- the question is dealing with fractions, percents, or other relational numbers

Here's How to Crack It

Plugging In works with both Word Problems and Plug and Chug questions. Question 43 may look like it requires a "content-based" approach, but let's see how much easier it is if we Plug In.

First, let's Plug In a number for the variable. The best numbers to Plug In are usually small and easy to deal with: numbers such as 2, 5, and 10. Let's try 2 in this problem. If $x = 2$,

$$4(2)^2 + 20(2) + 24 = 4(4) + 20(2) + 24$$
$$= 16 + 40 + 24$$
$$= 56 + 24$$
$$= 80$$

So if we Plug In 2 everywhere there's an x, the expression gives us 80. Now, since the question is merely asking for an equivalent expression, we will want the same result as we plug our value into the answer choices. In this case, 80 is our *target answer*. Let's go to the answer choices and see which one matches up:

43. $4(2)^2 + 20(2) + 24$ is equivalent to $\boxed{80}$.

   A. $(4(2) + 4)((2) + 6) = (12)(8) = 96$
   B. $(4(2) - 4)((2) - 6) = (4)(-4) = -16$
   C. $(4(2) - 24)((2) - 1) = (-16)(1) = -16$
   D. $2(2(2) - 4)((2) - 3) = 2(0)(-1) = 0$
   E. $2(2(2) + 4)((2) + 3) = 2(8)(5) = 80$

The only one that matches up is (E), the correct answer. No quadratic formula or difficult factoring required!

Let's review the steps:

> Once you've determined that you can Plug In, follow these steps.
>
> 1. Plug In an easy-to-use value for your variable or variables.
>
> 2. Work the information in the question using the numbers you've Plugged In to find a *target answer.*
>
> 3. Plug the variables into the answer choices to find the one that matches up with the target.
>
> 4. Make sure you check all the answer choices. If more than one answer choice works, Plug In a new set of numbers and try again.

Let's try another one.

———————○———————

28. As part of an analysis to determine how summer vacations affect students' retention of school materials, scientists conducted an experiment. As shown in the chart below, they showed the time, d days, since the student had finished and the number of facts, f, that the student remembered from the previous year.

d	1	3	5	7	9
f	96	72	48	24	0

Which of the following equations represents all the data found in this study?

F. $f = 9 - d$

G. $f = 3(9 - d)$

H. $f = 3d + 3$

J. $f = 3(36 - 4d)$

K. $f = 96d$

Here's How to Crack It

This problem looks very different from our last two, but notice that it has some important features in common with them. Most important for our purposes are the variables in the answer choices. With these we know that we can Plug In on this question.

This problem is much bulkier than the last two, though, and in many ways more intimidating. This is because it's a *Word Problem*. As we mentioned earlier in this chapter, even though Word Problems often use the same mathematical concepts, they ask about them in much more convoluted ways. Here's a simple Basic Approach for dealing with Word Problems.

When dealing with Word Problems on the ACT Math test

1. **Know the question.** Read the whole problem before calculating anything, and underline the actual question.

2. **Let the answers help.** Look for clues on how to solve and ways to use POE (Process of Elimination).

3. **Break the problem into bite-sized pieces.** Watch out for tricky phrasing.

Let's use these steps to solve this problem.

1. **Know the question.** We need to find an equation that can accommodate all of the information in the table for d and f. The question in this problem is below the chart. How much of the other stuff do we need? Not much.
2. **Let the answers help.** Remember how important the answers have been in what we've done so far in this chapter. If there are variables in those answer choices, we can usually Plug In. We have variables in these answer choices, so we'll plan to Plug In here.
3. **Break the problem into bite-sized pieces.** We know we need an equation that will work for all the points in this chart. Let's pick one set of points that will be easy to test, and then a second set to confirm our answers. Go easy on yourself! There's no reason to pick the biggest numbers. Let's try first the point to the far right of the chart: $d = 9$, $f = 0$. We want an equation that will work for these points, so let's try the answers:

    F. $0 = 9 - 9$ ✔

    G. $0 = 3(9 - 9)$ ✔

    H. $0 = 3(9) + 3$ ✗

    J. $0 = 3(36 - 4(9))$ ✔

    K. $0 = 96(9)$ ✔

Okay, we've eliminated two of the answer choices. Now let's try another set of points: $d = 7, f = 24$.

F. $24 = 9 - 7$ ✗
G. $24 = 3(9 - 7)$ ✗
H. $f = 3d + 3$
J. $24 = 3(36 - 4(7))$ ✔
K. $f = 96d$

Only one remains, and our best answer is (J). All using basic arithmetic in the formulas provided.

———————◯———————

PLUGGING IN THE ANSWERS

Now, what happens when we don't have the hallmarks of easy Plugging In problems: variables in the answer choices or in the problem? Like question 45:

———————◯———————

45. A high-school basketball player has shot 170 free throws and has made 100 of those free throws. Starting now, if she makes each free throw she attempts, what is the least number of free throws she must attempt in order to raise her free-throw percentage to at least 70% ?

A. 19
B. 20
C. 63
D. 64
E. 70

In this problem, there are no variables anywhere to be seen. Still, we're going to need to put together some kind of equation or something that will enable us to answer the question. For this one, we can *Plug in the Answers* (PITA).

PITA when

- the question asks for a specific amount. Look for "How many?" or "How much?" or "What is the value of?"

- there are no variables in the answer choices

Care for Some PITA?
Note that the PITA strategy is slightly different from just Plugging In. With PITA, you're specifically using the answer choices.

Question 45 is a Word Problem, so let's go through the steps:

1. **Know the question.** We need to figure out how many additional free throws this player will need to have a free-throw percentage of 70%. Also, when ACT italicizes or capitalizes a word, pay special attention. In this case, they've italicized the word *least*. Keep this in mind, it tells you that a number of the answer choices may work, but the correct will be the *least* of these. The phrase "What is the least number?" is the kind of very specific question that usually makes for a good PITA problem.

2. **Let the answers help.** There are no variables in these answer choices, and that coupled with the fact that it asks for a specific value is a good indication that we'll be using these answer choices to PITA. Notice the answer choices are listed in ascending order, which means it might be smart to start with the middle choice. That way we can eliminate answers that are too high or too low.

3. **Break the problem into bite-sized pieces.** With many PITA problems, it can help to create columns, building on the information given in the answer choices and the problem. Start with the question that's being asked: You've already got five possible answers to that question.

45. A high-school basketball player has shot 170 free throws and has made 100 of those free throws. Starting now, if she makes each free throw she attempts, <u>what is the least number of free throws she must attempt in order to raise her free-throw percentage to at least 70% ?</u>

Free-throws	Total free-throws	Total completed	Percentage free-throws
A. 19			
B. 20			
C. 63	233	163	69.9%
D. 64			
E. 70			

Here's How to Crack It

As (C) has shown, 63 additional free throws only raises the percentage to 69.9%. We know this is wrong because we want to raise it to 70%. Therefore, since (C) gives a value that is too small, (A) and (B) must be too small as well. Let's try (D).

Our best answer here is (D) because it produces a free-throw percentage of 70.1%. Choice (E) will produce a percentage greater than 70% as well, but remember, this question is asking for the *least*.

45. A high-school basketball player has shot 170 free throws and has made 100 of those free throws. Starting now, if she makes each free throw she attempts, <u>what is the least number of free throws she must attempt in order to raise her free-throw percentage to at least 70% ?</u>

	Free-throws	Total free-throws	Total completed	Percentage free-throws
~~A.~~	~~19~~	189	89	47.1
~~B.~~	~~20~~	190	90	47.4%
~~C.~~	~~63~~	233	163	69.9%
D.	64	234	164	70.1%
E.	70			

Let's review what we've learned about this type of question so far.

When you've identified a problem as a PITA problem, do the following:

- Start with the middle answer choice. This can help with POE (Process of Elimination).

- Label your answer choices—they answer the question you underlined in the problem.

- When you find the correct answer, stop! But make sure you're answering the right question.

- Make sure you account for all the relevant information. PITA is most effective in simplifying difficult Word Problems, but make sure you've got everything you need!

Let's try another problem.

18. The product of two distinct integers is 192. If the sum of those same two integers is 28, what is the value of the larger of the two integers?

F. 18
G. 16
H. 12
J. 10
K. 8

Here's How to Crack It
Let's go through the steps.

1. **Know the question.** "What is the value of the larger of the two integers?" The key word here is *larger*. The numbers in the answer choices will be possibilities for this *larger* value. Notice this is asking for a specific value, which means we can PITA.
2. **Let the answers help.** We've got a list of non-variable answers in ascending order. Each one offers a possible answer to the specific question posed in the problem. Let's PITA, and use the answers to work backwards through the problem.
3. **Break the problem into bite-sized pieces.** Even though this is a short problem, there's a lot of information here, so we should use columns to help us keep all the information straight. The problem says that the *sum* of the two integers is 28, so let's start there. Begin with (C) to help with Process of Elimination.

18. The product of two distinct integers is 192. If the sum of those same two integers is 28, <u>what is the value of the larger of the two integers?</u>

Larger integer	Smaller integer	(Larger × Smaller) = 192?
F. 18		
G. 16		
H. 12	16	CAN'T WORK
J. 10		
K. 8		

We can eliminate (H) right off the bat. Just from what we've found, 12 can't be the *larger* integer if 16 is the *smaller* integer. We will therefore need a number larger than 12, so we can eliminate (J) and (K) as well. Let's try (G).

18. The product of two distinct integers is 192. If the sum of those same two integers is 28, <u>what is the value of the larger of the two integers?</u>

Larger integer	Smaller integer	(Larger × Smaller) = 192?
F. 18		
G. 16	12	16 × 12 = 192 Yes!
~~**H.** 12~~	~~16~~	~~CAN'T WORK~~
~~**J.** 10~~		
~~**K.** 8~~		

Choice (G) works, so we can stop there. Notice how PITA and Plugging In have enabled us to do these problems quickly and accurately without getting bogged down in generating difficult algebraic formulas.

A NOTE ON PLUGGING IN AND PITA

Plugging In and PITA are not the only ways to solve these problems, and it may feel weird using these methods instead of trying to do these problems "the real way." You may have even found that you knew how to work with the variables in Plugging In problems or how to write the appropriate equations for the PITA problems. If you can do either of those things, you're already on your way to a great Math score.

But think about it this way. We've already said that ACT doesn't give any partial credit. So do you think doing it "the real way" gets you any extra points? It doesn't: On the ACT, a right answer is a right answer, no matter how you get it. "The real way" is great, but unfortunately, it's often a lot more complex and offers a lot more opportunities to make careless errors.

The biggest problem with doing things the real way, though, is that it essentially requires that you invent a new approach for every problem. Instead, notice what we've given you here: two strategies that will work toward getting you the right answer on any number of questions. You may have heard the saying, "Give a man a fish and you've fed him for a day, but teach a man to fish and you've fed him for a lifetime." Now, don't worry, our delusions of grandeur are not quite so extreme, but Plugging In and PITA are useful in a similar way. Rather than giving you a detailed description of how to create formulas and work through them for these problems that won't themselves ever appear on an ACT again, we're giving you a strategy that will help you to work through any number of similar problems in future ACTs.

Try these strategies on your own in the drill that concludes this chapter.

PLUGGING IN AND PITA DRILL 1

2. If $\dfrac{3n}{4} - 7 = 2$, then $n =$

   F. -9

   G. $-\dfrac{7}{3}$

   H. $\dfrac{7}{3}$

   J. 9

   K. 12

9. Which of the following expressions is equivalent to $(3x^2 - 2x + 4) + (2x - 1) - (x^2 - 3x + 2)$?

   A. $x^2 - 2x + 3$
   B. $x^2 + 2x - 1$
   C. $2x^2 - 3x - 5$
   D. $2x^2 - 3x - 1$
   E. $2x^2 + 3x + 1$

11. If b is a positive integer greater than 1, what is the smallest integer value of a for which there exists a value of b such that $\sqrt{a} - b^2 > 0$?

   A. 5
   B. 16
   C. 25
   D. 36
   E. 49

16. Which of the following expressions is equivalent to $\dfrac{p^2 - 3p}{2p} + \dfrac{1}{p^2}$?

   F. $\dfrac{p^2 - 3p + 1}{2p^3}$

   G. $\dfrac{2p^2}{p^3 - 3p^2 + 2}$

   H. $\dfrac{p^3 - 3p^2 + 2}{2p^2}$

   J. $\dfrac{p - 3p^2}{p^3 + 4}$

   K. $\dfrac{2 - p^2}{p^2 + p - 2}$

18. Amethyst's route to work is 48 miles long. Along the way, she stops for coffee and notices that the ratio of the number of miles she's driven so far to the number of miles left to go is 3:1. How many miles does she have left to drive?

   F.   6
   G.   12
   H.   24
   J.   30
   K.   36

23. If $\dfrac{w - 1}{2} = z$ and $\dfrac{w + z}{2} = 11$, then which of the following is equivalent to z ?

   A.   5
   B.   7
   C.   11
   D.   13
   E.   15

24. A salesman earns \$600 per week in base salary. For each successful sale, he receives \$125 in commission. Which of the following represents the amount of money, in dollars, the salesman earns in a given week in which he makes s successful sales?

   F. $725s$
   G. $125s - 600$
   H. $600s + 125$
   J. $600 - 125s$
   K. $600 + 125s$

27. The expression $(n^2 - 6n + 5)(n + 4)$ is equivalent to:

   A. $n^3 - 2n^2 - 19n + 20$
   B. $n^3 - n^2 + 9n + 20$
   C. $n^3 - 2n^2 - 7n + 20$
   D. $n^3 + 2n^2 - 24n + 20$
   E. $n^3 - 2n^2 - 29n + 20$

30. If $|2n + 6| = |3n + 4|$, then what are the possible values of n ?

   F.   0 and 2
   G.   0 and -2
   H. -2 and 2
   J.   2 only
   K. -2 only

32. If $f(a) = a^2 + 3$ and $g(a) = 3a - 1$, which of the following is an expression for $g(f(a))$?

    F. $a^2 + 3a + 2$
    G. $3a^2 - 3$
    H. $-a^2 + 3a - 2$
    J. $3a^2 + 9a - 3$
    K. $3a^2 + 8$

40. In a professional sports league consisting of x teams, y represents the number of teams that qualify for the playoffs in a given season. Which of the following could be used to determine the fraction of teams that does NOT make the playoffs in a given season?

    F. $\dfrac{x-y}{x}$

    G. $\dfrac{y-x}{x}$

    H. $\dfrac{y}{x}$

    J. $\dfrac{x-y}{y}$

    K. $\dfrac{x+y}{x}$

41. For positive real numbers x, y, and z such that $3x = 4y$ and $\dfrac{2}{3}y = \dfrac{1}{3}z$, which of the following inequalities is true?

    A. $x < y < z$
    B. $x < z < y$
    C. $y < x < z$
    D. $y < z < x$
    E. $z < y < x$

45. Which of the following gives the solution set for $\sqrt[3]{(n^2 - 6n)} = 3$?

    A. $\{3\}$
    B. $\{2 \pm \sqrt{3}\}$
    C. $\{-3, 9\}$
    D. $\{3, -9\}$
    E. $\{27\}$

46. If $x > y$, then $-|y - x|$ is equivalent to which of the following?

    F. $\sqrt{y - x}$
    G. $x - y$
    H. $|y - x|$
    J. $-(x - y)$
    K. $|x - y|$

48. If $-1 < x < 0$, then which of the following must be true?

    F. $0^x > 0$

    G. $-\dfrac{1}{x} > 1$

    H. $x + \dfrac{1}{x} = 0$

    J. $\dfrac{1}{x} > 0$

    K. $x^0 < 0$

49. If n is a real number, then what is the solution to the equation $27^{2n} = 81^{(n+1)}$?

    A. $n = 0$
    B. $n = 1$
    C. $n = 2$
    D. $n = 3$
    E. $n = 4$

55. Which of the following is an irrational value of n that is a solution to the equation $|n^2 - 30| - 6 = 0$?

    A. $\sqrt{6}$
    B. 6
    C. $2\sqrt{6}$
    D. $3\sqrt{6}$
    E. $4\sqrt{6}$

59. Consider all pairs of positive integers a and b whose sum is 6. For how many values of a does $a^b = b^a$?

    A. None
    B. 1
    C. 2
    D. 3
    E. 6

PLUGGING IN AND PITA DRILL 1 ANSWER KEY

2. K
9. E
11. C
16. H
18. G
23. B
24. K
27. A
30. H
32. K
40. F
41. C
45. C
46. J
48. G
49. C
55. C
59. D

PLUGGING IN AND PITA DRILL 1 EXPLANATIONS

2. **K**   Plug In the Answers on this one. No harm in starting with the middle answer choice, but if you want this problem to be as easy as possible (and it is question 2, so it should be relatively easy), you might try the whole numbers in the answers first. With (J), it means that $\frac{3(9)}{4} - 2 = 7$. Since $\frac{3(9)}{4} = 6.75$, you can eliminate it. Try (K): $\frac{3(12)}{4} - 2 = 7$. $\frac{3(12)}{4} = 9$, and $9 - 2 = 7$, so you've found your answer.

9. **E**   If the expressions confuse you, just plug in an easy number, such as $x = 2$. Substitute it into the equation: $(3(2)^2 - 2(2) + 4) + (2(2) - 1) - ((2)^2 - 3(2) + 2)$. Do the exponents and multiplication first: $(12 - 4 + 4) + (4 - 1) - (4 - 6 + 2)$. Now do the addition and subtraction: $12 + 3 - 0 = 15$. Our target is 15. Now plug 2 into each of the answers, and pick the one that equals 15. It's (E). Don't forget to check all five answers.

11. **C**   This is a tricky and confusing problem made simple by Plugging In the Answers. Since the problem asks for the smallest possible value of a, start with the smallest answer choice. Work your way up to 25, and the problem reads $\sqrt{25} - b^2 > 0$. The question becomes, "Is there a value of b (remember, b must be an integer greater than 1) that makes that equation true?" Sure there is: If $b = 2$, then $5 - 4 > 0$.

16. **H**   The algebra is fairly complicated here, so the best approach is to plug in a relatively small and simple number. If you say, for example, that $p = 3$, then the original expression comes out to $\frac{1}{9}$; this is your target answer. Now plug $p = 3$ into the expressions in the answer choices in order to determine which one matches your target answer. Choice (F) becomes $\frac{1}{54}$; (G) becomes 9; (H) becomes $\frac{1}{9}$; (J) becomes $-\frac{24}{31}$; and (K) becomes $-\frac{7}{10}$. Choice (H) is therefore the only one that matches your target, and thus is correct.

18. **G**   Note that the problem is asking for the number of miles left to go. Plug In the Answers starting with (H). If she has 24 miles left, then she's halfway there—that's not far enough along, so eliminate (H) and any answer with higher mileage. Plug in (G). If she's got 12 miles left to go, that means $48 - 12 = 36$, meaning she's driven 36 miles so far. Since the ratio of 36:12 is 3:1, (G) is your answer.

23. **B**   This question is best approached through PITA. Since all of the answer choices are integers, start with the one in the middle, (C). If $z = 11$, then $\frac{w-1}{2} = 11$. Multiply both sides by 2 and solve to determine that $w = 23$. If you put these two values into the left-hand side of the second equation provided in the question stem, you get $\frac{23+11}{2} = \frac{34}{2} = 17$. This is too big, so eliminate (C) and test (B). If $z = 7$, then $\frac{w-1}{2} = 7$. Multiply both sides by 2 and solve to determine that $w = 15$. If you put these two values into the left-hand side of the second equation provided in the question stem, you get $\frac{15+7}{2} = \frac{22}{2} = 11$. This matches the information in the question stem, and thus (B) is correct.

24. **K**   Plug In a small number for the number of sales he's completed so the math is as easy as possible. If he completed 2 sales, then he's made $250 commission to go with his $600 base salary, for total earnings of $850. Choice (K) gets you the same value.

27. **A**   Play it safe and Plug In 2. $(2^2 - 6(2) + 5)(2 + 4)$ means $(4 - 12 + 5)(6)$, which gives you -18 as a target answer. Choice (A) will read $2^3 - 2(2)^2 - 19(2) + 20$. Simplified, $8 - 8 - 38 + 20 = -18$.

30. **H**   This question is best approached through PITA. The answer choices are all different combinations of three numbers: 2, −2, and 0. So these numbers need to be plugged in. If $n = -2$, then the left-hand side of the equation is $|2(-2) + 6| = |-4 + 6| = |2| = 2$. If $n = -2$, then the right-hand side of the equation is $|3(-2) + 4| = |-6 + 4| = |-2| = 2$. This works, so any answer choice that does not have $n = -2$ as a solution can be eliminated; cross off (F) and (J). Now try the other solution from (H): if $n = 2$, then the left-hand side of the equation is $|2(2) + 6| = |4 + 6| = |10| = 10$. If $n = 2$, then the right-hand side of the equation is $|3(2) + 4| = |6 + 4| = |10| = 10$. This also works, so (H) is the correct answer.

32. **K**   When you have one function inside another, start with the one on the inside and work your way out. And of course, you should Plug In! So plug in 2, and start with $f(2) = 2^2 + 3$. That means $f(2) = 7$. That's now the value you can plug in to the other function: $g(7) = 3(7) - 1$, so your target answer is 20. Plug 2 into the answer choices, and (K) will read $3(2)^2 + 8$, which is 20.

40. **F**   Plug In values for the number of teams in the league and the number of teams that qualify for the playoffs. Say there are 15 teams in the league (represented by x) and 8 of them qualify (represented by y). That leaves 7 for the number of teams that do not qualify, which means that your target answer is $\frac{7}{15}$. Choice (F) becomes $\frac{15-8}{15}$, or $\frac{7}{15}$.

41. **C**   Plugging In is the easiest way to solve this problem, but we need to choose numbers that work with the given equations. Start with the first equation, $3x = 4y$. The easy thing to do here is choose $x = 4$ and $y = 3$ because $(3)(4) = (4)(3)$. Now we can solve the second equation: $\frac{2}{3}(3) = \frac{1}{3}z$, so $2 = \frac{1}{3}z$ and $z = 6$. Now it's a simple matter to put them in order: $3 < 4 < 6$, so $y < x < z$.

45. **C**   To make things a little easier, you can cube both sides to get rid of the radical. The right side of the equation is now 27. Now, Plug In the Answers and see which one works. In (C), $(-3)^2 - 6(-3) = 9 - (-18) = 27$, and $(9)^2 - 6(9) = 81 - 54 = 27$.

46. **J**   Plug In anything you want as long as $x > y$, such as $x = 3$ and $y = 2$. In the original problem, $-|2 - 3| = -|-1|$, so the target answer is -1. Try this out in the answer choices. Choice (J) works: $-(3 - 2) = -1$.

48. **G**   This question can be approached by thinking about abstract number properties, but it is easier to plug in a simple number for x and check whether the answer choices are true. Try an easy number, such as $x = -\frac{1}{2}$. Choice (F) becomes $0^{-\frac{1}{2}} = 0$, which is not greater than 0; eliminate (F). Choice (G) becomes $-\frac{1}{-\frac{1}{2}} = \frac{1}{\frac{1}{2}} = 2$, which is greater than 1, so keep (G) for now. Choice (H) becomes $-\frac{1}{2} + \frac{1}{-\frac{1}{2}} = -\frac{1}{2} + (-2) = -2\frac{1}{2}$, which is not equal to 0; eliminate (H). Choice (J) becomes $\frac{1}{-\frac{1}{2}} = -2$, which is not greater than 0; eliminate (J). Choice (K) becomes $\left(-\frac{1}{2}\right)^0 = 1$, which is not less than 0; eliminate (K) and choose (G).

49. **C**   This question is best approached by Plugging In the Answers. Start with (C): if $n = 2$, then the equation becomes $27^{2(2)} = 81^{2+1}$ or $27^4 = 81^3$. Put these numbers into your calculator to determine whether they are, in fact, equal. Both 27^4 and 81^3 are equal to 531,441, so (C) is correct.

55. **C**   The problem asks for an irrational solution, so while (B) would work, it is rational, so cross it off. Then Plug In the Answers. When you Plug In the value in (C), the equation reads $\left|(2\sqrt{6})^2 - 30\right| - 6 = 0$. When you square $2\sqrt{6}$, you get 24, so it's $|24 - 30| - 6 = 0$. The value inside the absolute value symbol becomes -6, the absolute value of which is 6. The final equation is now much simpler: $6 - 6 = 0$.

59. **D** First, figure out all the pairs of positive integers which add up to 6 and Plug In. 1^5 and 5^1 aren't equal, so try 2 and 4: $2^4 = 4^2$. Be sure to keep track of what the problem asks: How many values of a satisfy the equation? Consider that a could occupy the place of either the 2 or the 4, so those are 2 possible values for a. The last pair of numbers is 3 and 3. Since $3^3 = 3^3$, 3 is the third value for a.

PLUGGING IN AND PITA DRILL 2

3. Which of the following expressions is equivalent to $a^2 - 8a + 16$?

   A. $(a-4)(a-4)$
   B. $(a-4)(a+4)$
   C. $(a-2)(a-8)$
   D. $(a-2)(a+8)$
   E. $(2a-4)(2a-4)$

6. A 62-centimeter-long string is cut into 4 pieces such that the first piece is twice as long as the second piece, the second piece is three times as long as the third piece, and the third piece is three times as long as the fourth piece. How many centimeters in length is the longest of the 4 pieces?

   F. 2
   G. 8
   H. 18
   J. 26
   K. 36

7. The expression $-w[x-(y+z)]$ is equivalent to:

   A. $-wx - wy - wz$
   B. $-wx + wy - wz$
   C. $-wx + wy + wz$
   D. $-wx - y + z$
   E. $wx - y + z$

9. Jenna is swimming laps in a pool on 5 consecutive days. If the numbers below represent the number of laps she swims each day, what 3 numbers should be placed in the blanks below so that the difference between the laps Jenna swims on consecutive days remains the same?

   $$5, \underline{\quad}, \underline{\quad}, \underline{\quad}, 53$$

   A. 12, 24, 36
   B. 16, 32, 48
   C. 17, 29, 41
   D. 20, 30, 40
   E. 21, 29, 37

18. Teddy, Harry, and Obie are buying baseball cards. Teddy always buys cards in packs of 15, Harry always buys cards in packs of 10, and Obie always buys cards in packs of 25. What is the smallest number of cards all three could buy such that they all have the same number of cards?

    F. 25
    G. 150
    H. 250
    J. 750
    K. 3,750

19. Which of the following variable expressions would represent the area of a parallelogram if its base is represented by $a+3$ and its height is represented by $a-5$?

    A. $2a-2$
    B. $a^2 - 15$
    C. $a^2 - 8a - 15$
    D. $a^2 - 2a - 15$
    E. $a^2 - 2a + 15$

20. The expression $(2x+5y)-(3x-2y)$ is equivalent to:

    F. $-x-3y$
    G. $-x+7y$
    H. $x-3y$
    J. $x+7y$
    K. $5x-3y$

21. For all positive integers a, b, and c, which of the following expressions is equivalent to $\dfrac{a-b}{b}$?

    A. $\dfrac{a+b+c}{b+c}$
    B. $\dfrac{a \cdot c - b \cdot c}{b \cdot c}$
    C. $\dfrac{a - b \cdot c}{b \cdot c}$
    D. $\dfrac{a \cdot c + b \cdot c}{b \cdot c}$
    E. $\dfrac{-a - b \cdot c}{-b \cdot c}$

22. Sheldon has 30 comic books. Some of the comic books were originally 10¢, and the others were originally 45¢. The original value of all 30 comic books is $9.65. How many 45¢ comic books does Sheldon have?

  F. 11
  G. 13
  H. 15
  J. 19
  K. 21

23. Let a be a real number. Which of the following is a value of a such that $a^2 + 9a = 0$?

  A. 18
  B. 6
  C. 3
  D. −3
  E. −9

26. Given $7a - b = 2a + 3b$, which of the following is an expression for b ?

  F. $-\left(\dfrac{2a+3b}{7a}\right)$

  G. $-\dfrac{5a}{4}$

  H. $\dfrac{5a}{4}$

  J. $\dfrac{5a}{2}$

  K. $\dfrac{2a+3b}{7a}$

27. The height of a parallelogram is 7 inches shorter than the base from which the height is measured. If the area of the parallelogram is 60 square inches, what is the height, in inches?

  A. 5
  B. 9
  C. 12
  D. 24
  E. 53

33. For all real values y, $\dfrac{\left[4(y-3)\right]^2}{8} = ?$

  A. $\dfrac{1}{2}y^2 - 3y + \dfrac{9}{2}$

  B. $y^2 - 9$

  C. $2y^2 - 18$

  D. $2y^2 - 12y - 18$

  E. $2y^2 - 12y + 18$

35. Brian and Miguel decide to have a race. Miguel decides to give Brian a 20-meter lead at the beginning of the race. Brian runs at a speed of $2\dfrac{1}{2}$ meters per second. Miguel runs at a speed of 5 meters per second. If they start running at the same time, in how many seconds will it take for Miguel to catch Brian?

  A. $2\dfrac{1}{2}$

  B. 4

  C. 8

  D. $12\dfrac{1}{2}$

  E. 20

47. If b is an integer, then the difference of $3b$ and $7b$ is *always* divisible by which of the following?

  A. 3
  B. 4
  C. 7
  D. 10
  E. 21

49. Luree is measuring a quilt that is in the shape of a parallelogram. She discovers that the area of the quilt is A feet squared, and the base is b feet. The height of the parallelogram is y feet longer than its base. Which of the following equations would give Luree the length y in terms of A and b ?

  A. $y = A - 2b$

  B. $y = \dfrac{A}{2} - b$

  C. $y = \dfrac{A}{b}$

  D. $y = \dfrac{A}{b} - b$

  E. $y = \dfrac{A}{b} - 2b$

50. Party Hats X and Y are both right circular cones. The radius of the base of Hat X is 6 times the radius of the base of Hat Y, and the height of Hat X is 3 times the height of Hat Y. The volume of Hat X is how many times the volume of Hat Y ? (Note: $V_{cone} = \dfrac{1}{3}\pi r^2 h$)

  F. 9
  G. 18
  H. 36
  J. 54
  K. 108

51. What real value of x satisfies the equation $27^{x+2} = \dfrac{3^2}{9^{x-3}}$?

A. -1

B. $\dfrac{2}{5}$

C. $\dfrac{3}{2}$

D. 2

E. 3

53. Let x and y be real numbers. If $(x-y)^2 = -2xy$, it *must* be true that:

A. both x and y are zero.
B. both x and y are negative.
C. both x and y are fractions.
D. either x or y is zero.
E. x is positive and y is negative.

PLUGGING IN AND PITA DRILL 2 ANSWER KEY

3. A
6. K
7. C
9. C
18. G
19. D
20. G
21. B
22. J
23. E
26. H
27. A
33. E
35. C
47. B
49. D
50. K
51. B
53. A

PLUGGING IN AND PITA DRILL 2 EXPLANATIONS

3. **A**   If you're not sure how to factor this expression, choose a value for a and find the value of the expression. Then substitute the same value for a to see which of the answer choices has the same value. Try an easy number to avoid complicated calculations, such as $a = 2$. In the original expression, $a^2 - 8a + 16 = (2)^2 - 8(2) + 16 = 4 - 16 + 16 = 4$. When you plug $a = 2$ into each of the answer choices, only (A) gives a value of 4: $(2 - 4)(2 - 4) = (-2)(-2) = 4$.

6. **K**   The question asks for the length of the longest piece of string, so use the provided answers as a guideline. Start in the middle with (H), so the longest piece of string would be 18 centimeters. The second piece of string would be half that length, or 9 centimeters. The third piece of string is one-third the length, or 3 centimeters, and the fourth piece is one-third of that, or 1 centimeter. The sum of these lengths would be 18 + 9 + 3 + 1 = 31, which does not agree with the 62 centimeters given in the question. Eliminate (F) and (G), which will also be too low. With (K), the longest piece of string would have a length of 36 centimeters, the second piece would be 18 centimeters, the third would be 6 centimeters, and the fourth would be 2 centimeters. The total length of all four pieces would be 36 + 18 + 6 + 2 = 62, which agrees with the total given in the question.

7. **C**   Because the distributing in this problem can be difficult, try picking a few values. Keep them simple: let's say $w = 2$, $x = 3$, $y = 4$, and $z = 3$. In the given expression, this will mean $-2\left[3 - (4 + 5)\right] = -2[3 - 9] = -2[-6] = 12$. Plug these numbers in to the answer choices to see which gives a value of 12. Only (C) works, so it is the correct answer.

9. **C**   You can use the answer choices to help solve this question. If you start with (C), the sequence of numbers would be 5, 17, 29, 41, 53. According to the question, the difference between consecutive numbers should remain the same. So, since $17 - 5 = 12$, all the other differences between consecutive numbers should also be 12: $29 - 17 = 12$, $41 - 29 = 12$, and $53 - 41 = 12$, so this is the correct answer. The other choices each have the same difference between the three numbers in the choices themselves, but none of them carries that difference to the 5 and 53 given in the problem. Make sure that you check every pair of consecutive numbers when trying each answer choice, and don't forget the numbers from the problem!

18. **G**   To find the smallest number of cards that all three can buy, use the answer choices. The correct answer will need to be divisible by 10, 15, and 25. Remember, though, that even if an answer choice works, you need to find the *smallest* number, so start with (F). Since 25 is not divisible by either 10 or 15, (F) is not correct. Choice (G) is divisible by 10, 15, and 25, so it is the answer. Choices (H), (J), and (K) are larger than (G), so it is irrelevant whether they are divisible by our numbers or not.

19. **D**   Assign a number to represent the value of a. When choosing a value for a, make sure that the number you choose does not cause either dimension of the parallelogram to be negative. Try $a = 10$, which

means that the base would be 13, and the height would be 5. The formula for area of a parallelogram is $A = bh$, so $A = 13 \times 5 = 65$. When you substitute $a = 10$ into each of the answer choices, only (D) gives has a value of 65.

20. **G**   Since the distributing and subtraction can be complex, try picking values for x and y. If $x = 2$ and $y = 3$, then $(2(2) + 5(3)) - (3(2) - 2(3)) = (4 + 15) - (6 - 6) = 19 - 0 = 19$. Plug these x and y values in to the answer choices to find that only (G) yields a value of 19. If you chose (J), be careful: You may have forgotten to distribute the negative sign.

21. **B**   Choose values for a, b, and c, and substitute those values into the given equation. Then substitute the same values into the answer choices and figure out which choice has the same value. Try $a = 2$, $b = 3$, and $c = 4$. This makes the original expression $\dfrac{a-b}{b} = \dfrac{2-3}{3} = -\dfrac{1}{3}$. Only (B) has the same value: $\dfrac{a \cdot c - b \cdot c}{b \cdot c} = \dfrac{2 \cdot 4 - 3 \cdot 4}{3 \cdot 4} = \dfrac{8-12}{12} = -\dfrac{1}{3}$. If you chose (C) be careful: The c will not divide out of the equation equally if it is not multiplied by the a as well as the b.

22. **J**   Use the provided answer choices to determine the correct number of 45¢ comic books. Start in the middle: this will help with POE. With (H), the total value of the 45¢ comic books would be $0.45 \times 15 = \$6.75$. Since 15 of the comic books are 45¢, the other 15 would be 10¢ comics. So, the total value of the 10¢ comic books would be $0.10 \times 15 = \$1.50$, and the total value for all 30 comic books would be $\$6.75 \times \$1.50 = \$8.25$, which is less than $9.65, the value given in the problem. Therefore, there must be more comic books at 45¢. For (J), the total value would be $\$0.45 \times 19 + \$0.10 \times 11 = \$6.65$. If you chose (F), be careful: This is the number of 10¢ comics.

23. **E**   If you're not sure how to factor this problem, try the numbers from the answer choices. Start in the middle to help with POE. If $a = 3$, then $(3)^2 + 9(3) = 36 \neq 0$, so eliminate (C). You can also eliminate (A) and (B) because those values will be too large. Try (E). If $a = -9$, then $(-9)^2 + 9(-9) = 0$, which works. Choice (E) is therefore the only possible answer.

26. **H**   You can isolate b in the given equation, but you can also plug in a value for a and find the corresponding value for b. Try $a = 4$. If $a = 4$, then $7(4) - b = 2(4) + 3b$, $28 - b = 8 + 3b$, $-4b = -20$, and $b = 5$. Now, plug in 4 for a in each answer choice. Choices (F) and (K) are incorrect because if you want to solve for b, you cannot have b in your expression. Choice (G) forgets to divide by a negative, and (J) results from incorrectly combining the b terms. Only (H) correctly yields the target value of 5.

27. **A**   Use the formula for area of a parallelogram, $A = bh$. Since the answer choices are all possible values for the height of the parallelogram, substitute each choice to figure out which value yields an area of 60 in². With (C), the height would be 12 in., which means that the base is 19 in. because the height is 7 in. shorter than the base. Use the formula for area of a parallelogram to find $A = b \cdot h = 19 \cdot 12 = 228 \text{ in}^2$, which is greater than the target area of 60. Eliminate (C), (D), and

(E), because you'll need a shorter height. Choice (A) gives a height of 5, which results in a base of 12 and an area of $12 \cdot 5 = 60$. If you chose (C), be careful: This is the base of the parallelogram, and the problem is asking for the height.

33. **E**   If you substitute a value for y, you can avoid some of the common algebraic errors. Let $y = 2$. Substitute this into the given expression to get $\dfrac{[4(2-3)]^2}{8} = \dfrac{[4(-1)]^2}{8} = \dfrac{[-4]^2}{8} = \dfrac{16}{8} = 2$. When you substitute $y = 2$ into each of the answer choices, only (E) has a value of 2. If you got one of the other answers, make sure you applied the square to the 4 in the numerator.

35. **C**   To figure out when Miguel will catch Brian, you need to know the time at which their total distances will be the same. Use the numbers in the answer choices to figure out how far each of them traveled and see whether the totals are equivalent. If you try (C), they both have run for 8 seconds. In that time, traveling at 5 meters per second, Miguel will have traveled $8 \times 5 = 40$ meters. Brian, given a 20–meter lead and running at a speed of $2\frac{1}{2}$ meters per second, will have traveled $20 + \left(8 \times 2\frac{1}{2}\right) = 20 + 20 = 40$ meters as well. Since their total distances are equal, Miguel needs 8 seconds to catch Brian. If you chose (B), you may have found only the time it takes Miguel to run 20 m, but remember, Brian is moving also.

47. **B**   Since the question only tells you that b has to be an integer, choose any integer for b and then solve the problem. Try $b = 2$. The two values are then $3(2) = 6$ and $7(2) = 14$, which have a difference of $14 - 6 = 8$. The correct answer must divide evenly into 8, so the answer is (B). If you're not convinced, try another value for b. You'll find that it yields the same final answer.

49. **D**   First, to make the question easier to understand, replace the values for the base and height with actual numbers. Set $b = 3$ and $y = 2$. This means that the base of the parallelogram is 3 feet, and the height of the parallelogram is $b + y = 2 + 3 = 5$ feet. Using the formula for the area of a parallelogram, the resulting area should be $A = b \cdot h = 3 \cdot 5 = 15$ square feet. Substitute the values into the answer choices, and the only equation that is true is the one given in (D).

50. **K**   You can solve this question by choosing values for the dimensions of each hat. Make sure to obey the relationships given in the question. Since Hat Y is the smaller hat, choose the radius and height for Hat Y first. For Hat Y, let $r_Y = 3$ and $h_Y = 2$. Using the given formula for volume of a cone,

$V_Y = \frac{1}{3}\pi(3)^2 \cdot 2 = \frac{1}{3}\pi \cdot 9 \cdot 2 = 6\pi$. The problem states that the base of Hat X is 6 times the radius of the base of Hat Y, so $r_X = 18$. The problem then states that the height of Hat X is 3 times the height of Hat Y, so $h_X = 6$. With these values, $V_Y = \frac{1}{3}\pi(18)^2 \cdot 6 = \frac{1}{3}\pi \cdot 324 \cdot 6 = 648\pi$. To compare V_X to V_Y, divide the two volumes: $\frac{648\pi}{6\pi} = 108$. Choice (F) is the total of the two numbers given in the question, and (G) is their product. If you picked (J), you may have squared the height instead of the radius.

51. **B** You can use the answer choices and your calculator to help you find the value of x. When using your calculator, remember to use parentheses correctly! Start in the middle with (C). Substitute $x = \frac{3}{2}$ into the equation to find $27^{\frac{3}{2}+2} = \frac{3^2}{9^{\frac{3}{2}-3}}$. You'll notice that this gives a *huge* number on the left side of the equation, so let's eliminate (C), (D), and (E), and try something smaller. In (B), if $x = \frac{2}{5}$, then the equation will read $27^{\frac{2}{5}+2} = \frac{3^2}{9^{\frac{2}{5}-3}}$. Calculate these values to find that the two sides are equal, and the correct answer is (B).

53. **A** Find values for x and y that work in the given equation. Let the answers help if you're not sure where to start. If $x = 0$ and $y = 0$, the equation works: $(0 - 0)^2 = -2(0)(0)$ and $0 = 0$. Because these two values work, we can keep (A) and eliminate (B), (C), and (E). Test (D) by plugging in a few values, and you'll find that no other values can work. Only (A) gives the values that *must* be true.

Chapter 9
Geometry

We've seen in the Algebra chapter that a smart test-taking strategy, in and of itself, can improve your Math score. That is no less true for Geometry problems, but for these you typically have to bring a bit more to the table. ACT doesn't give you the formulas like SAT does, so you need to have them stored in your brain (or your calculator) when test day rolls around. Remember, counting Trigonometry, Geometry makes up about half of any given ACT Math test.

THE BASIC APPROACH

Let's try a straightforward geometry problem.

22. In right triangle $\triangle STU$ shown below, V is the midpoint of $\overline{TU}$. In inches, what is the length of $\overline{UV}$?

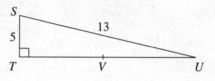

F. 6
G. 9
H. 12
J. 72
K. 144

Step 1: Ballpark

First, ACT has actually done us a big favor on this problem. While they claim that "illustrative figures are NOT necessarily drawn to scale," it's usually safe to assume that they are at least close. Remember what we're looking for here, the length of $\overline{UV}$. Look closely at this figure: You can tell just by looking at it that the longest side is $\overline{SU}$, which has a length of 13, so it's not likely that any smaller part of the triangle will have a longer length, eliminating (J) and (K). We can probably eliminate (H) as well because $\overline{SU}$ is so much longer than $\overline{UV}$. This way, if we were running short on time and had to guess, we have improved our chances of guessing from 20% to 50%. Not bad for no work, huh?

Step 2: Write on the Figure

Now, let's dig in to get our final answer. Rather than trying to keep everything in your mind, make sure you are writing all over your figure. The problem says that V is the midpoint of $\overline{TU}$, so make sure you mark that on your figure. It's probably worth emphasizing the portion, $\overline{UV}$, that you are looking for as well.

Step 3: Write Down Formulas

As for the formulas, get those down before you begin working the problem as well. For this problem, you are dealing with the sides of a right triangle, so it is likely that you will need the Pythagorean theorem: $a^2 + b^2 = c^2$, where c is the longest side. Plug in the information you have, and write anything new that you find on the figure:

$$a^2 + b^2 = c^2$$

$$(5)^2 + \left(\overline{TU}\right)^2 = (13)^2$$

$$\left(\overline{TU}\right)^2 = (13)^2 - (5)^2$$

$$\left(\overline{TU}\right)^2 = 169 - 25$$

$$\left(\overline{TU}\right)^2 = 144$$

$$\overline{TU} = 12$$

Don't make your brain work any harder than it needs to! Make sure you're writing everything down. Hopefully by now your scratch paper looks something like this:

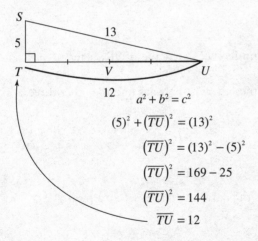

Now, once you've got all the information on the figure, it's probably very clear that the answer is (F) because $\overline{TU}$ is 12, and $\overline{UV}$ is one-half of this value. If you know your Pythagorean triples, you may have found $\overline{TU}$ even more quickly, but make sure you're reading the question carefully. If you don't read all the way, you might fall into the trap and pick (H).

So let's review the basic approach for Geometry problems.

The Basic Approach for Geometry

1. Use ballparking to eliminate wrong answers on questions in which a figure is given.

2. Write any information given by the question on the provided figure.

3. Write down any formulas you need and Plug In any information you have.

4. If the question doesn't provide a figure, draw your own.

THE FORMULAS

Here are some of the formulas you may find useful on Geometry questions.

Circles

Think CArd! (Circumference, Area, radius, diameter)

If you have one of these, you can always find the other three.

$$d = 2r \qquad C = \pi d = 2\pi r \qquad A = \pi r^2$$

When dealing with the parts of a circle, set up a ratio.

$$\frac{part}{whole} = \frac{central\ angle}{360°} = \frac{arc}{2\pi r} = \frac{sector\ area}{\pi r^2}$$

For Coordinate Geometry, be able to recognize the equation of a circle:

$$(x - h)^2 + (y - k)^2 = r^2$$

where (h,k) is the center of the circle, and (x,y) is any point on the circle.

Triangles

$$\text{Area} = A = \frac{1}{2}bh$$

Perimeter: P = sum of the sides

Sum of all angles: $180°$

Similar triangles have congruent angles and proportional sides.

Right Triangles

The Triangle rules apply, but there are some special rules for right triangles.

Pythagorean theorem, where a, b, and c are the sides of the triangle, and c is the hypotenuse:

$$a^2 + b^2 = c^2$$

SOHCAHTOA (ratios between sides and angles of right triangles)

$$\sin\theta = \frac{\text{Opposite}}{\text{Hypotenuse}} \qquad \cos\theta = \frac{\text{Adjacent}}{\text{Hypotenuse}} \qquad \tan\theta = \frac{\text{Opposite}}{\text{Adjacent}}$$

Special Right Triangles

When you've determined the angles of your right triangle, use the following ratios to bypass the Pythagorean theorem:

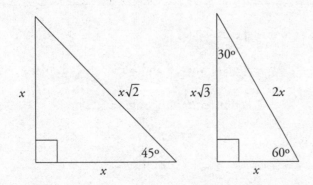

If a triangle problem contains a $\sqrt{2}$ or a $\sqrt{3}$, you can most likely use one of these special triangles.

If you don't know the angles, you can often bypass the Pythagorean theorem with the Pythagorean triples:

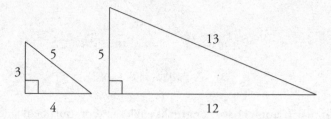

These Pythagorean triples are basic ratios, so they can be multiplied to be used with larger numbers.

6:8:10 is commonly cited as a Pythagorean triple, but it is just the 3:4:5 multiplied by 2.

Four-Sided Figures (Quadrilaterals)

Parallelogram: Opposite sides are parallel, opposite sides and angles are equal

Rhombus: Opposite sides parallel, ALL sides equal, opposite angles equal A rhombus is a *parallelogram* in which all four sides are equal.

Rectangle: Opposite sides parallel, opposite sides equal, ALL angles 90° A rectangle is a *parallelogram* with four right angles.

Square: Opposite sides parallel, ALL sides equal, ALL angles 90° A square is a type of *parallelogram*, *rhombus*, and *rectangle*.

For any of these four shapes:

Area: $A = bh$, where b and h are perpendicular

Perimeter: $P =$ the sum of all sides

Coordinate Geometry Formulas

All points are written (x,y), where x gives the x-coordinate and y gives the y-coordinate.

Two lines *intersect* when they meet at a single point.

$$\text{Slope: } \frac{\text{rise}}{\text{run}} = \frac{y_2 - y_1}{x_2 - x_1}$$

where (x_1,y_1) and (x_2,y_2) are two points on a line.

$$\text{Slope-intercept formula: } y = mx + b$$

where (x,y) is a point on the line, m is the slope, and b is the y-intercept, or the point at which the line crosses the y-axis.

Use the slope-intercept form when a question asks for the slope of a *perpendicular* line. The slope of a line perpendicular to it will be the opposite reciprocal or $-\frac{1}{m}$. That is, if slope of a line is 2, the slope of a perpendicular will be $-\frac{1}{2}$.

Parallel lines have equal slopes.

THE PROBLEMS

Plane Geometry

Let's use these formulas and the Basic Approach to solve some problems.

44. A circle has a diameter of 8 inches. What is the area of the circle, to the nearest 0.1 square inch?

    F.   12.6
    G.   25.1
    H.   50.3
    J.   64.0
    K. 201.1

Here's How to Crack It

Remember the Basic Approach. There's no figure, so draw your own. Once you've done that, mark it up with information from the problem, and get all your formulas down. Think CArd!

Your paper should look something like this:

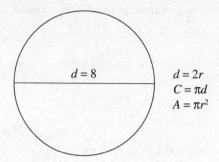

$d = 8$

$d = 2r$
$C = \pi d$
$A = \pi r^2$

Now work the formulas to get the answer. We know that the diameter of this circle is 8, which means its radius is 4. Use the radius in the Area formula, and use your calculator to find this Area:

$$A = \pi r^2$$
$$A = \pi(4)^2$$
$$A = 16\pi$$
$$A \approx 50.3$$

This matches up nicely with (H). If you don't have a calculator, or you're not especially handy with it, no problem. Use ballparking. You know that π is roughly equivalent to 3, so your answer will need to be close to 16×3 or 48. Only (H) is close enough.

Coordinate Geometry

Let's try a Coordinate Geometry problem. ACT likes to make a big deal about the distinction between Plane and Coordinate Geometry, but as we'll see, your approach won't really differ at all.

23. In the standard (x,y) coordinate plane, point G lies at $(-3,-4)$, and point H lies at $(2,5)$. What is the length of $\overline{GH}$ in coordinate units?

    A. 7
    B. 4
    C. $\sqrt{14}$
    D. $\sqrt{45}$
    E. $\sqrt{106}$

Here's How to Crack It

Your first impulse here will probably be to whip out the distance formula and complete this problem in lightning-fast time. The only problem is that the distance formula looks like this:

$$d = \sqrt{(x_2 - x_1)^2 + (y_2 - y_1)^2}$$

Yikes. If you've got this formula stored away in the RAM of your brain, great. Unfortunately, for most of us, this is a really easy formula to forget, or worse, to remember incorrectly. What you'll find about ACT Geometry is that for 90% of the problems, you're best off just dealing with the basics. For weird shapes in Plane Geometry, this will mean carving things up into recognizable shapes and working from there. On Coordinate Geometry, you will find that simple formulas and the Basic Approach can get you plenty of points.

Let's use the Basic Approach. First and foremost, this is a Geometry problem, and they haven't given you a figure. Draw your own. It should look something like this:

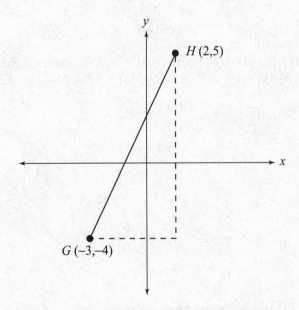

Now, look carefully at the line you've drawn for $\overline{GH}$. Remind you of anything? How about the hypotenuse of a right triangle? Remember, you want to work with the basics, and you know your triangles, so let's turn this thing into a right triangle.

Draw in the sides and find the lengths of those sides. To find the base of the triangle, figure out how much you're moving from one *x*-coordinate to the other. The points are (–3,–4) and (2,5), so the *x*-coordinate will go from –3 to 2, or 5 units. The *y*-coordinate will go from –4 to 5, or 9 units. After you've drawn all this in and marked up your figure, you should have something like this:

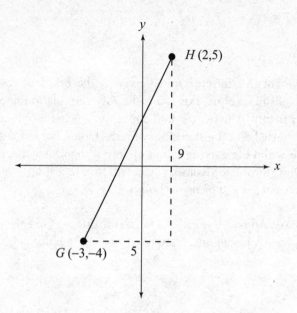

And now this is just a plain old ("plane" old?) Plane Geometry problem. You know two sides of a right triangle and need the third. Sounds like a job for the Pythagorean theorem.

$$a^2 + b^2 = c^2$$
$$(5)^2 + (9)^2 = \left(\overline{GH}\right)^2$$
$$\left(\overline{GH}\right)^2 = 25 + 81$$
$$\left(\overline{GH}\right)^2 = 106$$
$$\overline{GH} = \sqrt{106}$$

The answer is (E). And no distance formula required.

Trigonometry

There's a common misconception about the ACT regarding Trigonometry. Many believe that if you don't have a solid foundation in Trigonometry, you can't get a good score on the ACT Math test. However, let's think back to the chart from the beginning of this lesson. Remember, there are only 4 trig questions on any given ACT.

What's more, two of these questions will deal with basic SOHCAHTOA, which you clearly don't need a whole semester or year of trig to learn. The other two questions may deal with radians, or the unit circle, or some of the trig identities, but you shouldn't worry about these until you've solidified a math score of at least 28.

So let's have a look at one of these basic SOHCAHTOA questions.

42. According to the measurements given in the figure below, which of the following expressions gives the distance, in meters, from the house to the garage?

F. $40 \tan 38°$

G. $40 \cos 38°$

H. $40 \sin 38°$

J. $\dfrac{40}{\cos 38°}$

K. $\dfrac{40}{\sin 38°}$

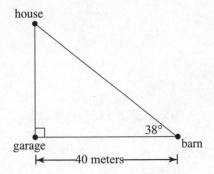

Here's How to Crack It

They've already written most of the information you'll need on the figure, but it can be worth noting the side that you are looking for: the side that shows the distance from the house to the garage.

Let the answer choices help. These choices tell you a lot more than you may think: First of all, they offer the main indication that this will be a SOHCAHTOA problem by showing that you will need to choose sine, cosine, or tangent. Next, they tell you that you'll only be dealing with one angle, the 38° one. Finally, they tell you that you won't need to do any weird rounding with decimals because they just want the sine, cosine, or tangent expression.

Have a close look at the sides you're dealing with. Where are they relative to the 38° angle? The base of the triangle is touching the 38° angle, so it's *adjacent*, and

Trig Tip

Don't worry about Advanced Trigonometry concepts unless you are consistently scoring a 28 or higher on the ACT Math test. It's way too much to learn for only two questions!

the side you're looking for is *opposite* the 38° angle. It looks like we won't be dealing with the *hypotenuse* at all. So which trig function deals with the *opposite* and *adjacent* sides? Remember SOHCAHTOA. The function we'll need is tangent. And don't do more work than you need to. Only (F) offers an expression featuring the tangent function, so it must be the correct answer.

Shapes Within Shapes: What's the Link?

ACT's favorite way to ask hard Geometry questions is to put shapes within shapes. You know the drill: Some shape inscribed in some other shape, or two shapes share a common side. They've got all kinds of ways to ask these questions. But when you see a shape drawn within another shape, there's usually one question that will blow the question wide open: *What's the link between the two shapes?* Let's try a few.

1. A square inscribed in a circle

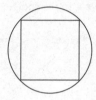

2. A triangle inscribed in a rectangle

3. A square overlapping with a circle

So, what's the link?

1. What's the link? The diagonal of the square is the diameter of the circle.

2. What's the link? The base of the triangle is the long side of the rectangle, and the height of the triangle is the short side of the rectangle.

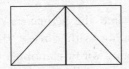

3. What's the link? The side of the square is equivalent to the radius of the circle.

Let's try a problem that deals with these concepts.

37. In the square shown below, points *E* and *F* are the midpoints of sides $\overline{AB}$ and $\overline{CD}$, respectively. Two semicircles are drawn with centers *E* and *F*. What is the perimeter, in feet, of the shaded region?

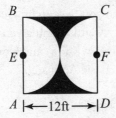

   A. $12 + 12\pi$
   B. $24 + 12\pi$
   C. $24 + 24\pi$
   D. $48 + 12\pi$
   E. $48 + 24\pi$

Here's How to Crack It

Make sure you write everything you need on the figure, including the relevant square and circle formulas. Since you are dealing with shapes within shapes, now is also a good time to figure out what the link is, what these two (or three, in this case) shapes have in common. Don't worry about digging up a formula for the perimeter of that hourglass-shaped thing. Stick with the shapes you know.

For this problem, the links occur on the right and left sides of the figure: The left and right sides of the square are the same as the diameters of each of the semicircles. We can therefore say that if all sides of a square are equal, each of these sides is 12. Since the diameter of each semicircle is equivalent to a side of the square, then the diameters of both semicircles must also be 12.

Let's use this information to find the perimeters of each of these semicircles. Remember, when you're dealing with circles, the perimeter is called the *circumference*, which can be found with the formula $C = \pi d$. Since you're dealing with a semi-circle here, you'll need to divide its circumference in half. Let's find the circumference of the semicircle with center E.

$$\frac{C_E}{2} = \frac{\pi d}{2}$$
$$= \frac{\pi (12)}{2}$$
$$= 6\pi$$

The semicircle with center F will have the same circumference because it has the same diameter. Now all we need to do is add up our perimeters to find our answer. You know the sides of the square will each be 12 and the circumference of each semicircle will be 6π, so the total perimeter of the shaded region will be $12 + 12 + 6\pi + 6\pi = 24 + 12\pi$, as in (B).

So let's hear it once more:

> Don't do more work than you have to on Geometry problems by trying to remember every weird formula you've ever learned. Stick to the formulas you know, and work with the Basic Approach.

Now go ahead and give some of these concepts a try in the following drills.

GEOMETRY DRILL 1

Plane Geometry

8. In the figure below, $\overline{AB} \parallel \overline{CD}$. What is the value of y ?

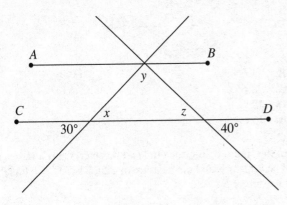

   F. 110°
   G. 120°
   H. 135°
   J. 140°
   K. 170°

14. The 8-sided figure below is divided into 6 congruent squares. The total area of the 6 squares is 96 square centimeters. What is the perimeter, in centimeters, of the figure?

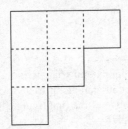

   F. 16
   G. 28
   H. 48
   J. 56
   K. 96

22. The base of triangle M is four times the base of triangle N, while the height of triangle N is half the height of triangle M. The area of triangle M is how many times that of triangle N ?

   F. 2
   G. 4
   H. 8
   J. 10
   K. 16

26. A rectangular horse corral is built along one side of a square barn whose area is 5,776 square feet. The length of the corral is the same as the length of the side of the barn, while the width of the corral is one-fourth the length of the side of the barn. What is the area of the horse corral, in square feet?

   F. 76
   G. 1,016
   H. 1,284
   J. 1,444
   K. 5,776

27. In right triangle $\triangle FHK$ below, $\overline{GJ}$ is parallel to $\overline{FK}$, and $\overline{GJ}$ is perpendicular to $\overline{HK}$ at J. The length of $\overline{HK}$ is 12 inches, the length of $\overline{GJ}$ is 6 inches, and the length of $\overline{GH}$ is 10 inches. What is the length, in inches, of $\overline{FK}$?

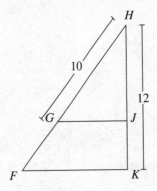

   A. 7
   B. 8
   C. 9
   D. 10
   E. 11

30. The diameter of circle A is twice that of circle B. If the area of circle A is 36π, then what is the circumference of circle B ?

　F.　π
　G.　3π
　H.　6π
　J.　9π
　K.　18π

36. In the figure below, the distance from A to B is $\dfrac{1}{3}$ the distance from B to C. The area of $\triangle BDE$ is what fraction of the area of rectangle $ACDE$?

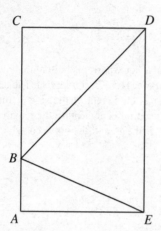

　F.　$\dfrac{1}{6}$

　G.　$\dfrac{1}{3}$

　H.　$\dfrac{1}{2}$

　J.　$\dfrac{3}{5}$

　K.　$\dfrac{2}{3}$

39. The circle with center E is inscribed in square $ABCD$ as shown in the figure below. If line $\overline{AC}$ (not shown) has a length of $8\sqrt{2}$, then what is the area of the circle?

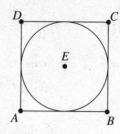

　A.　π
　B.　4π
　C.　8π
　D.　12π
　E.　16π

48. In the figure below, the circle with center X has a radius of 8 centimeters, and the measure of $\angle SRX$ is 70°. What is the measure of $\overline{RS}$?

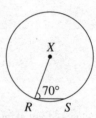

　F.　20°
　G.　40°
　H.　50°
　J.　55°
　K.　70°

54. The side of an equilateral triangle is s inches longer than the side of a second equilateral triangle. How many inches longer is the altitude of the first triangle than the altitude of the second triangle?

　F.　$\dfrac{\sqrt{3}}{2}s$

　G.　$\sqrt{2}s$

　H.　$2s$

　J.　$3s$

　K.　s^3

55. In the figure below, the circles' centers at *N* and *O* intersect at *X* and *Y*, and points *N, X, Y,* and *O* are collinear. The lengths of $\overline{MN}$, $\overline{OP}$, and $\overline{XY}$ are 10, 8, and 3 inches, respectively. What is the length, in inches, of $\overline{NO}$?

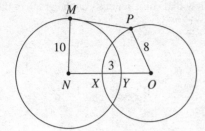

A. 10
B. 11
C. 12
D. 15
E. 18

57. The five semicircles in the figure below touch only at their corners. If the distance from *A* to *F* along the diameters of the semicircles is 60 inches, what is the distance, in inches, from *F* to *A* along the arcs of these semicircles?

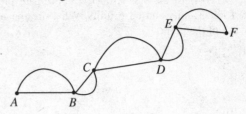

A. 30π
B. 40π
C. 60π
D. 72π
E. 90π

Coordinate Geometry

3. A point at $(5,-4)$ in the standard (x,y) coordinate plane is shifted left 3 units and up 6 units. What are the new coordinates of the point?

 A. $(11, 7)$
 B. $(8, 2)$
 C. $(8,10)$
 D. $(2, 2)$
 E. $(2,10)$

13. The points $A(-6,8)$ and $B(10,2)$ lie in the standard (x,y) coordinate plane. What is the midpoint of $\overline{AB}$?

 A. $(-3, 4)$
 B. $(2, 5)$
 C. $(4,10)$
 D. $(5, 1)$
 E. $(8,-3)$

19. What is the x-intercept of the line $y = 5x + 2$?

 A. $\left(0, -\dfrac{2}{5}\right)$

 B. $\left(0, \dfrac{2}{5}\right)$

 C. $(2, 0)$

 D. $\left(\dfrac{2}{5}, 0\right)$

 E. $\left(-\dfrac{2}{5}, 0\right)$

24. Points $O(5,3)$ and $P(-3,8)$ lie in the standard (x,y) coordinate plane. What is the slope of a line that is perpendicular to line of $\overline{OP}$?

 F. $-\dfrac{8}{5}$

 G. $-\dfrac{5}{8}$

 H. $\dfrac{5}{8}$

 J. 1

 K. $\dfrac{8}{5}$

33. What are the quadrants of the standard (x,y) coordinate plane below that contain points on the graph of the equation $8x + 4y = 12$?

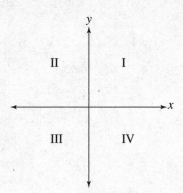

Quadrants of the standard
(x,y) coordinate plane

 A. II and IV only
 B. I, II, and III only
 C. I, II, and IV only
 D. I, III, and IV only
 E. II, III, and IV only

39. On a map in the standard (x,y) coordinate plane, the cities of Everton and Springfield are represented by the points $(-3,-5)$ and $(-6,-8)$, respectively. Each unit on the map represents an actual distance of 20 kilometers. Which of the following is closest to the distance, in kilometers, between these 2 cities?

 A. 316
 B. 120
 C. 85
 D. 60
 E. 49

41. The figure below shows the graph in the standard (x,y) coordinate plane of one of the following functions. Which function is shown?

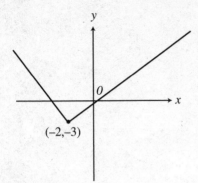

(–2,–3)

A. $y = |x + 2| + 3$

B. $y = |x - 2| - 3$

C. $y = |x + 2| - 3$

D. $y = |x + 3| - 2$

E. $y = |x - 3| + 2$

47. The figure below shows the graph of line ℓ in the standard (x,y) coordinate plane. Which of the following could be the equation of line ℓ ?

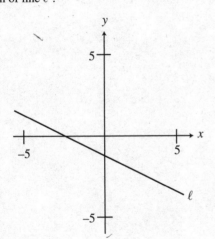

A. $y = -\dfrac{5}{2}x - 1$

B. $y = \dfrac{5}{2}x + 1$

C. $y = -\dfrac{2}{5}x - 1$

D. $y = -\dfrac{2}{5}x + 1$

E. $y = \dfrac{2}{5}x - 1$

48. The graph of $f(x) = x^3$ is shown in the standard (x,y) coordinate plane below. For which of the following equations is the graph of the cubic function shifted 4 units to the left and 3 units up?

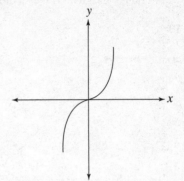

F. $f(x) = (x - 4)^3 - 3$

G. $f(x) = (x - 4)^3 + 3$

H. $f(x) = (x + 3)^3 - 4$

J. $f(x) = (x + 4)^3 + 3$

K. $f(x) = (x + 4)^3 - 3$

50. If a circle in the standard (x,y) coordinate plane has the equation $(x + 3)^2 + (y - 5)^2 = 16$, then which of the following points represents the center of the circle?

F. (–5, 3)

G. (–3,–5)

H. (3, 5)

J. (–5,–3)

K. (–3, 5)

56. The graph below shows the distance a hot-air balloon is from the ground for a period of 10 minutes. A certain order of 3 of the following 5 actions describes the balloon's movement in relation to the position of the ground. Which order is it?

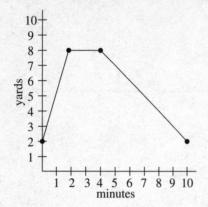

I.   Remains stationary for 2 minutes
II. Moves away at 3 yards per minute
III. Moves toward at 3 yards per minute
IV. Moves away at 1 yard per minute
V.   Moves toward at 1 yard per minute

F. I, II, II
G. II, I, V
H. III, I, IV
J. IV, I, III
K. V, I, II

Trigonometry

21. In right triangle $\triangle LMN$ below, $\sin L = \dfrac{3}{8}$. Which of the following expressions is equal to $\sin M$?

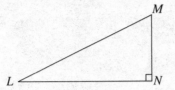

A. $\dfrac{8}{3}$

B. $\dfrac{\sqrt{73}}{3}$

C. $\dfrac{\sqrt{55}}{3}$

D. $\dfrac{\sqrt{73}}{8}$

E. $\dfrac{\sqrt{55}}{8}$

23. In isosceles right triangle ABC (not shown), $\overline{AB} = \overline{AC} = 3$. Which of the following represents the value of $\cos \angle ABC$?

A. $\dfrac{\sqrt{2}}{2}$

B. $\dfrac{\sqrt{3}}{2}$

C. $\sqrt{2}$

D. $\sqrt{3}$

E. 2

25. A painter leans a 10-foot ladder against a wall at an angle of 65° relative to the ground. How far away from the wall is the base of the ladder?

A. $10 \tan 65°$

B. $10 \sin 65°$

C. $10 \cos 65°$

D. $\dfrac{10}{\sin 65°}$

E. $\dfrac{10}{\cos 65°}$

29. For the polygon below, which of the following represents the length, in inches, of $\overline{FK}$?

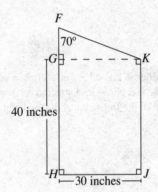

A. 10

B. 30

C. $\dfrac{10}{\sin 70°}$

D. $\dfrac{30}{\sin 70°}$

E. $\sin 70°$

35. A right triangle is shown in the figure below. Which of the following expressions gives θ ?

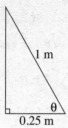

0.25 m

A. $\cos^{-1}\left(\dfrac{1}{4}\right)$

B. $\sin^{-1}\left(\dfrac{1}{4}\right)$

C. $\tan^{-1}\left(\dfrac{1}{4}\right)$

D. $\cos^{-1}(4)$

E. $\tan^{-1}(4)$

37. A straight ladder is leaned against a house so that the top of the ladder is 12 feet above level ground, as shown in the figure below. Which of the following gives the length, in feet, of the ladder?

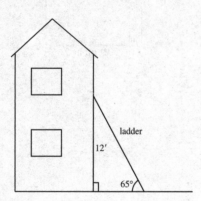

A. $x = 12\cos 65°$

B. $x = 12\sin 65°$

C. $x = \dfrac{12}{\cos 65°}$

D. $x = \dfrac{12}{\sin 65°}$

E. $x = \dfrac{12}{\tan 65°}$

53. In $\triangle XYZ$, the measure of $\angle X$ is 57°, the measure of $\angle Y$ is 72°, and the length of $\overline{XZ}$ is 12 inches. Which of the following is an expression for the length, in inches, of $\overline{YZ}$?

(Note: The law of sines states that for any triangle, the ratios of the lengths of the sides to the sines of the angles opposite those sides are equal.)

A. $\dfrac{\sin 57°}{12\sin 72°}$

B. $\dfrac{\sin 72°}{12\sin 57°}$

C. $\dfrac{12\sin 72°}{\sin 57°}$

D. $\dfrac{12\sin 57°}{\sin 72°}$

E. $\dfrac{(\sin 57°)\,(\sin 72°)}{12}$

56. If $\cos\theta = \dfrac{3}{4}$ and $0 < \theta < \dfrac{\pi}{2}$, which of the following is equal to $\sin\theta\tan\theta$?

F. $\dfrac{7}{12}$

G. $\dfrac{4}{3\sqrt{7}}$

H. $\dfrac{4}{3}$

J. $\dfrac{4\sqrt{7}}{3}$

K. $\dfrac{12}{7}$

58. The angle in the standard (*x*,*y*) coordinate plane shown below has its vertex at the origin. One side of this angle includes the positive *x*-axis, and the other side with measure θ passes through (−12,5). What is the sine of θ ?

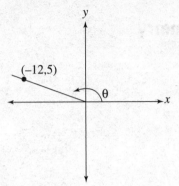

F. $-\dfrac{13}{5}$

G. $-\dfrac{12}{13}$

H. $-\dfrac{5}{13}$

J. $\dfrac{5}{13}$

K. $\dfrac{12}{5}$

59. The domain of the function $f(x) = 4\sin(3x − 1) + 2$ is all real numbers. Which of the following is the range of the function $f(x)$?

A. $-4 \le f(x) \le 4$

B. $-6 \le f(x) \le 2$

C. $-5 \le f(x) \le 3$

D. $-2 \le f(x) \le 6$

E.   All real numbers

GEOMETRY DRILL 1 ANSWER KEY

Plane Geometry

8. F
14. H
22. H
26. J
27. C
30. H
36. H
39. E
48. G
54. F
55. D
57. A

Coordinate Geometry

3. D
13. B
19. E
24. K
33. C
39. C
41. C
47. C
48. J
50. K
56. G

Trigonometry

21. E
23. A
25. C
29. D
35. A
37. D
53. D
56. F
58. J
59. D

GEOMETRY DRILL 1 EXPLANATIONS

Plane Geometry

8. **F**   According to the figure, the angle opposite x is 30°, so $x = 30$. Similarly, the angle across from z is 40°, so $z = 40$. Since x, y, and z form a triangle, the sum of these three angles must be 180°. The value of y is therefore $180 - 30 - 40 = 110°$, which is (F).

14. **H**   Since the area of the six congruent squares is 96, the area of each square is $\frac{96}{6} = 16$. It might be tempting to select (F) here, but remember you're looking for the perimeter of the entire figure, not the area of each square. The area of a square is equal to s^2, so the length of the side of each square is $\sqrt{16} = 4$. The perimeter of the figure consists of 12 sides of congruent squares, so the perimeter is $12 \times 4 = 48$. Choice (G) confuses the sides of the square with the sides of the figure. Choice (J) misuses the fact that the figure is 8-sided; (K) finds the perimeter if all 4 sides of the 6 squares were exposed.

22. **H**   This question can be approached algebraically or by plugging in your own numbers. If you plug in some small numbers for the base and height of triangle N, such as 2 and 3, respectively, the base and height of triangle M would then be four times as big and twice as big, or 8 and 6, respectively. The area of triangle M would be $\frac{1}{2}bh = \frac{1}{2}(8)(6) = 24$, while the area of triangle N would be $\frac{1}{2}bh = \frac{1}{2}(2)(3) = 3$. Triangle M is therefore 8 times larger than triangle N, which is (H).

26. **J**   If the area of the barn is 5,776 square feet, you can take the square root of that number on your calculator to determine that the sides of the barn have a length of 76 feet. This is also the length of the corral. The width of the corral is one-fourth its length, so $\frac{76}{4} = 19$ feet. The area of the corral is thus $76 \times 19 = 1,444$ square feet, so (J) is the answer.

27. **C**   Given $\overline{GJ}$ is parallel to $\overline{FK}$, $\triangle FHK$ and $\triangle GHJ$ are similar triangles, so they have proportional sides. $\triangle GHJ$ is a right triangle, so you can either use the Pythagorean theorem or identify the sides as the Pythagorean triplet 6:8:10 to determine $\overline{HJ}$ is 10. Then set up the proportion $\frac{\overline{FK}}{\overline{GJ}} = \frac{\overline{HK}}{\overline{HJ}}$ to determine $\overline{FK}$: $\frac{\overline{FK}}{6} = \frac{12}{8}$, so $\overline{FK}$ is 9 inches.

30. **H** If the area of circle A is 36π, and the area of any circle is πr^2, then the radius of circle A must be 6. The diameter of circle A is therefore 12, and the diameter of circle B is half that, or 6. The circumference of any circle is $2\pi r$ or πd, so the circumference of circle B is 6π. Choice (H) is correct.

36. **H** Plug in some numbers for the sides of the rectangle. Let's say $AB = 2$. Since AB is $\frac{1}{3}$ of BC, $BC = 6$, and $AC = DE = 8$. There are no restrictions on AE, so let's say $AE = CD = 3$. The area of $ACDE = (8)(3) = 24$. To find the area of $\triangle BCD$, subtract the areas of triangles ABE and CBD. The area of $ABE = \frac{1}{2}(3)(2) = 3$, and the area of $CBD = \frac{1}{2}(3)(6) = 9$, so the area of $BDE = 24 - (3 + 9) = 12$. Therefore, BDE is $\frac{1}{2}$ the area of $ACDE$.

39. **E** If the length of $\overline{AC}$ is $8\sqrt{2}$, then the sides of the square must be 8 (splitting a square in half gives you two 45-45-90 triangles with ratios $1:1:\sqrt{2}$). The radius of the circle is half the length of the side of the square, so the radius is 4. The area of the circle is $\pi r^2 = \pi(4^2) = 16\pi$. Therefore, the answer is (E).

48. **G** Both $\overline{RX}$ and $\overline{SX}$ are radii of the circle, making them congruent. The triangle $\triangle RSX$, therefore, is isosceles, and $\angle SRX$ and $\angle RSX$ are congruent, each measuring 70°. The third angle $\angle RSX = 180° - 2(70°) = 40°$ and is equal to the measure of $\overset{\frown}{RS}$. Choices (J) and (K) make the incorrect pair of angles congruent.

54. **F** Plug in values for the sides of the triangles: Triangle 1 can have a side length of 8 and triangle 2 can have a side length of 6, making $s = 2$. Equilateral triangles can be split into two 30-60-90 triangles, thus their altitudes are $\frac{1}{2}$(side length)$\times \sqrt{3}$. Triangle 1's altitude is $4\sqrt{3}$, and triangle 2's altitude is $3\sqrt{3}$, making the answer $4\sqrt{3} - 3\sqrt{3} = \sqrt{3}$. Choice (G) confuses 30-60-90 with 45-45-90, and (H), (J), and (K) do not have a $\sqrt{3}$.

55. **D** $\overline{MN}$ and $\overline{OP}$ are the radii of their respective circles, so the radius $\overline{NY}$ of circle N is 10 inches, and radius $\overline{OP}$ of circle O is 8 inches. Given $\overline{XY}$ is 3 inches long, $\overline{NX}$ is $10 - 3 = 7$ inches and $\overline{OY}$ is $8 - 3 = 5$ inches. Adding the three segments $\overline{NX}$, $\overline{XY}$, and $\overline{OY}$, the length of $\overline{NO}$ is $7 + 3 + 5 = 15$ inches. Choices (A) and (B) are too small, (C) calculates the length with $\overline{XY}$, and (E) doesn't consider the radii overlapping in $\overline{XY}$.

57. **A** The problem gives us no information about the relative lengths of the different diameters, so it must not matter, and the easiest thing to do is to make them all the same. There are five diameters, so $\frac{60}{5} = 12$. A circle with diameter 12 has a circumference of 12π, so a semicircle with diameter 12 will have a length of $\frac{1}{2}(12\pi) = 6\pi$. There are 5 semicircles, so the total distance from F to A along the semicircles is $(5)(6\pi) = 30\pi$.

Coordinate Geometry

3. **D** To shift left, subtract from the x-coordinate: $5 - 3 = 2$; to shift up, add to the y-coordinate: $-4 + 6 = 2$. Choice (A) confuses the x- and y-coordinates, and (B), (C), and (E) confuse the addition and subtraction.

13. **B** The coordinates for midpoint are the averages of the endpoints: $\left(\dfrac{x_1 + x_2}{2}, \dfrac{y_1 + y_2}{2} \right)$. For segment $\overline{AB}$, the midpoint is at $\dfrac{-6 + 10}{2} = 2, \dfrac{8 + 2}{2} = 5$. Choices (A) and (D) incorrectly take half the coordinate of one of the endpoints. Choice (C) adds, rather than averages, the endpoints. Choice (E) subtracts, rather than adds, the endpoint coordinates.

19. **E** The x-intercept is the point at which a line crosses the x-axis, so the y-value of that point will always be 0. Plug in 0 for the y in the equation, and solve for x: $0 = 5x + 2 \rightarrow -2 = 5x \rightarrow -\dfrac{2}{5} = x$. The x-intercept is thus $\left(-\dfrac{2}{5}, 0 \right)$, which is (E).

24. **K** Use the point-slope formula to determine the slope of line $\overline{OP}$: $\dfrac{y_2 - y_1}{x_2 - x_1} = \dfrac{8 - 3}{-3 - 5} = -\dfrac{5}{8}$. The slope of a line perpendicular to this one will have a negative reciprocal slope: $\dfrac{8}{5}$, so (K) is correct.

33. **C** To determine the graph of the equation, you must isolate the y by subtracting $8x$ and dividing by 4. The resulting equation is $y = -2x + 3$, which is a line with a slope of -2 and a y-intercept of 3. Because the y-intercept is positive, the line crosses the y-axis from Quadrant II to Quadrant I and extends into Quadrant IV. The line never passes through Quadrant III, eliminating (B), (D), and (E). Choice (A) is a partial answer and does not include Quadrant I. Alternatively, once the equation is in slope-intercept form, just plug it into your graphing calculator and look at the graph.

39. **C** Find the distance between the points using the distance formula: $d = \sqrt{(x_1 - x_2)^2 + (y_1 - y_2)^2} = \sqrt{[(-3) - (-6)]^2 + [(-5) - (-8)]^2} = \sqrt{(3)^2 + (3^2)} = \sqrt{18} = 3\sqrt{2}$. Multiply the coordinate distance by 20 to get the distance in kilometers. Choices (A) and (E) incorrectly calculate the distance by adding the coordinates and forgetting to square the differences, respectively. Choices (B) and (D) result when the distance formula is not used. If you have trouble remembering the distance formula, sketch a figure, and use the Pythagorean theorem as detailed in the introductory chapter.

41. **C**   The correct answer is (C). There are two good ways to solve this question. Even if you don't know anything about absolute value questions, you can still get this right by plugging the given point into the answer choices. Here's what you get:

A. $-3 = |-2 + 2| + 3$, which simplifies to $-3 = 3$. Incorrect.

B. $-3 = |-2 - 2| - 3$, which simplifies to $-3 = 1$. Incorrect.

C. $-3 = |-2 + 2| - 3$, which simplifies to $-3 = -3$. **Correct.**

D. $-3 = |-2 + 3| - 2$, which simplifies to $-3 = -1$. Incorrect.

E. $-3 = |-2 - 3| + 2$, which simplifies to $-3 = 7$. Incorrect.

A slightly faster way to do this question is to memorize the basic form of an absolute value equation. For the equation $y = |x - a| + b$, the vertex is (a, b). Plugging the vertex $(-2, -3)$ into this formula gives us $y = |x - (-2)| - 3$, which simplifies to $y = |x + 2| - 3$.

47. **C**   This question is best done with POE and a little bit of ballparking. First, deal with the y-intercept. Since the line crosses the y-axis below the origin, the y-intercept must be negative, so eliminate (B) and (D). Next, deal with the sign of the slope. A line that slopes down from left to right has a negative slope, so eliminate (E). Finally, decide whether the numerator is more or less than the denominator. Remember, slope is rise over run. The total run of this line (distance from left to right) is 10, but the rise is considerably less than that, so the numerator must be less than the denominator. Eliminate (A), leaving only (C).

48. **J**   For any function $f(x + h) + k$, h indicates horizontal shifts, and k indicates vertical shifts. Because the horizontal shift is 4, not 3, you can eliminate (H). A negative h indicates a shift right, not left, eliminating (F) and (G). A negative k indicates a shift down, not up, eliminating (K).

50. **K**   The standard equation for a circle is $(x - h)^2 + (y - k)^2 = r^2$, where the center of the circle is the point (h, k). Therefore, the center of this circle is at the point $(-3, 5)$, which makes (K) the correct answer.

56. **G**   The balloon remains stationary in the middle stage, so action (I) should be second in the order of events, eliminating (F). In the first stage, the graph is increasing, which means the distance between the balloon and the ground increases, so the balloon is moving away, eliminating (H) and (K). The rate of increase is greater than the rate of decrease in the third stage, so (J) is incorrect. Only (G) gives the correct actions in the correct order.

Trigonometry

21. **E**   Draw a triangle and use SOHCAHTOA to label the known sides: leg $\overline{MN}$ is 3, and hypotenuse $\overline{LM}$ is 8. Use the Pythagorean theorem to determine the third side: $\overline{LN}^2 + 3^2 = 8^2$, so $\overline{LN} = \sqrt{55}$, eliminating (B) and (D). Since $\sin = \dfrac{\text{opposite}}{\text{adjacent}}$, $\sin M = \dfrac{\overline{LN}}{LM} = \dfrac{\sqrt{55}}{8}$. Choice (A) gives $\cos M$, and (C) gives $\tan M$.

23. **A**   Since no diagram is provided, make your own. The triangle will look something like this:

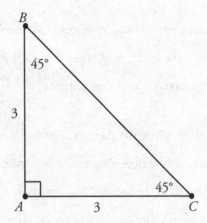

You can solve this question on your calculator, but that will give you a decimal. Based on the formatting of the answer choices, it is easier to figure out the length of $\overline{BC}$. Because this is a 45-45-90 triangle with ratios $1{:}1{:}\sqrt{2}$, $\overline{BC}$ is $3\sqrt{2}$. Since cosine is defined as $\dfrac{\text{adjacent}}{\text{hypotenuse}}$, $\cos \angle ABC = \dfrac{3}{3\sqrt{2}}$, which simplifies to $\dfrac{\sqrt{2}}{2}$. Therefore, (A) is correct.

25. **C**   Since no diagram is provided, make your own. The figure will look something like this:

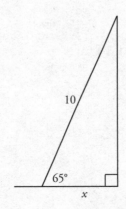

Since you are looking for the distance between the base of the ladder and the wall, represented by x, you are dealing with the side that is adjacent to the 65° angle as well as the hypotenuse. Since cosine is defined as $\dfrac{\text{adjacent}}{\text{hypotenuse}}$, $\cos 65 = \dfrac{x}{10}$. Multiply both sides by 10 to get $x = 10 \cos 65$, which is (C).

29. **D**   Because quadrilateral *GHJK* has four right angles, it is a rectangle, and $\overline{GK}$ measures 30 inches. We must use SOHCAHTOA to determine the side lengths of right triangle *FGK*, eliminating (A) and (B). Since we know the measure of $\angle F$, use SOH: $\sin 70° = \dfrac{30}{FK}$, which rearranges to give $\overline{FK} = \dfrac{30}{\sin 70°}$.

35. **A**   We know the side adjacent to angle θ and the hypotenuse, so use CAH to set up the problem: $\cos\theta = \dfrac{0.25}{1} = \dfrac{1}{4}$. To determine the measure of angle θ, use the inverse function $\cos^{-1}$, eliminating (B), (C), and (E). Choice (D) incorrectly uses the reciprocal of $\dfrac{\text{adjacent}}{\text{hypotenuse}}$.

37. **D**   Remember SOHCAHTOA! We're given the side *opposite* the 65° angle, and we want to find the *hypotenuse*, so we need the sine function. Plug the information you have into the function: $\sin 65° = \dfrac{12}{x}$ (where x is the length of the ladder). Multiply both sides by x to get $x \sin 65° = 12$. Then divide by $\sin 65°$ to get $x = \dfrac{12}{\sin 65°}$. The correct answer is (D).

53. **D**   Draw the triangle to determine that side $\overline{YZ}$ is opposite $\angle X$, and side $\overline{XZ}$ is opposite $\angle Y$. Using the law of sines, set up the proportion: $\dfrac{12 \text{ inches}}{\sin 72°} = \dfrac{\overline{YZ}}{\sin 57°}$. Multiply both sides by $\sin 57°$ to get $\overline{YZ} = \dfrac{12 \sin 57°}{\sin 72°}$. Choice (C) does not use the correct angle-side pairs, and (A), (B), and (E) use the incorrect proportions.

56. **F** The correct answer is (F). We can use SOHCAHTOA and a right triangle to defeat this seemingly hard problem. Draw a right triangle and mark in angle θ. If $\cos\theta = \dfrac{3}{4}$, that means the adjacent side is 3, and the hypotenuse is 4. Now use the Pythagorean theorem to find the third side: $3^2 + b^2 = 4^2$, so $9 + b^2 = 16$, which simplifies to $b^2 = 7$ and finally to $b = \sqrt{7}$. Your sketch should look something like this:

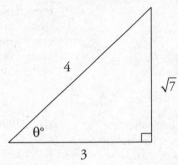

Now just plug your dimensions into the functions: $\sin\theta\tan\theta = \dfrac{\sqrt{7}}{4} \cdot \dfrac{\sqrt{7}}{4} = \dfrac{7}{12}$.

58. **J** In the standard (x,y) coordinate plane, the sine of an angle in Quadrant II is always positive, eliminating (F), (G), and (H). Make a right triangle with the x-axis, which gives you a 5-12-13 triangle. The angle θ is at the origin, so the leg opposite the angle is 5 and the hypotenuse is 13. Sine is defined as "opposite over hypotenuse," which in this case gives $\dfrac{5}{13}$, so the answer is (J).

59. **D** The range of $\sin x$ is normally between -1 to 1, inclusive; however, the range can change depending on the graph's amplitude and vertical shift. In the general form $A\sin(Bx+C)+D$, amplitude is indicated by A, vertical shift is indicated by D, and the range is between $-A + D$ and $A + D$. The range for this function, therefore, is $-4+2 \le f(x) \le 4+2$. Choice (A) neglects the vertical shift of the graph; (B) subtracts rather than adding the vertical shift of $+D$; (C) uses the horizontal rather than vertical shift value; and (E) gives the domain, not the range of the function.

GEOMETRY DRILL 2

Plane Geometry

7. What is the perimeter, in meters, of a parallelogram with side lengths of 12 m and 10 m ?

A. 22
B. 44
C. 48
D. 60
E. 120

15. Kayla is mowing her lawn and the lawn of her neighbor. She discovers that the two lawns have the same area. Her lawn is a triangle with a base of 90 feet, and the height of the triangle is 80 feet. If her neighbor's lawn is a square, what is the length, in feet, of a side of the square?

A. $\sqrt{170}$
B. 30
C. 60
D. 170
E. 240

17. In the figure below, parallel lines M_1 and M_2 intersect transversal l. What is the value of $x + y$?

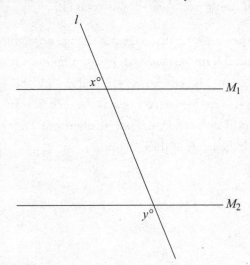

A. 60
B. 90
C. 120
D. 180
E. 360

18. Brandie bought a few cans of paint, and each can contains enough paint to cover 300 square meters. She is painting a triangular mural on a wall that is 6 meters tall. She opens 1 can of paint and starts painting. Before Brandie needs to open another can of paint, she can paint a triangle that is the height of the wall and is how many meters long?

F. 6
G. 50
H. 100
J. 294
K. 1,800

27. The ratio of the lengths of corresponding sides of 2 similar isosceles triangles is 3:5. One of the equal sides in the larger isosceles triangle is 30 centimeters long. How many centimeters long is one of the equal sides in the smaller isosceles triangle?

A. 18
B. 38
C. 45
D. 50
E. 90

32. The radius of a circle is 12 inches. What is the area of the circle, in square inches?

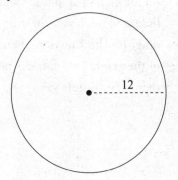

F. 12π
G. 24π
H. 48π
J. 144π
K. 576π

35. The perimeter of an isosceles triangle is 57 centimeters, and one side measures 22 centimeters. If it can be determined, what is one possibility for the lengths, in centimeters, of the other two sides?

A. 13, 22
B. 13, 44
C. 19, 22
D. 22, 35
E. Cannot be determined from the given information

37. Triangle *XYZ* below has an area of 72 square inches. Circle *O* is tangent to the triangle at *W*, and the height of the triangle is equal in length to the base. If the line *WY* is a diameter of circle *O*, what is the area, in square inches, of the circle?

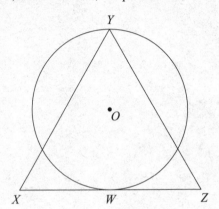

A. 6π
B. 12π
C. 24π
D. 36π
E. 144π

Use the following information to answer questions 38–40.

Shown below is a rectangular pool with a ramp leading up to one side. A water pump fills the pool at an average rate of 70 cubic yards per hour as it fills the pool. The pool is a rectangular box of length of 20 yards, width of 10 yards, and height of 3 yards. Also shown below is a ramp that leads to the top of the pool. The ramp is attached to the top of the pool and has an angle of elevation of 48°.

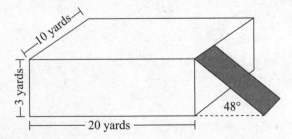

38. Which of the following is closest to the length of the ramp, to the nearest 0.1 yards?

(Note: $\sin 48° \approx 0.74$; $\cos 48° \approx 0.67$; $\tan 48° \approx 1.11$)

F. 2.7
G. 3.3
H. 3.0
J. 4.1
K. 4.5

39. The water pump starts to fill a completely empty pool and continues until the pool is completely filled. To the nearest 0.1 hours, for how many hours does the pump fill the pool with water?

A. 8.5
B. 8.6
C. 14.3
D. 103.0
E. 114.3

40. Rosie wants to build a pool that is geometrically similar to the pool shown in the figure. The new pool will have a height of $4\frac{1}{2}$ yards. What will be the length, in yards, of the longest side of the new pool?

F. 10
G. $13\frac{1}{3}$
H. 15
J. $21\frac{1}{2}$
K. 30

---

41. Triangle *ABC* shown below is isosceles, and line segment *DE* is parallel to *AC*. What is the perimeter, in inches, of the quadrilateral *ADEC* ?

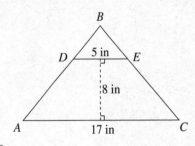

A. 20
B. 22
C. 30
D. 38
E. 42

42. A rectangular box is 20 inches high, 14 inches long, and 8 inches wide. What is the surface area, in square inches, of the rectangular box?

    F.   552
    G.   672
    H. 1,104
    J.   1,680
    K. 2,240

43. Jackie decides to draw shapes using chalk on the sidewalk. The first shape Jackie decides to draw is a rectangle. Her rectangle has a perimeter of 32 inches, and the length of the rectangle is three times its width. What is the area, in square inches, of the rectangle?

    A.   32
    B.   36
    C.   48
    D.   64
    E. 144

50. In the figure below, a table in the shape of an equilateral triangle is placed on top of 3 circular stands. The length of each side of the table is 20 inches. The stands are congruent, and each stand is tangent to the other 2 stands. Each vertex of the table lies on the center of a circle. The region that is interior to the table and exterior to all 3 stands is shaded. What is the area, to the nearest square inch, of the shaded region?

    F.   16
    G.   52
    H. 121
    J.   157
    K. 173

60. In a regular octagon, all 8 interior angles are congruent. What is the measure of each interior angle of a regular octagon?

    F.   45°
    G.   90°
    H. 108°
    J.   135°
    K. 180°

Coordinate Geometry

12. What is the slope–intercept form of $-3x - y + 7 = 0$?

    F. $y = -3x - 7$
    G. $y = -3x + 7$
    H. $y = 3x - 7$
    J. $y = 3x + 7$
    K. $y = 7x + 3$

21. What is the slope–intercept form of $6x + 2y - 4 = 12$?

    A. $y = 3x + 8$

    B. $y = 3x - 8$

    C. $y = -3x + 8$

    D. $y = -3x - 8$

    E. $y = -8x + 3$

22. What is the slope of any line perpendicular to the line $2x + 5y = -10$?

    F. $-\dfrac{5}{2}$

    G. $-\dfrac{2}{5}$

    H. $\dfrac{2}{5}$

    J. $\dfrac{1}{2}$

    K. $\dfrac{5}{2}$

23. A line in the standard (x,y) coordinate plane has equation $-5x + 3y = -9$. What is the slope of this line?

    A. -3

    B. $-\dfrac{5}{3}$

    C. $\dfrac{3}{5}$

    D. $\dfrac{5}{3}$

    E. 3

31. What is the y-coordinate of the point in the standard (x,y) coordinate plane at which the lines $y = 4x + 7$ and $y = 6x - 3$ intersect?

    A. 5
    B. 6
    C. 7
    D. 10
    E. 27

36. What is the slope of the line that passes through both of the points $(3,7)$ and $(9,11)$ in the standard (x,y) coordinate plane?

    F. $-\dfrac{3}{2}$

    G. $-\dfrac{2}{3}$

    H. $\dfrac{2}{3}$

    J. $\dfrac{3}{2}$

    K. 10

41. Which of the following equations, when graphed in the standard (x,y) coordinate plane, would cross the x-axis at $x = -3$ and $x = 5$?

    A. $y = -3(x - 3)(x + 5)$

    B. $y = -3(x + 3)(x - 5)$

    C. $y = 3(x + 3)(x + 5)$

    D. $y = 5(x - 3)(x - 5)$

    E. $y = 5(x - 3)(x + 5)$

Use the following information to answer questions 44–45.

The points $P(-5,6)$, $Q(-3,4)$, $R(-3,12)$, and $S(4,4)$ are shown in the standard (x,y) coordinate plane below.

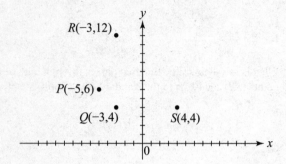

44. What is the slope of $\overleftrightarrow{PR}$?

F. 3

G. $-\dfrac{2}{9}$

H. -1

J. $-\dfrac{9}{4}$

K. -4

45. What is the tangent of the smallest angle in right triangle QRS ?

A. $\dfrac{7}{15}$

B. $\dfrac{7}{\sqrt{105}}$

C. $\dfrac{8}{\sqrt{105}}$

D. $\dfrac{7}{8}$

E. $\dfrac{8}{7}$

59. Which of the following equations describes a line that is parallel to a line with equation $-4x+3y=24$?

A. $-8x+6y=36$

B. $-4x-3y=12$

C. $-3x+4y=18$

D. $4x+3y=9$

E. $8x+6y=21$

Trigonometry

24. The right triangle shown below has a hypotenuse of 9 centimeters. The measure of the angle indicated is 78°. Which of the following is closest to the length, in centimeters, of the side opposite the 78° angle?

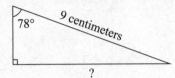

(Note: $\sin 12° \approx 0.2079$ $\sin 78° \approx 0.9781$

$\cos 12° \approx 0.9781$ $\cos 78° \approx 0.2079$

$\tan 12° \approx 0.2126$ $\tan 78° \approx 4.7046$)

F. 0.978
G. 1.871
H. 8.800
J. 8.803
K. 42.342

28. Mario is standing on the ground and looking at the top of a flagpole. He knows that the flagpole is exactly 18 feet high and that $\sin\theta = \dfrac{5}{13}$, where θ is the angle indicated in the figure below. About how many feet long is the indicated distance from Mario on the ground to the top of the flagpole?

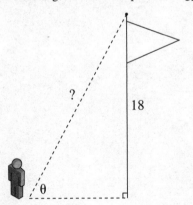

F. 46.8
G. 43.2
H. 19.5
J. 13.0
K. 6.9

35. A right triangle is given in the figure below. Which of the following expressions gives θ ?

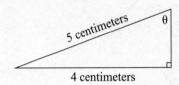

A. $\cos^{-1}\left(\dfrac{4}{5}\right)$

B. $\tan^{-1}\left(\dfrac{4}{5}\right)$

C. $\sin^{-1}\left(\dfrac{4}{5}\right)$

D. $\tan^{-1}\left(\dfrac{5}{4}\right)$

E. $\cos^{-1}\left(\dfrac{5}{4}\right)$

48. Tommy lives on the edge of a lake and wants to travel by boat to his friend Sherrie's house. Tommy travels the 550 yards from his house to Sherrie's house along a straight line in a direction (shown below) that is 33° clockwise from due east. To the nearest yard, Sherrie's house is how many yards due south and how many miles due east from Tommy's house?

(Note: $\sin 33° \approx 0.545$, $\cos 33° \approx 0.839$)

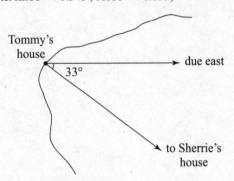

	due south	due east
F.	275	476
G.	300	461
H.	325	550
J.	389	389
K.	461	300

52. An angle with measure θ such that $\cos\theta = \dfrac{24}{25}$ is in standard position with its terminal side extending into Quadrant IV, as shown in the standard (x,y) coordinate plane below. What is the value of $\tan\theta$?

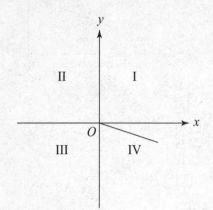

F. $\dfrac{24}{7}$

G. $\dfrac{24}{25}$

H. $-\dfrac{7}{25}$

J. $-\dfrac{7}{24}$

K. $-\dfrac{24}{25}$

GEOMETRY DRILL 2 ANSWER KEY

Plane Geometry

7. B
15. C
17. D
18. H
27. A
32. J
35. A
37. D
38. J
39. B
40. K
41. E
42. H
43. C
50. F
60. J

Trigonometry

24. J
28. F
35. C
48. G
52. J

Coordinate Geometry

12. G
21. C
22. K
23. D
31. E
36. H
41. B
44. F
45. D
59. A

GEOMETRY DRILL 2 EXPLANATIONS

Plane Geometry

7. **B**   To solve for the perimeter of a parallelogram, recall that the opposite sides of a parallelogram are equal in length. The lengths of the four sides of this parallelogram are therefore 12 m, 10 m, 12 m, and 10 m. The perimeter of the parallelogram is the sum of these four values, 44 m. If you picked (A), you may have found the sum of the given two sides.

15. **C**   Since you know that the two lawns have equal areas, you can use the area of Kayla's lawn to find the length of the sides of her neighbor's lawn. The formula for area of a triangle is $A = \frac{1}{2}bh$, which means that the area of Kayla's triangular lawn is $A = \frac{1}{2}(90)(80) = \frac{1}{2}(7,200) = 3,600$ ft^2. Using that as the total area of the square lawn, use the formula for the area of a square to solve for each side. The formula for the area of a square is $A = s^2$, where s is the length of each side of the square. Use the area of Kayla's lawn to find $s^2 = 3,600$, and $s = 60$. If you chose (E), be careful: this is the perimeter of the square, not its side length.

17. **D**   When two parallel lines are intersected by a transversal, it forms small angles and big angles. Any small angle is equal to any other small angle, and any big angle is equal to any other big angle. Lastly, any small angle and any big angle are supplementary, and their measures sum to 180°. In the figure, the angle measuring $x°$ is a small angle, and the angle measuring $y°$ is a big angle, so their sum equals 180°. The other choices make specific assumptions about the angles, which can't be supported by the information given in the problem.

18. **H**   The question gives the height and total area of Brandi's triangular wall. To find the length of the base, use the formula for area of a triangle, which is $A = \frac{1}{2}bh$. Substitute the given information to find $300 = \frac{1}{2}b(6)$, 300 = 3b, and b = 100 meters, or (H). If you picked (G), you may have forgotten the fraction $\frac{1}{2}$ in the area formula.

27. **A**   Similar triangles have corresponding sides that are proportional to one another. In this question, you are given that the corresponding sides in two similar triangles are in a ratio of 3:5, or $\frac{3}{5}$. Since the length of one of the equal sides in the larger isosceles triangle is 30 centimeters, set up a proportion to find the length of one of the equal sides in the smaller triangle. If x is the length of the side in the smaller triangle, then $\frac{3}{5} = \frac{x}{30}$. Cross-multiplying gives 5x = 90, and x = 18, as in (A). If you chose (D), you may have reversed the numbers in the proportion and treated 30 cm as a side of the *smaller* triangle.

32. **J** To find the area of a circle, use the area formula $A = \pi r^2$. Given that the radius of the circle is 12 inches, you can substitute 12 into the formula to find that $A = \pi(12)^2 = 144\pi$. Choice (F) multiplies the radius by π. Choice (G) is the diameter of the circle, and (H) is twice that. Choice (K) finds the diameter of 24 inches and uses that as the radius in the area formula.

35. **A** Since two sides of an isosceles triangle have equal lengths, the given side, 22 centimeters, could be one of the equal sides, or it could be the third side of the triangle. If it were the third side of the isosceles triangle, the lengths of the other two sides would be equal. Using the perimeter, we know that the last two sides must total $57 - 22 = 35$ cm in length. So each side would measure $\frac{35}{2} = 17.5$ cm, which is not in the answer choices. Therefore, you can conclude that the side of 22 centimeters must be one of the two equal sides, and the third side is $57 - 22 - 22 = 13$ cm, as in (A). Choice (E) is rarely correct on the ACT, and in this case, we were able to solve directly for our answer.

37. **D** Given that triangle XYZ has the same base and height, you can solve for the height and base by using the area formula for a triangle, which is $A = \frac{1}{2}bh$. Since base and height are the same, the equation then becomes $A = \frac{1}{2}h \cdot h$, or $A = \frac{1}{2}h^2$. Therefore, since the area of the triangle is 72 square inches, $\frac{1}{2}h^2 = 72$, and $h = 12$. Since the circle is tangent to the triangle at point W, the line WY is both the height of the triangle and the diameter of circle O. Therefore, the radius of the circle is 6, and you can plug this radius in to the formula for area of a circle, which is $A = \pi r^2$. So, $A = \pi(6)^2$, and $A = 36\pi$. If you chose (B), be careful: this is the circumference of the circle. If you chose (E), you may have forgotten to halve the diameter before finding the area of the circle.

38. **J** The length of the ramp is the hypotenuse of the right triangle formed by the height of the ramp, the height of the pool, and the ground. The only length you are given is the height of the pool, which is 3 yards. The length of the ramp will be the hypotenuse of this triangle, so use SOHCAHTOA. In this case, $\sin 48° = \frac{3}{\text{ramp}}$. Substitute the approximation $\sin 48° \approx 0.74$ into your equation to get $0.74 = \frac{3}{\text{ramp}}$, or $\text{ramp} = \frac{3}{0.74} \approx 4.1$ yards when rounded to the nearest 0.1 yards.

39. **B** First, find the volume of the pool to figure out how much water needs to be pumped into the pool. The formula for volume of a rectangular box is $V = l \cdot w \cdot h$, so $V_{Pool} = 20 \cdot 10 \cdot 3 = 600$ cubic yards. In the explanation above the figure, you are given that the water pump fills the pool at an average rate of 70 cubic yards per hour. So, to find the amount of time it takes to fully fill the pool, divide the entire volume by the rate given, which is $\frac{600}{70} \approx 8.6$ hours, which is (B). If you selected (A), you may not have rounded correctly.

40. **K** Shapes that are geometrically similar to one another have sides that are proportional in length. Since you know that the height of the original pool is 3 yards, and the length of the longest side is 20 yards, you can set up the proportion $\frac{3}{4.5} = \frac{20}{x}$, where x is the length of the longest side in the new pool. Cross-multiplying gives you $3x = 90$, and $x = 30$ yards for the length of the longest side of the new pool. If you chose (G), be careful: you may have reversed the terms in the proportion, and if you chose (H), you may have found the new length of the wrong side.

41. **E** To find the perimeter of the quadrilateral $ADEC$, find the lengths of sides AD and EC. Since DE is parallel to AC, draw a line from point D perpendicular to AC and a line from point E also perpendicular to AC. The lengths of each of these segments is 8 inches because parallel lines are always the same distance apart from each other. Therefore, this rectangle has length 8 inches and width 5 inches with two smaller right triangles on either side. Since triangle ABC is isosceles, the base of each of the right triangles is exactly half of the remaining length of the base of triangle ABC, or $\frac{17-5}{2} = \frac{12}{2} = 6$. Given two sides of each smaller right triangle, you can use the Pythagorean theorem, $a^2 + b^2 = c^2$, to find the length of the third side. In this case, that third side is the hypotenuse, c, and plugging the given values into the equation gives $(6)^2 + (8)^2 = c^2$, or $c^2 = 100$, which means that the hypotenuse is exactly 10 inches. The perimeter is the sum $AD + DE + EC + AC = 5 + 10 + 17 + 10 = 42$ inches, or (E).

42. **H** Draw a figure to help you visualize this problem. To find the surface area of a rectangular box, add the areas of all the faces of the box. In a rectangular box, faces that are opposite one another are equal, so you can find the area of the front, top, and side of the box and multiply that result by 2. The area of the front face is $14 \times 20 = 280$. The area of the top face is $14 \times 8 = 112$, and the area of the right side of the box is $8 \times 20 = 160$. The total of those three sides is $280 + 112 + 160 = 552$, which is (F). However, this value gives only three of the faces of the box, so multiply 552 by 2 to get 1,104 square inches, which is (H). If you picked (K), you may have found the volume of the box rather than its surface area.

43. **C** The formula for perimeter of a rectangle is $P = 2l + 2w$. For this rectangle, the length is three times the width, or $l = 3w$. Substituting $3w$ for l and 32 for P into the formula for perimeter gives $32 = 2(3w) + 2w$, or $32 = 6w + 2w$, $8w = 32$, and $w = 4$. So since the width of the rectangle is 4 inches, using the relationship $l = 3w$, the length is 12 inches. To find the area, use the formula for area of a rectangle: $A = l \cdot w = 12 \cdot 4 = 48$ square inches, or (C).

50. **F** Since you're looking for the area of the shaded region of the triangular table, you first need to find the area of the table and then subtract the areas of the circular stands on the inside of the

table. The area of the triangle is $A = \frac{1}{2}bh$, so you first need to find the height. Draw a line from one vertex perpendicular to the opposite side, to form two 30-60-90 triangles. Since the sides of this triangle have a ratio of $x : x\sqrt{3} : 2x$, and the value of x for this triangle is 10, so the height of the equilateral triangle is $x\sqrt{3}$, or $10\sqrt{3}$ inches. Substitute the base and height into the formula to get $A = \frac{1}{2}bh = \frac{1}{2}(20)(10\sqrt{3}) = (10)(10\sqrt{3}) = 100\sqrt{3}$ square inches. Now find the areas of the three circle sectors, which are all equal because the circles all have the same radius. Each of the angles of an equilateral triangle is 60°, so the three sectors have central angles of 60°. The radius of each circle is exactly half of the side length of the equilateral triangle, or $\frac{1}{2}(20) = 10$ inches. The area of one sector of the circle is $\frac{60°}{360°} = \frac{1}{6}$ of the entire circle, so the area of a sector is $A = \frac{1}{6}\pi r^2 = \frac{1}{6}\pi(10)^2 = \frac{1}{6}(100\pi) = \frac{50}{3}\pi$ square inches. Therefore, the total area of the three sectors is $3\left(\frac{50}{3}\pi\right) = 50\pi$ square inches. Now subtract the area of the sectors from the area of the triangle: $100\sqrt{3} - 50\pi \approx 16$, or (F). If you picked (H), you may have subtracted the area of only one of the sectors.

60. **J** The total degrees in any n-sided polygon is given by the equation $(n-2)\cdot 180°$. You use this equation to figure out that for an octagon, the total number of degrees is $(8-2)\cdot 180° = 6\cdot 180° = 1{,}080°$. Divide the total number of degrees by 8 to find the measure of each interior angle: $\frac{1.080°}{8} = 135°$. If you picked any of the other answers, you may have been using an incorrect value for the total degrees in the octagon.

Coordinate Geometry

12. **G** The slope-intercept form of a line is $y = mx + b$. To put an equation in this form, isolate y on the left-hand side of the equation. First, add $3x$ to each side to get $-y = 3x - 7$, and then subtract 7 from each side to get $-y = 3x - 7$. Now, you just need to multiply (or divide) both sides by -1 to get $7 = -3x + 7$, so the answer is (G). Choices (F), (H), and (J) are similar versions of the correct answer that each make an error involving a negative sign, either when adding or subtracting terms from the left side or when multiplying the final equation by -1.

21. **C** To find the slope-intercept form of a line, rewrite the equation in the form $y = mx + b$. Begin by subtracting $6x$ from each side of the equation to get $2y - 4 = -6x + 12$. Next, add 4 to each side to get $2y = -6x + 16$. Finally, divide each side by 2 to get $y = -3x + 8$. Choices (A), (B), and (D) all make mistakes involving negative signs, and (E) switches the coefficient of x with the constant on the right side of the equation.

22. **K** First, find the slope of the line by writing it in slope-intercept form. Subtract $2x$ from each side and then divide each side by 5 to get $y = -\dfrac{2}{5}x - 2$. Perpendicular lines have opposite reciprocal slopes. Since the slope of the original line is $-\dfrac{2}{5}$, the negative reciprocal would be $\dfrac{5}{2}$, as in (K). Choice (F) forgets to take the *negative* reciprocal. Choice (G) is the slope of a parallel line, and (H) gives the negative of the original slope, but not the negative reciprocal.

23. **D** When finding the slope of a line given in the standard (x,y) coordinate plane, rewrite the equation in slope-intercept form, which is $y = mx + b$. In this case, start by adding $5x$ to each side of the equation to isolate y, which results in $3y = 5x - 9$. Now divide both sides by 3, giving $y = \dfrac{5}{3}x - 3$. In this case, the slope is the coefficient of x, which is $\dfrac{5}{3}$. If you chose (B), be careful: You may have switched some negative signs.

31. **E** To find the y-coordinate of the point of intersection of two lines, you need to find values for x and y that satisfy both equations. Both equations are equal to y, so set the right side of the first equation equal to the right side of the second equation: $4x + 7 = 6x - 3$. Then solve for x to get $-2x = -10$, and $x = 5$. To find the value of y, substitute $x = 5$ into either of the original equations. If you use the first equation, for example, $y = 4(5) + 7 = 20 + 7 = 27$. If you chose (A) be careful: this is the x-coordinate!

36. **H** To find the slope of a line given two points in the standard (x,y) coordinate plane, use the slope formula: $\text{slope} = \dfrac{\text{rise}}{\text{run}} = \dfrac{y_2 - y_1}{x_2 - x_1}$. Using the points $(3,7)$ and $(9,11)$, $\text{slope} = \dfrac{11 - 7}{9 - 3} = \dfrac{4}{6} = \dfrac{2}{3}$, or (H). If you chose (F) or (G), be careful: You may have forgotten one of the negatives in the slope formula. If you chose (J), you might have found $\dfrac{\text{run}}{\text{rise}}$ rather than $\dfrac{\text{rise}}{\text{run}}$.

41. **B** In the standard (x,y) coordinate plane, when a function crosses the x-axis, y will be equal to 0. So, you are looking for an equation in which, when $x = -3$ and when $x = 5$, $y = 0$. When you plug in $x = -3$ to all the equations, only (B) and (C) result in $y = 0$. When you plug in $x = 5$ to those two remaining answer choices, only (B) still gives you $y = 0$. Choices (A) and (E) give equations that, when graphed, cross the x-axis at $x = 3$ and $x = -5$, and (D) gives an equation that, when graphed, crosses the x-axis when $x = -3$ and $x = -5$.

44. **F**   To find the slope of a line given two points on the standard (x, y) coordinate plane, use the formula for slope: slope $= \dfrac{\text{rise}}{\text{run}} = \dfrac{y_2 - y_1}{x_2 - x_1}$. Plug in the given coordinate points into the equation to get $\dfrac{12 - 6}{-3 - (-5)} = \dfrac{6}{2} = 3$, as in (F). If you chose (H) or (J), you may have found the slope of a different line. Choice (H) is the slope of $\overleftrightarrow{PQ}$, and (G) is the slope of $\overleftrightarrow{PS}$.

45. **D**   Start by drawing the three sides of the right triangle QRS and find the lengths of its legs. Since QR is a vertical segment, the length of QR is the difference between the y-coordinates, or 8 units. Since QS is a horizontal segment, the length of QS is the difference between the x-coordinates, or 7 units. In all triangles, the shortest side is always opposite the smallest angle. Therefore, $\angle R$ is the smallest angle because it is opposite the shortest side. To find the tangent of $\angle R$, use SOHCAHTOA, which tells you that $\tan \theta = \dfrac{\text{opposite}}{\text{adjacent}}$. So $\tan R = \dfrac{7}{8}$, which is (D). If you chose one of the other answers, make sure you are solving for the correct function. Choice (E) is the tangent of $\angle S$. Choice (B) is the sine of $\angle R$, and (C) is the cosine of $\angle R$.

59. **A**   To find which line is parallel to the given line, begin by writing the original equation in slope-intercept form, or $y = mx + b$. Start by adding $4x$ to each side of the equation, giving you $3y = 4x + 24$, and then divide each side by 3 to get $y = \dfrac{4}{3}x + 6$. The slope of this equation is $\dfrac{4}{3}$, and any line parallel to this line must also have a slope of $\dfrac{4}{3}$. Convert each answer choice to slope-intercept form to find the equation that also has a slope of $\dfrac{4}{3}$. Choice (A) is the answer because the equation in slope-intercept form is $y = \dfrac{4}{3}x + 6$. Choices (B), (C), and (E) all have slopes of $-\dfrac{4}{3}$, and (C) has a slope of $-\dfrac{3}{4}$, which is the slope of a line perpendicular to the original equation.

Trigonometry

24. **J**   Since you are asked to find the *opposite* side of a particular angle, and you are given the *hypotenuse*, use the first part of SOHCAHTOA, which indicates that $\sin \theta = \dfrac{\text{opposite}}{\text{hypotenuse}}$. Substitute the given information to find $78° = \dfrac{x}{9}$. Multiply each side of the equation by 9, so $x = 9 \cdot \sin 78°$. Using the provided approximation for $\sin 78°$, $x = 9 \times 0.9781 = 8.8029$, which rounds to 8.803. Choice (H) is close, but it isn't the closest approximation. If you picked (K), you may have found the tangent instead of the sine.

28. **F**   First, since the hypotenuse of the triangle must be its longest side, eliminate (H), (J), and (K). Given that $\sin\theta = \dfrac{5}{13}$, use SOHCAHTOA. This means that $\sin\theta = \dfrac{\text{opposite}}{\text{hypotenuse}}$, so you can set up a proportion to find the length of the hypotenuse. Let x be the length of the hypotenuse, and $\sin\theta = \dfrac{18}{x}$. Set the two values for $\sin\theta$ equal to each other to get $\dfrac{5}{13} = \dfrac{18}{x}$. Solve the equation by multiplying each side by $13x$ to $5x = 234$, or $x = 46.8$ feet. If you picked (G), be careful: This is the horizontal distance between Mario and the flagpole.

35. **C**   In the figure, you are given the hypotenuse of the right triangle, as well as the side that is opposite the indicated angle θ. Therefore, use SOHCAHTOA, specifically the relationship of $\sin\theta = \dfrac{\text{opposite}}{\text{hypotenuse}}$. Substitute the information given in the question to find $\sin\theta = \dfrac{4}{5}$. To solve for the value of θ, take the inverse sine of each side of the equation, which would give $\sin^{-1}(\sin\theta) = \sin^{-1}\left(\dfrac{4}{5}\right)$. The inverse sine function and sine function cancel each other out, leaving you with $\theta = \sin^{-1}\left(\dfrac{4}{5}\right)$.

48. **G**   Redraw the right triangle with a 33° angle and a hypotenuse of length 550 yards. The length of the leg adjacent to the 33° angle is the distance due east, and the length of the leg opposite the 33° angle is the distance due south. To figure out the lengths of those legs, choose one and use SOHCAHTOA. To find the distance due south, or the distance *opposite* the given angle, use $\sin\theta = \dfrac{\text{opposite}}{\text{hypotenuse}}$, so $\sin 33° = \dfrac{\text{south}}{550}$. Using the provided information, $\dfrac{\text{south}}{550} = 0.545$, and $\text{south} = 0.545 \cdot 550 \approx 300$. Choice (G) is the only answer choice with the correct due south distance, so you can stop there. If you prefer to start by finding the distance due east, use $\sin\theta = \dfrac{\text{adjacent}}{\text{hypotenuse}}$, so $\sin 33° = \dfrac{\text{east}}{550}$. Using the provided information, $\dfrac{\text{east}}{550} = 0.839$, and $\text{east} = 0.839 \cdot 550 \approx 461$. If you picked (K), be careful: The sides are reversed in this answer choice.

52. **J**   This is a difficult problem, but it is easy to solve if you know a few basic trig facts. First, remember "All Students Take Calculus." This is a helpful reminder of which quadrants have positive functions. In Quadrant I, *all* trig functions are positive. In Quadrant II, *sine* is positive. In Quadrant III, *tangent* is positive. In Quadrant IV, *cosine* is positive. This is helpful because it tells us that a tangent value in Quadrant IV must be negative, eliminating (F) and (G). Then, because $\tan\theta = \dfrac{\text{opposite}}{\text{adjacent}}$, our final value cannot include the hypotenuse 25, eliminating (H) and (K) and leaving only (J).

Chapter 10
Math Practice Test 1

ACT MATHEMATICS TEST
60 Minutes—60 Questions

DIRECTIONS: Solve each problem, choose the correct answer, and then darken the corresponding oval on your answer document.

Do not linger over problems that take too much time. Solve as many as you can; then return to the others in the time you have left for this test.

You are permitted to use a calculator on this test. You may use your calculator for any problems you choose, but some of the problems may best be done without using a calculator.

Note: Unless otherwise stated, all of the following should be assumed:

1. Illustrative figures are NOT necessarily drawn to scale.
2. Geometric figures lie in a plane.
3. The word *line* indicates a straight line.
4. The word *average* indicates arithmetic mean.

DO YOUR FIGURING HERE.

1. Bob's Burgers charges $8 dollars for a hamburger and $5 for an order of French fries. Last month, h hamburgers and f orders of fries were purchased. Which of the following expressions gives the total amount of money, in dollars, Bob's Burgers earned on hamburgers and fries last month?

    A. $5h + 8f$
    B. $8h + 5f$
    C. $13(h + f)$
    D. $40(h + f)$
    E. $8(h + f) + 5f$

2. If $a = 8$, $b = -2$, and $c = 3$, what does $(a - b + c)(b + c)$ equal?

    F. -65
    G. -13
    H. 9
    J. 13
    K. 65

3. An artist at the State Fair paints 40 portraits per day. A second artist paints 50 portraits per day. The second artist opens for business three days after the first. Both remain open until the Fair closes, which is 11 days after the first artist began. Together, the two artists have painted how many portraits?

    A. 400
    B. 440
    C. 720
    D. 840
    E. 900

4. Josh has been a professional baseball player for four years. His home run totals each year have been 30, 39, 51, and 44, respectively. In order to maintain his current average number of home runs per season, how many home runs must Josh hit next year?

    F. 31
    G. 39
    H. 41
    J. 44
    H. 51

GO ON TO THE NEXT PAGE.

5. A craftswoman is paid $9.00 per necklace for making up to 30 necklaces per week. For each necklace over 30 that she is asked to make in a week, she is paid 1.5 times her regular pay. How much does she earn in a week in which she is asked to make 34 necklaces?

A. $162
B. $270
C. $306
D. $324
E. $459

6. Which of the following mathematical expressions is equivalent to the verbal expression "The square root of a number, n, is 19 less than the value of 5 divided by n" ?

F. $n^2 = \dfrac{5}{n} - 19$

G. $n^2 = \dfrac{n}{5} - 19$

H. $\sqrt{n} = 19 - \dfrac{n}{5}$

J. $\sqrt{n} = \dfrac{y}{n} - 19$

K. $\sqrt{n} = \dfrac{5}{n} - 19$

7. If $12(y - 3) = -7$, then $y = $?

A. $-\dfrac{43}{12}$

B. $-\dfrac{10}{12}$

C. $-\dfrac{7}{12}$

D. $\dfrac{29}{12}$

E. $\dfrac{43}{12}$

8. At a department store, purses sell for $12 each during a one-day sale. Rita spent $84 on purses during the sale, $38.50 less than if she had bought the purses at the regular price. How much do purses cost at the regular price?

F. $ 5.50
G. $15.50
H. $16.00
J. $17.50
K. $20.00

GO ON TO THE NEXT PAGE.

9. $(2a - 5b^2)(2a + 5b^2) =$

   A. $4a^2 - 25b^4$
   B. $4a^2 - 10b^4$
   C. $4a^2 + 25b^4$
   D. $2a^2 - 25b^4$
   E. $2a^2 - 10b^4$

DO YOUR FIGURING HERE.

10. A rectangle's perimeter is 18 feet, and its area is 18 square feet. What is the length of the longest side of the rectangle?

   F. 10
   G. 8
   H. 6
   J. 3
   K. 2

11. In $\triangle XYZ$, $\angle X$ is 64°. What is the sum of $\angle Y$ and $\angle Z$?

   A. 26°
   B. 64°
   C. 116°
   D. 126°
   E. 128°

12. Each morning, a glee club member chooses her outfit among 4 plaid skirts, 5 pairs of argyle socks, 3 sweaters, and 4 headbands. How many different outfits are possible for her to put together on any given morning consisting of one skirt, one pair of socks, one sweater, and one headband?

   F. 4
   G. 15
   H. 16
   J. 120
   K. 240

13. Positive integers x, y, and z are consecutive such that $x < y < z$. The sum of x, $2y$, and $\frac{z}{2}$ is 59. What are the values of x, y, and z, respectively?

   A. 10, 11, 12
   B. 11, 12, 13
   C. 14, 15, 16
   D. 16, 17, 18
   E. 18, 19, 20

14. A function $h(x)$ is defined as $h(x) = -5x^3$. What is $h(-2)$?

   F. −1,000
   G. −40
   H. 30
   J. 40
   K. 1,000

GO ON TO THE NEXT PAGE.

DO YOUR FIGURING HERE.

15. If $z = \sqrt[4]{97}$, then which of the following must be true?

    A. $2 < z < 3$
    B. $3 < z < 4$
    C. $4 < z < 5$
    D. $5 < z < 6$
    E. $6 < z$

16. What is the greatest common factor of 96, 108, and 144 ?

    F. 12
    G. 18
    H. 24
    J. 36
    K. 48

17. Cowan Cola is holding a contest to develop a new, more environmentally efficient can for its soft drink. The winning can is a cylinder ten inches tall, with a volume of 40π in^3. What is the radius, in inches, of the can?

    A. 1
    B. 2
    C. 4
    D. 5
    E. 8

18. A clock has 12 numbered points. Four points W, X, Y, Z lie on the clock representing certain numbers. W represents 3:00. X is 4 units clockwise from W. Y is 9 units counterclockwise from W. Z is 5 units counterclockwise from W and 7 units clockwise from W. What is the order of points, starting with W and working clockwise around the circle?

    F. W, X, Y, Z
    G. W, X, Z, Y
    H. W, Y, X, Z
    J. W, Y, Z, X
    K. W, Z, Y, X

19. Tribbles reproduce at a rate described by the function $f(a) = 12(3)^a$, where a represents the number of days and $f(a)$ represents the number of tribbles. At this rate, how many tribbles will there be at the end of Day Four?

    A. 48
    B. 96
    C. 240
    D. 972
    E. 1,296

GO ON TO THE NEXT PAGE.

20. The height of a triangle is half the height of a larger triangle. The two triangles have the same base. The area of the larger triangle is Y square feet. The area of the smaller triangle is xY square units. Which of the following is the value of x ?

F. $\dfrac{1}{4}$

G. $\dfrac{1}{2}$

H. 1

J. 2

K. 4

DO YOUR FIGURING HERE.

21. $(2x+3y+4z)-(6x-7y+8z)$ is equivalent to:

A. $-4x+10y-4z$

B. $-4x+10y+12z$

C. $-4x-4y-4z$

D. $-8x+10y+12z$

E. $-8x-4y+12z$

22. The right triangle shown below has lengths measured in inches. What is $\cos\theta$?

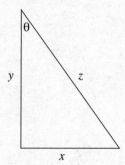

F. $\dfrac{x}{y}$

G. $\dfrac{x}{z}$

H. $\dfrac{y}{x}$

J. $\dfrac{y}{z}$

K. $\dfrac{z}{y}$

GO ON TO THE NEXT PAGE.

DO YOUR FIGURING HERE.

23. On a dead-end street, 8 houses are evenly spaced around a circular cul-de-sac. A newspaper delivery person bikes around the cul-de-sac and tosses the newspapers onto the driveway of each house. The delivery person bikes rapidly enough that the person can only toss to every third house. On which lap around the cul-de-sac will the delivery person have delivered newspapers to all 8 houses on the street?

    A. 2nd
    B. 3rd
    C. 4th
    D. 8th
    E. 11th

24. Lines q and m are in the standard (x,y) coordinate plane. The equation for line q is $y = 23x + 500$. The y-intercept of line m is 10 less than the y-intercept of line q. What is the y-intercept of line m ?

    F. 2.3
    G. 13
    H. 50
    J. 490
    K. 510

25. The expression $-9a^5(8a^7 - 4a^3)$ is equivalent to:

    A. $-36a^9$
    B. $-72a^{12} + 36a^8$
    C. $-72a^{12} - 36a^8$
    D. $-72a^{35} + 36a^{15}$
    E. $-72a^{35} - 36a^{15}$

26. $-4|-9 + 2| = ?$

    F. -44
    G. -28
    H. 3
    J. 28
    K. 44

GO ON TO THE NEXT PAGE.

27. In right triangle $\triangle WYZ$ shown below, $\overline{XV}$ is perpendicular to $\overline{WZ}$ at point V and is parallel to $\overline{YZ}$. Line segments $\overline{WY}$, $\overline{XV}$, and $\overline{WV}$ measure 30 inches, 6 inches, and 8 inches, respectively. What is the measurement, in inches, of $\overline{YZ}$?

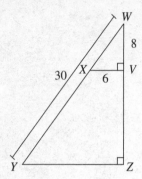

DO YOUR FIGURING HERE.

- A. 15
- B. 18
- C. 20
- D. 24
- E. 27

28. As an experiment in botany class, students tracked a plant growing at a constant rate upward, perpendicular to the ground. As shown in the table below, they measured the height, h inches, of the plant at 1-week intervals from $w = 0$ weeks to $w = 4$ weeks.

w	0	1	2	3	4
h	7	10	13	16	19

Which of the following equations expresses this data?

- F. $h = w + 7$
- G. $h = 3w + 4$
- H. $h = 3w + 7$
- J. $h = 7w + 3$
- K. $h = 10w$

29. The inequality $4(n-3) < 5(n+2)$ is equivalent to which of the following inequalities?

- A. $n > -22$
- B. $n > -14$
- C. $n > -13$
- D. $n > -2$
- E. $n > 2$

GO ON TO THE NEXT PAGE.

30. The sides of an equilateral triangle are 4 inches long. One vertex of the triangle is at (1,1) on a coordinate graph labeled in inch units. Which of the following could give the coordinates of another vertex of the triangle?

   F. (–4, 1)
   G. (0, 1)
   H. (2, 3)
   J. (1,–3)
   K. (5,–3)

DO YOUR FIGURING HERE.

31. For △*LMN*, shown below, which of the following expresses the value of *m* in terms of *n* ?

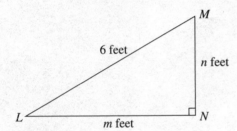

   A. $6-n$
   B. $\sqrt{6-n}$
   C. $\sqrt{12+n^2}$
   D. $\sqrt{36-n^2}$
   E. $\sqrt{36+n^2}$

32. A jar holds 10 pear jellybeans, 16 cherry jellybeans, and 19 watermelon jellybeans. How many extra pear jellybeans must be added to the 45 jellybeans currently in the jar so that the probability of randomly selecting a pear jellybean is $\frac{3}{8}$?

   F. 9
   G. 11
   H. 21
   J. 35
   K. 45

GO ON TO THE NEXT PAGE.

33. The graph of the equation $6x + 3y = 12$ is found in which quadrants of the standard (x,y) coordinate plane below?

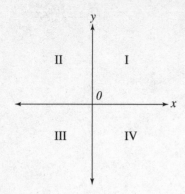

    A. II and IV only
    B. I, II, and III only
    C. I, II, and IV only
    D. I, III, and IV only
    E. II, III, and IV only

34. The graph of $y = -2x^2 + 10$ contains the point $(3, 4n)$ in the standard (x,y) coordinate plane. What is the value of n ?

    F.   7
    G.   1
    H. −2
    J. −4
    K. −8

35. Jennifer, Kelly, and Meredith split their apartment rent. Jennifer paid $\frac{2}{3}$ of the rent, Kelly paid $\frac{1}{4}$ of the rent, and Meredith paid the rest. What is the ratio of Jennifer's contribution to Kelly's contribution to Meredith's contribution?

    A. 1:3:8
    B. 3:8:1
    C. 3:1:8
    D. 8:3:1
    E. 8:1:3

GO ON TO THE NEXT PAGE.

36. In the standard (x,y) coordinate plane, a circle has an equation of $x^2 + (y+4)^2 = 28$. Which of the following gives the center and radius of the circle, in coordinate units?

	center	radius
F.	$(0,-4)$	$\sqrt{28}$
G.	$(0,-4)$	14
H.	$(0,-4)$	28
J.	$(0, 4)$	$\sqrt{28}$
K.	$(0, 4)$	14

37. An equilateral triangle and 2 semicircles have dimensions as shown in the figure below. What is the perimeter, in inches, of the figure?

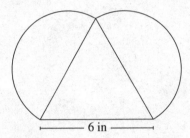

— 6 in —

- **A.** $3 + 3\pi$
- **B.** $6 + 6\pi$
- **C.** $6 + 12\pi$
- **D.** $18 + 6\pi$
- **E.** $18 + 12\pi$

38. In the figure below, points H, J, K, and L bisect the sides of rhombus $DEFG$, and point M is the intersection of $\overline{HK}$ and $\overline{JL}$. The area enclosed by $DEFG$ except the area enclosed by $HEFM$ is shaded. What is the ratio of the area of $HEFM$ to the area of the shaded area?

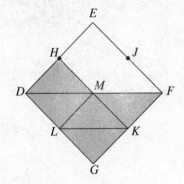

- **F.** 1:2
- **G.** 3:4
- **H.** 3:5
- **J.** 3:8
- **K.** Cannot be determined from the given information

GO ON TO THE NEXT PAGE.

39. In the standard (x,y) coordinate plane, the endpoints of $\overline{FG}$ lie on the coordinates $(-6,10)$ and $(8,-2)$. What is the y-coordinate of the midpoint of $\overline{FG}$?

A. 1
B. 2
C. 4
D. 6
E. 8

DO YOUR FIGURING HERE.

40. What is the volume, in cubic feet, of a cube with a side of length 9 feet?

F. 729
G. 486
J. 243
H. 81
K. 27

41. The system below has linear equations, in which r, s, t, and v are positive integers.

$$rx + sy = t$$
$$rx + sy = v$$

Which of the following best describes a possible graph of such a system of equations in the standard (x,y) coordinate plane?

  I.   2 lines intersecting at only 1 point
 II.   1 single line
III.   2 parallel lines

A. I only
B. III only
C. I and II only
D. II and III only
E. I and III only

GO ON TO THE NEXT PAGE.

42. Given the dimensions in the figure below, which of the following expresses the distance, in feet, from the tree to the house?

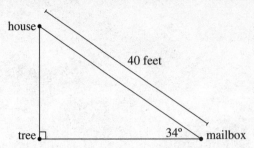

F. $40 \sin 34°$

G. $40 \cos 34°$

H. $40 \tan 34°$

J. $\dfrac{40}{\sin 34°}$

K. $\dfrac{40}{\cos 34°}$

43. The chart below shows the percentage of students, by grade, enrolled in a school. A student is picked randomly in a lottery to win a new graphing calculator. What are the odds (in the grade:not in the grade) that the winning student is in Grade 6 ?

Grade	5	6	7	8	9
Percentage of total number of students	12	22	25	27	14

A.   1:4
B.   1:5
C.   7:25
D.   11:39
E.   11:50

GO ON TO THE NEXT PAGE.

DO YOUR FIGURING HERE.

Use the following information to answer questions 44–46.

The figure below shows the pattern of a square tile mosaic to decorate the wall of Chelsea's Mexican Café. Grout fills the small spaces between individual tile pieces. All white triangular tiles are equilateral and share a vertex with each adjacent triangular piece. A green square piece is at the center of the mosaic. The length of the mosaic is 3 meters.

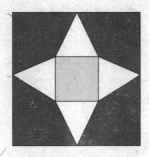

44. How many lines of symmetry in the plane does the pattern of the tile mosaic have?

   F. 2
   G. 3
   H. 4
   J. 8
   K. Infinitely many

45. What is the length of the diagonal of the mosaic, to the nearest 0.1 meters?

   A. 2.4
   B. 3.0
   C. 3.4
   D. 4.2
   E. 5.7

46. Joe wants to put a tile mosaic on the wall of his office. The pattern of the mosaic will be identical to that in the restaurant. The length of the office wall is 20% shorter than the length of the mosaic. The office wall is how many meters long?

   F. 0.6
   G. 2.4
   H. 2.8
   J. 3.6
   K. 6.0

GO ON TO THE NEXT PAGE.

47. In the figure below, $\overline{DE} \parallel \overline{FG}$, $\overline{DG}$ bisects $\angle HDE$, and $\overline{HG}$ bisects $\angle FGD$. If the measure of $\angle EDG$ is 68°, what is the measure of $\angle DHG$?

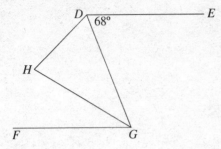

- A. 68°
- B. 78°
- C. 80°
- D. 82°
- E. Cannot be determined from the given information

48. In the figure shown below, points A, B, and C lie on the circle with an area of 16π square meters and center O (not shown). $\overline{AC}$ is the longest chord in the circle, and the measure of $\overline{AB}$ is 4 meters. What is the degree measure of minor arc BC ?

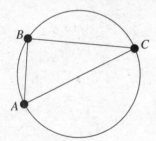

- F. 60°
- G. 90°
- H. 120°
- J. 145°
- K. Cannot be determined from the given information

49. For which of the following values of b would the system of equations below have no solutions?

$$12x + 8y = 16$$

$$3x + by = 2$$

- A. 2
- B. 4
- C. 8
- D. 16
- E. 32

GO ON TO THE NEXT PAGE.

Use the following information to answer questions 50–52.

Rebecca and Scott make and sell pies and cookies for school bake sales. It takes them 1 hour to make a dozen cookies and 3 hours to make a pie. The shaded triangular region shown below is the graph of a system of inequalities representing weekly constraints Rebecca and Scott have on their baking. For making and selling d dozen cookies and p pies, they make a profit of $12d + 25p$ dollars. They sell all the goods they bake.

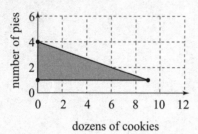

dozens of cookies

50. The constraint represented by the horizontal line segment containing (9,1) means that each school-week, Rebecca and Scott make a minimum of:

F. 1 pie
G. 9 pies
H. 1 dozen cookies
J. 9 dozen cookies
K. 10 dozen cookies

51. What is the maximum profit Rebecca and Scott can earn from the baking they do in 1 school-week?

A. $100
B. $109
C. $122
D. $133
E. $237

52. During the third week of October each year, school is closed for Fall Break, and Rebecca and Scott have more time than usual to bake. During that week, for every hour that they spend baking, they donate $2 to the school's fund for after-school reading programs. This year, they baked 5 pies and 3 dozen cookies during Fall Break. Which of the following is closest to the percent of that week's profit they donated to the reading program fund?

F. 5%
G. 9%
H. 15%
J. 18%
K. 22%

GO ON TO THE NEXT PAGE.

DO YOUR FIGURING HERE.

53. The *determinant* of a matrix $\begin{bmatrix} a & c \\ b & d \end{bmatrix}$ equals $ad - bc$. What must be the value of w for the matrix $\begin{bmatrix} w & w \\ w & 10 \end{bmatrix}$ to have a determinant of 25 ?

   A. 5

   B. $\dfrac{10}{3}$

   C. $\dfrac{5}{2}$

   D. $-\dfrac{5}{3}$

   E. -5

54. Henry discovers that the population of the bacterial colony in his lab can be calculated using the equation $x = B(1 + .2g)^n$, where x is the current population, B is the original number of bacteria, g is a growth rate constant for that species, and n is the number of days elapsed. Which of the following is an expression for B in terms of g, n, and x ?

   F. $x - .2g^n$

   G. $x + .2g^n$

   H. $\left(\dfrac{x}{1 + .2g} \right)^n$

   J. $\dfrac{x}{\left(1 - .2g\right)^n}$

   K. $\dfrac{x}{\left(1 + .2g\right)^n}$

55. If m and n are real numbers such that $m < -1$ and $n > 1$, then which of the following inequalities *must* be true?

   A. $\dfrac{n}{m} > 1$

   B. $|n|^2 > |m|$

   C. $\dfrac{n}{7} + 2 > \dfrac{m}{7} + 2$

   D. $n^2 + 1 > m^2 + 1$

   E. $n^{-2} > m^{-2}$

GO ON TO THE NEXT PAGE.

56. Triangles *TVW* and *XYZ* are shown below. The given side lengths are in inches. The area of △*TVW* is 45 square inches. What is the area of △*XYZ* in square inches?

DO YOUR FIGURING HERE.

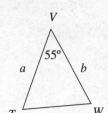

F. 22.5
G. 27
H. 30
J. 45
K. 50

57. Triangle *JKL* is shown in the figure below. The measure of ∠*K* is 50°, *JK* = 9 cm, and *KL* = 6 cm. Which of the following is the lengths, in centimeters, of *LJ* ?

(Note: For a triangle with sides of length *a*, *b*, and *c* opposite angles ∠*A*, ∠*B*, and ∠*C*, respectively, the law of sines states $\dfrac{\sin \angle A}{a} = \dfrac{\sin \angle B}{b} = \dfrac{\sin \angle C}{c}$, and the law of cosines states $c^2 = a^2 + b^2 - 2ab\cos \angle C$.)

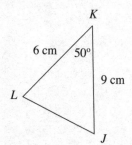

A. $9 \sin 50°$

B. $6 \sin 50°$

C. $\sqrt{9^2 - 6^2}$

D. $\sqrt{9^2 + 6}$

E. $\sqrt{9^2 + 6^2 - 2(9)(6)\cos 50°}$

58. What is the sum of the first 3 terms of the arithmetic sequence in which the 7th term is 13.5, and the 11th term is 18.3 ?

F. 15.9
G. 22.5
H. 25.5
J. 32.4
K. 43.5

GO ON TO THE NEXT PAGE.

59. In the equation $w^2 - pw + q = 0$, p and q are integers. The *only* possible value for w is 8. What is the value of p ?

- A. 8
- B. −8
- C. 16
- D. −16
- E. 64

DO YOUR FIGURING HERE.

60. The solution set of which of the following equations is the set of real numbers that are 4 units from −1 ?

- F. $|x+1| = 4$
- G. $|x-1| = 4$
- H. $|x+4| = 1$
- J. $|x-4| = 1$
- K. $|x+4| = -1$

END OF TEST.
STOP! DO NOT TURN THE PAGE UNTIL TOLD TO DO SO.

Chapter 11
Math Practice Test 1: Answers and Explanations

MATH SCORING DIRECTIONS

Score Your Practice Test

Step A

Count the number of correct answers: _____. This is your *raw score*.

Step B

Use the score conversion table below to look up your raw score. The number to the left is your *scale score*: _____.

Math Scale Conversion Table

Scale Score	Raw Score	Scale Score	Raw Score	Scale Score	Raw Score
36	60	27	45–47	18	24–25
35	59	26	42–44	17	21–23
34	58	25	40–41	16	17–20
33	56–57	24	37–39	15	14–16
32	55	23	35–36	14	11–13
31	54	22	33–34	13	9–10
30	52–53	21	31–32	12	7–8
29	50–51	20	29–30	11	6
28	48–49	19	26–28	10	5

MATH PRACTICE TEST 1 ANSWER KEY

1. B	31. D
2. J	32. G
3. D	33. C
4. H	34. H
5. D	35. D
6. K	36. F
7. D	37. B
8. J	38. H
9. A	39. C
10. H	40. F
11. C	41. D
12. K	42. F
13. D	43. D
14. J	44. H
15. B	45. D
16. F	46. G
17. B	47. B
18. H	48. H
19. D	49. A
20. G	50. F
21. A	51. D
22. J	52. K
23. B	53. A
24. J	54. K
25. B	55. C
26. G	56. J
27. B	57. E
28. H	58. G
29. A	59. C
30. J	60. F

MATH PRACTICE TEST 1 EXPLANATIONS

1. **B** Since *h* represents the number of hamburgers, multiply it by $8 to get the total amount of money paid for burgers; since *f* represents the number of orders of fries, multiply it by $5 to get the total amount of money paid for fries. You want the total amount of money earned, so you need to add the two expressions together: $8h + 5f$. You can also just plug in values for *h* and *f* and see which answer choice matches the target answer you get for those values—only (B) will work for all values of *h* and *f*.

2. **J** Plug in the values given in the question. The problem should then read $(8 - [-2] + 3)(-2 + 3)$. Follow the order of operations and do the arithmetic within each parenthesis individually before multiplying: $(13)(1) = 13$.

3. **D** Figure out the two artists separately, and then combine. The first one paints 40 portraits a day for 11 days, so 440 total. The second paints 50 per day for 8 days, so 400 total. Add them up, and there are 840 portraits.

4. **H** If you add together all the home runs, you get 164. Divide that by four seasons, and his average number of home runs per season is 41. The question is simply asking you how to keep a 41 home run average going after a fifth year. Simple: Hit 41 home runs exactly in year five.

5. **D** The trick here is that you must calculate the first 30 necklaces at the regular rate of $9.00 each: She makes $270 for the first 30. Then figure out what 1.5 times her usual rate is (it's $13.50), and multiply that by the extra four necklaces. She gets $54 for the extras; add that to the $270, and she makes a total of $324 for the week.

6. **K** This question is about translating English into math. The trickiest part is remembering to subtract 19 from $\frac{5}{n}$ instead of the other way around. Read closely and make sure you take the square root and not the square of *n*.

7. **D** Those answer choices are ugly, but if you have a good calculator and are comfortable with all the fractions and parentheses, you can PITA. Otherwise, just solve for the variable. First, distribute the 12 on the left side, and you get $12y - 36 = -7$. Add 36 to both sides and you get $12y = 29$. Divide both sides by 12, and you're done.

8. **J** First, calculate how many $12 purses you get for $84—you can buy seven of them. The difference between the prices is $38.50, so divide this by 7, and you get the value of the discount per purse, which turns out to be $5.50. Now add that to the sale price of a single purse, and you get $17.50 as the non-discount price.

9. **A**   You can Plug In, though the numbers will get fairly large once you start taking things to the 4th power. Or you can solve it as a quadratic, using FOIL. You may recognize it as a twist on $(x + y)(x - y)$. You know that when one binomial is a sum and the other a difference, their product will be the difference of two squares, so eliminate (C). After that, just make sure everything gets squared, coefficients as well as variables, and you wind up with (A).

10. **H**   The formula for a rectangle's area is base × height. PITA to find which answer choice fits the parameters in the question. Remember to start with the middle value! If we use 6 for the longer side of the rectangle, that means the short side will be 3 because we need an area of 18. Adding all four sides together gives us 6 + 6 + 3 + 3 = 18, the perimeter given in the question, so (H) is the correct answer.

11. **C**   The sum of all the angles in any triangle is 180. Since $\angle X$ is 64°, the sum of $\angle Y$ and $\angle Z$ is calculated by subtracting 64° from 180°, leaving 116°.

12. **K**   Every possibility must be accounted for. For each of the four skirts, there are five sock options. $4 \times 5 = 20$, so there are 20 skirt/sock combinations. For each of those 20 combinations, there are three sweater options: $20 \times 3 = 60$, so there are 60 skirt/sock/sweater combinations. Finally, for each of these 60 combinations, there are 4 headband options: $60 \times 4 = 240$ total outfit combinations.

13. **D**   Use PITA. Start with the middle answer, (C), and you'll get $14 + 2(15) + \dfrac{16}{2} = 52$, so you know you need a higher set of numbers. Go to (D), and you'll get $16 + 2(17) + \dfrac{18}{2} = 59$.

14. **J**   When ACT gives you a function and then identifies a number inside the parentheses, it means to plug that number in for x every time it appears in the question. In this case, $x = -2$, so the function will end up reading $h(x) = -5(-2)^3$. Then you get $h(x) = -5(-2)^3$. $(-2)^3 = -8$, and when you multiply that by -5, you get 40. Watch out for the traps in (F) and (K), which involve cubing the -5 along with the x.

15. **B**   Don't overcomplicate here. Grab your calculator to see what the 4th root of 97 is (it's in the "Math" menu of your graphing calculator). Another approach would be to recognize that $z = \sqrt[4]{97}$ could be altered to read $z^4 = 97$. This way, you can PITA. Since $3^4 = 81$, and $4^4 = 256$, the value of z must be between 3 and 4.

16. **F**   The simplest approach is to PITA. Grab your calculator and divide each of the numbers in the question by each answer choice, starting with the highest answer choice because the question asks for

the greatest. 24 and 48 are factors of 96 and 144, but not of 108, so (H) and (K) must be eliminated. 18 and 36 are factors of 108 and 144, but not of 96, so (G) and (J) must be eliminated. That leaves (F) as the correct answer because 12 divides evenly into all three numbers.

17. **B** You'll need to know the formula for volume of a cylinder: $V = \pi r^2 h$. So plug the known height (10") into the formula, and set it equal to the known volume: $40\pi = \pi r^2(10)$. $6\pi = \pi r^2(4)$. Solve from here, and you will find that $r = 2$. You can also PITA because the answer choices represent the radius in that formula.

18. **H** This problem is very difficult to visualize, so make sure you draw a figure. Since W represents 3:00, count the hours in the directions indicated in the problem, and mark the points that you reach. X will be 7:00; Y will be 6:00, and Z will be 10:00. So the order, clockwise, will be W, Y, X, Z.

19. **D** The trouble with this problem is that it looks more complicated than it is. Since a represents the number of days and the problem asks you about Day Four, plug 4 in for a, and solve the equation. 3^4 is 81 and 81(12) is 972 tribbles.

20. **G** The best approach is to Plug In. You need the formula for area of a triangle: $\frac{1}{2}bh$. The two triangles have the same base, so start there—plug in 5, for instance. Then Plug In for the heights; try 4 for the larger and 2 for the smaller. Now you can compute the respective areas. For the larger, $\frac{1}{2}(5)(4) = 10$ square feet (the problem calls this y), and for the smaller, $\frac{1}{2}(5)(2) = 5$ square feet. So the final step is to re-read the problem and confirm what you're being asked for. $Y = 10$, and $xY = 5$, so $x = \frac{1}{2}$.

21. **A** To simplify the expression, distribute the negative to every term in the second set of variables and drop the parentheses: $2x + 3y + 4z - 6x + 7y - 8z$. Combine like terms to get $-4x + 10y - 4z$. Choices (B), (C), (D), and (E) forget to distribute the negative to at least one of the terms.

22. **J** Use SOHCAHTOA for right triangles: CAH means $\cos\theta = \dfrac{adjacent}{hypotenuse}$, which is $\dfrac{y}{z}$. Remember to identify the adjacent and opposite legs of the triangle relative to angle θ. Choice (G) incorrectly gives the adjacent leg as x rather than y; (F) gives $\tan\theta$; (H) gives $\cot\theta$; and (K) gives $\sec\theta$.

23. **B** Draw a diagram with numbers 1–8 evenly spaced around a circle. On the first run, the paper is delivered to houses 1, 4, and 7; on the second run, the paper is delivered to houses 2, 5, and 8; and on the third run, the paper is delivered to houses 3 and 6. Therefore, by the third lap, the paper has been delivered to all the houses.

24. **J**   In the equation of a line, $y = mx + b$, the y-intercept is given by constant b, thus line q has a y-intercept of 500. The y-intercept of line m is 10 less than line q, so subtract 10 from 500 to get 490. Choice (K) incorrectly adds 10; (H) calculates the y-intercept as 10 *times* less, rather than 10 less than that of line m. Choices (F) and (G) use the slope rather than the y-intercept.

25. **B**   Simplify the expression by multiplying $-9a^5$ to each term in the parentheses. Remember MADSPM. When bases are multiplied, exponents are added. Therefore, the equation should look like this: $-9a^5(8a^7 - 4a^3) = -72a^{(5+7)} + 36a^{(5+3)} = -72a^{12} + 36a^8$. Choices (D) and (E) incorrectly multiply the exponents. Choice (C) doesn't distribute the negative sign to the second term. Choice (A) incorrectly subtracts non-combinable terms inside the parentheses and then multiplies $-9a^5$.

26. **G**   Consider PEMDAS and first combine the terms inside the absolute value: $-4|-9 + 2| = -4|-7|$. Then take the absolute value of -7, which is $+7$, and multiply by -4 to get -28. Choices (F) and (K) incorrectly take the absolute value of -9 and 2 first and then combine. Choice (H) adds rather than multiplies -4 and $+7$. Choice (J) neglects to take the absolute value of -7.

27. **B**   Given YZ is parallel to XV, ΔWXV and ΔWYZ are similar triangles, thus they have proportional sides. First, use Pythagorean theorem $WX^2 = 6^2 + 8^2$ to calculate WX is 10, or remember that this is one of the special right triangles. Then set up the proportion $\dfrac{WX}{WY} = \dfrac{XV}{YZ}$ to find YZ: $\dfrac{10}{30} = \dfrac{6}{YZ}$, and YZ is 18 inches. Choices (A), (C), and (E) do not use the correct proportions; (D) is the length of WZ, not YZ.

28. **H**   Plug in a w value from the table, and eliminate equations that do not give the corresponding h value. When you plug in $w = 0$, (G), (J), and (K) do not give $h = 7$. When you plug in $w = 1$, (F) gives $h = 8$, not 10, so it can also be eliminated.

29. **A**   Simplify the expression by distributing the coefficients on both sides of the inequality: $4(n - 3) < 5(n + 2)$ becomes $4n - 12 < 5n + 10$. Combine like terms to get $-n < 22$ and divide by -1, remembering to flip the inequality sign. Choices (B), (C), (D), and (E) all result from either neglecting to distribute the coefficient completely through the parentheses or mixing up the positive and negative signs.

30. **J**   The other vertices of the triangle must be 4 inches from $(1,1)$. Use POE. Choice (F) is 5 units to the left, and (G) is only 1 unit to the left. Using either right triangles or the distance formula, you can determine (H) is not long enough, and (K) is too long. Choice (J) is 4 units due south from $(1,1)$. If you have trouble remembering the distance formula, just sketch and ballpark!

31. **D** Use the Pythagorean theorem: $m^2 + n^2 = 6^2$. Isolate m by subtracting n^2 and square rooting both sides. Choices (A), (B), and (C) do not correctly square each side length before isolating m. Choice (E) treats side m as the hypotenuse rather than one of the legs of the right triangle. If you get stuck with the algebra, plug in a value for n, and use your calculator.

32. **G** Probability is the fraction of what you want (pear jellybeans) over total number of possibilities (all jellybeans). Use PITA. There are currently $10 + 16 + 19 = 45$ jellybeans in the jar. Start with (H). If 21 pear jellybeans are added, then there will be a total of 66 jellybeans in the jar. The probability of selecting a pear jellybean will be $\frac{21}{66}$, which is too low. Go to (G). If 11 jellybeans are added, there will be a total of 56 jellybeans in the jar. The probability of selecting a pear jellybeans will be $\frac{21}{56}$, which simplifies to $\frac{3}{8}$, making (G) the correct answer.

33. **C** To determine the graph of the equation, you must isolate the y by subtracting $6x$ *and* dividing by 3. The resulting equation is $y = -2x + 4$, which is a line with a slope of -2 and a y-intercept of $+4$. Because the y-intercept is positive, the line crosses y-axis from Quadrant II to Quadrant I and extends into Quadrant IV. The line never passes through Quadrant II, eliminating (B), (D), and (E). Choice (A) is a partial answer and does not include Quadrant I. Remember, in order to avoid doing any figuring, once you've got the equation in slope-intercept form, you can just plug it in to your graphing calculator.

34. **H** Substitute the values $(3, 4n)$ in for (x, y) in the equation to get $4n = -2(3)^2 + 10$. Remember PEMDAS: $4n = -2(9) + 10$, so $4n = -8$, and $n = -2$. Choice (F) results when you mix up the positive and negative signs. Choices (G) and (J) result when you do not use PEMDAS correctly. Choice (K) is a partial answer and gives the value of $4n$, not n.

35. **D** Plug In! Make sure you choose a value for the rent that divides evenly by 3 and 4. Let's say the rent is $24. In that case, Jennifer pays $16, Kelly pays $6, and Meredith pays the remainder, or $2. The ratio of Jennifer's contribution to Kelly's contribution to Meredith's contribution is then 16:6:2, which simplifies to 8:3:1, or (D).

36. **F** The general equation of a circle is $(x - h)^2 + (y - k)^2 = r^2$, for which (h, k) are the coordinates for the center of the circle, and r gives the radius length. For the given equation, the $h = 0$ and $k = -4$; (J) and (K) confuse the sign in front of k. Since $r^2 = 28$, the radius of the circle is $\sqrt{28}$. Choice (G) divides by 2 rather than square rooting 28. Choice (H) gives the value of r^2, not r.

37. **B** The perimeter of the figure consists of one side of the equilateral triangle and the arc length of two semicircles. You can immediately eliminate (A), (D), and (E) because the length of one side of the equilateral triangle is 6 inches. Both semicircles have a diameter of 6 and given $C = d\pi = 6\pi$, each

semicircle has an arc length of 3π. With the exposed side of the triangle, the perimeter of the figure should be $P = 6 + 3\pi + 3\pi = 6 + 6\pi$. If you selected (C), you may have found the circumferences of two full circles rather than two semicircles.

38. **H**   Because *DEFG* is a rhombus, which has equal sides and equal angles, all 8 triangles formed by drawing the diagonals in the figure are equivalent. *HEFM* encloses the area of 3 triangles and the shaded region the area of 5 triangles, thus the ratio is 3:5. Choice (J) is the ratio of the unshaded area to the total area.

39. **C**   The midpoint is the average of the endpoints, so the *y*-coordinate of the midpoint is $\frac{y_1 + y_2}{2} = \frac{10 + (-2)}{2} = 4$. Choice (A) is the *x*-coordinate of the midpoint. Choices (B) and (E) only find the sum of the endpoint coordinates. Choice (D) confuses the negative sign and finds the average of 10 and 2.

40. **F**   The volume of a cube is s^3, so this cube is $9^3 = 729$ cubic feet. Choice (G) gives the surface area of the cube. Choice (J) the area of 3 faces of the cube, (H) gives the area of 1 face, and (J) confuses the side as 3 feet rather than 9.

41. **D**   Rearrange both equations into $y = mx + b$ form to compare their slopes and *y*-intercepts. The first equation, $rx + sy = t$, becomes $y = -\frac{r}{s}x + \frac{t}{s}$. The second equation, $rx + sy = v$, becomes $y = -\frac{r}{s}x + \frac{v}{s}$. Both functions have the slope of $-\frac{r}{s}$, so they cannot intersect at only 1 point, eliminating (I), and thus (A), (C), and (E). A system of two linear functions can give a single line graph if the equations have the same slope and *y*-intercept, which occurs if $t = v$. Lines with same slope and different *y*-intercepts are parallel and never intersect, so when *t* and *v* are not equal, you'll get two parallel lines, so the answer must be (D).

42. **F**   Because you are finding the side *O*pposite the 34° angle and are given the *H*ypotenuse, use SOHCAHTOA or the *sine* function, eliminating (G), (H), and (K). Since $\sin 34° = \frac{\text{opposite}}{40}$, you solve for the distance by multiplying 40, not dividing and thus eliminating (J).

43. **D**   Because 6th graders comprise 22% of the total number of students, $100 - 22 = 78\%$ of the students are not in 6th grade. The odds is the ratio of 22:78, which reduces to 11:39. Choice (E) incorrectly calculates the ratio of 6th graders to the total number of students. Choices (A), (B), and (C) are approximations of 22%; however, not as accurate as (D).

44. **H** Lines of symmetry cut the figure into two mirror images.

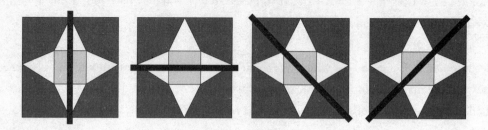

Since each of the divisions above creates two mirror images, the figure has four lines of symmetry.

45. **D** Because a square has right angles, you can determine the diagonal length using the Pythagorean theorem: $3^2 + 3^2 = d^2$. The diagonal is $3\sqrt{2}$ meters ≈ 4.2 meters. Choices (A) and (C) take the square root of 6 and 12, rather than 18. Choices (B) and (E) incorrectly calculate the diagonal without the Pythagorean theorem.

46. **G** Because the office wall is shorter, you can eliminate (J) and (K) immediately. Calculate 20% of the length of the current mosaic: 0.20×3 meters = 0.6 meters. Since the length is 20% shorter, subtract 0.6 meters from the original 3 meters. Choice (F) is a partial answer, but it does not give the actual length of the office wall. Choice (H) subtracts 0.2 rather than 20%.

47. **B** Because $\overline{DG}$ bisects $\angle HDE$, $\angle HDG = \angle EDG = 68°$. Since $\overline{DE} \parallel \overline{FG}$, $\angle FGD = \angle EDG = 68°$. Since $\overline{HG}$ bisects $\angle FGD$, $\angle DGH = 34°$ and $\angle DHG + \angle HDG + \angle DGH = 180°$, thus $\angle DHG = 78°$.

48. **H** Given the area of the circle is 16π square meters, the radius is 4 meters. $\overline{AC}$ is the longest chord in the circle, which is the diameter of the circle, so O can be labeled as the midpoint. $\overline{OA}$ and $\overline{OB}$ are each 4 meters, so ΔOAB is an equilateral triangle whose angles measure 60°. $\angle AOB + \angle BOC = 180°$, so $\angle BOC$ measures 120°, making the arc degree also 120°. Choice (F) gives the measure of arc AB rather than BC. Choices (G) and (J) use an incorrect triangle.

49. **A** A system of equations has no solutions if the equations have the same slope and different y-intercepts. Two linear equations have the same slope if they have the same ratio of coefficients for x and y. Set up a proportion of the coefficients: $\dfrac{12}{8} = \dfrac{3}{b}$. $12b = 24$, so $b = 2$. Choices (B), (C), (D), and (E) do not give slopes equal to that of the first equation.

50. **F**   The shading above the horizontal line segment means that the y-values, which represent the number of pies Rebecca and Scott make, are never less than 1. In other words, they always make at least 1 pie, which is (F).

51. **D**   The best way to approach this question, since it asks about the *maximum*, is check the endpoints or extremes of the graph: (9,1) and (0,4). Using the provided expression for weekly profit, $12(9) + 25(1)$ = \$133, which is (B). Check the other extreme to see that $12(0) + 25(4) = \$100$, which is less than \$133.

52. **K**   If Rebecca and Scott made 5 pies at 3 hours each and 3 dozen cookies at 1 hour each, then they spent 18 hours baking that week. They donated \$2 for every hour they spent baking, so they donated \$36. The question asks what percent of that week's profit they donated, so calculate that week's profit. According to the provided expression for weekly profit, $12(3) + 25(5) = \$161$. The \$36 donated, out of \$161 earned, is approximately 22%, which is (K).

53. **A**   Following the formula provided, $(w)(10) - (w)(w) = 25$. Rearranging, $10w - w^2 = 25$ becomes $w^2 - 10w + 25 = 0$. Factoring the quadratic into $(w - 5)(w - 5) = 0$, the only possible value for w is 5, so the answer is (A).

54. **K**   This formula may look complicated, but if you're careful with the pieces, this will be basic golden-rule algebra. If $x = B(1 + .2g)^n$, then divide both sides by $(1 + .2g)^n$ to get $\dfrac{x}{\left(1 + .2g\right)^n} = B$, which is (K). If you find the algebra daunting, you can also plug in simple numbers and find a target value for B.

55. **C**   The main things you know for sure about m and n are that m is negative, and n is positive. The least complicated option is to plug in values for m and n that adhere to the rules you're given, making m negative and n positive. Testing each answer choice using those values allows you to eliminate any that don't work out to be true. Even if you have several answer choices remaining after crossing out the ones that don't work with those numbers, picking a second set of numbers—still playing by the rules!—and testing each of your *remaining* answer choices with your new values should help you narrow it down to one. Alternatively, consider your answer choices. For (A), a positive number divided by a negative number will produce a negative number, not something greater than 1. Cross this answer out. For (B), remember that absolute value makes the inside result positive, and this will happen to both n and m. Then $|n|$ is squared, which will still be positive. A positive number, $|n|^2$, may or may not be bigger than another positive number, $|m|$, so cross this answer out. In (C), subtract

2 from both sides, and then multiply both sides by 7, so the expression becomes simply $n > m$, which you know to be true. Keep this answer. In (D), squaring both m and n make both values positive, without any sense of how large or small these newly positive numbers are. Thus, even after adding 1, there's still no way to say for sure which side is larger or smaller. As for (E), n^{-2} and m^{-2}, which are $\frac{1}{n^2}$ and $\frac{1}{m^2}$, are both positive numbers, but again you're given no sense of which is larger or smaller. The only answer that *must* be true is (C).

56. **J**

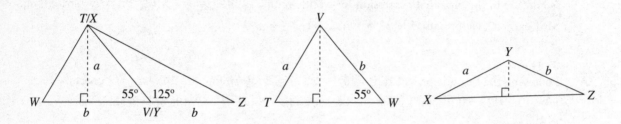

There are several ways to think about this question. There's not a lot of information to go on, so it becomes really important to pay very careful attention to what you do know and, since you're being asked to compare two things, any relationships you can discern. Noticing that the 55° angle and the 125° angle were supplementary might lead you to match up the a-sides to make the big triangle pictured above on the left. If Area $= \frac{1}{2} bh$, then for ΔTVW, $\frac{1}{2} bh = 45$, so $bh = 90$. Looking at ΔTZW, Area $= \frac{1}{2}(2b)(h) = bh = 90$. If the area of ΔTZW is 90, and the area of ΔTVW is 45, then $90 - 45 = 45$, so the area of ΔXYZ is also 45, so the answer is (J). Alternatively, consider the two triangles side by side, as pictured above on the right. Given that a and b are the legs of both triangles, to go from the 55° angle to the 125° angle requires dropping the height and lengthening the base proportionally. Because the base and height are inversely related this way, the area will stay constant even as the height and base shift.

57. **E** The first decision you have to make is which one (or both) of these laws is useful to you. You're trying to solve for a side where you have the opposite angle, but you don't have angles to match up with either of the other two sides you know. The sides are not equivalent, so you can't assume that the angles are

equivalent. Consequently, you may not have enough information to use the law of sines. The law of cosines, on the other hand, would let you solve for the missing side, c, knowing only the other sides and the opposite angle. Line up each piece of the formula to find that $LJ^2 = 9^2 + 6^2 - 2(9)(6) \cos 50°$. Before you start calculating this value, glance at your answer choices—they aren't asking you to solve completely, just to match up the filled-in formula. Take the square root of both sides to find $LJ = \sqrt{9^2 + 6^2 - 2(9)(6) \cos 50°}$, or (E).

58. **G** Break this problem up into little pieces. An arithmetic sequence has a common difference between terms, so the same number is being added to get from one term to the next. If the 7th term is 13.5 and the 11th term is 18.3, the 9th term must be exactly halfway between them at 15.9. Halfway between the 7th term and the 9th term is the 8th term, which would be at 14.7. If the 7th term is 13.5 and the 8th term is 14.7, then the common difference between terms is 1.2. Working backward from the 7th term, the 6th term is 12.3, the 5th term is 11.1, the 4th term is 9.9, the 3rd term is 8.7, the 2nd term is 7.5, and the 1st term is 6.3. Adding up the first three terms, $6.3 + 7.5 + 8.7 = 22.5$, which is (G). There is a formula for arithmetic sequences, but when you're dealing with relatively small numbers in relatively small quantities, sometimes the most reliable thing to do is simply write it out.

59. **C** If the *only* possible value for w is 8, then the quadratic in factored form is $(w - 8)(w - 8) = 0$. Expanding this by FOILing gives you $w^2 - 16w + 64 = 0$. Line this up with the original equation to find that p must be 16, and q must be 64. With your answer choices, make sure you know what you're looking for—if you picked (E), you may have solved for q instead of p.

60. **F** The simplest thing to do is to start by determining which values the problem is describing. Since it wants the numbers that are 4 units from −1, only two points satisfy that: −5 and 3. If you're having trouble thinking about that, simply draw a number line and count it out.

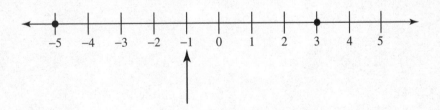

If the answer choices describe the solution set of −5 and 3, then you can test these values in each of the answer choices to eliminate ones that don't work. In (F), $|3 + 1| = 4$, and $|-5 + 1| = 4$. Both values work, so this will be your answer. In (G), $|3 - 1| \neq 4$, so eliminate that. In (H), $|3 + 4| \neq 1$, so eliminate that. In (J), $|-5 - 4| \neq 1$, so eliminate that, too. In (K), $|3 + 4| \neq 1$, so eliminate that.

Chapter 12
Math Practice Test 2

ACT MATHEMATICS TEST
60 Minutes—60 Questions

DIRECTIONS: Solve each problem, choose the correct answer, and then darken the corresponding oval on your answer document.

Do not linger over problems that take too much time. Solve as many as you can; then return to the others in the time you have left for this test.

You are permitted to use a calculator on this test. You may use your calculator for any problems you choose, but some of the problems may best be done without using a calculator.

Note: Unless otherwise stated, all of the following should be assumed:

1. Illustrative figures are NOT necessarily drawn to scale.
2. Geometric figures lie in a plane.
3. The word *line* indicates a straight line.
4. The word *average* indicates arithmetic mean.

---

1. Four railroad lines, A, B, C, and D, are pictured below, such that the pair of lines A and B and C and D run parallel to each other, respectively. If the obtuse angle created by the intersection of line A and C measures 110°, what is the measure of the obtuse angle at which line B intersects line D ?

DO YOUR FIGURING HERE.

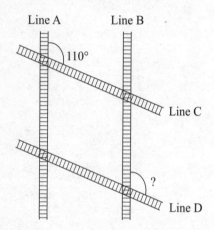

A. 110°
B. 120°
C. 170°
D. 210°
E. 250°

2. Which of the following is the simplified form of the expression $5(x-3)-3x+10$?

F. $2x-5$
G. $5x+7$
H. $8x-5$
J. $12x+10$
K. $22x$

GO ON TO THE NEXT PAGE.

3. In the standard (x,y) coordinate plane, a point lies at $(4,-7)$. If the point is shifted up 4 units and left 10 units, what are the new coordinates of the point?

   A. $(-14,-9)$
   B. $(\ -3,-9)$
   C. $(\ -6,-9)$
   D. $(\ -6,-3)$
   E. $(\ \ 0,\ 3)$

4. At a certain golf club, participants in a tournament must pay \$13 if they belong to the club and \$15 if they do not belong to the club. What is the total cost, in dollars, for x participants who belong to the club and 30 members who do not belong to the club?

   F. $13x + 15(30)$

   G. $(13 + 15)x$

   H. $13(x + 15)$

   J. $13(x + 30)$

   K. $x + 30$

5. If a new computer has its price increased from \$500 to \$650, by what percent did the computer's price increase?

   A. 5%
   B. 15%
   C. 23%
   D. 28%
   E. 30%

6. In the parallelogram $WXYZ$, $\angle W$ and $\angle Y$ are congruent, the measure of $\angle X$ is $112°$. What is the measure of $\angle Y$?

   F. $56°$
   G. $68°$
   H. $90°$
   J. $112°$
   K. $136°$

DO YOUR FIGURING HERE.

GO ON TO THE NEXT PAGE.

7. Nathan will choose one marble randomly from a sack containing 32 marbles that are in the colors and quantities shown in the table below. Each of the marbles is one color only.

Color	Quantity
White	5
Purple	1
Indigo	2
Cyan	8
Maroon	6
Tan	10

DO YOUR FIGURING HERE.

What is the probability that Nathan will choose a tan or maroon marble?

A. $\frac{3}{16}$

B. $\frac{5}{16}$

C. $\frac{7}{16}$

D. $\frac{1}{2}$

E. $\frac{1}{3}$

8. If a speedboat is travelling 100 miles in the span of $1\frac{1}{3}$ hours, what is the speedboat's average speed, in miles per hour?

F. 25
G. 33
H. 75
J. 100
K. 133

9. In order to calculate an employee's overall performance review value, Mr. Donovan removes the lowest value and then averages the remaining values. Shawna was evaluated 6 times with the following results: 22, 23, 26, 31, 35, and 43. What was Shawna's overall performance review value as determined by Mr. Donovan?

A. 27.4
B. 30.0
C. 31.0
D. 31.4
E. 31.6

GO ON TO THE NEXT PAGE.

10. Which of the following gives x in terms of P and q, given the equation $\dfrac{3x}{p} = q$?

   F. $\dfrac{q}{3p}$

   G. $\dfrac{p}{3q}$

   H. $\dfrac{pq}{3}$

   J. $pq - 3$

   K. $q + p - 3$

DO YOUR FIGURING HERE.

11. What is the value of $5x$ if $3x - 16 = 5$?

   A. 7
   B. 21
   C. 35
   D. 56
   E. 72

12. If the area of a square is 25 square feet, what is the perimeter of the square, in feet?

   F. 5
   G. 10
   H. 20
   J. 25
   K. 100

13. What is 11% of 3.22×10^4 ?

   A. 354,200
   B. 3,542
   C. 35.42
   D. 1.123
   E. 0.1123

14. Of the following expressions, which is a factor of the expression $x^2 + 3x - 18$?

   F. $x - 6$
   G. $x + 3$
   H. $x + 6$
   J. $x + 9$
   K. $x + 15$

15. Of the following real numbers, v, w, x, y, and z such that $v < w$, $y > x$, $y < v$, and $z > w$, which of the numbers if the smallest?

   A. v
   B. w
   C. x
   D. y
   E. z

GO ON TO THE NEXT PAGE.

16. A new operation, ♣, is defined as follows: (w,x) ♣ $(y,z) = (wz - yx)(wx - yz)$. What is the value of $(3,2)$ ♣ $(5,0)$?

    F.   −120
    G.   −60
    H.   0
    J.   6
    K.   60

DO YOUR FIGURING HERE.

17. A team of artists requires 2 types of structures—spheres and pyramids—for a collaborative art piece. The 2 types of structures are created by overlapping 5-inch squares made of 3 different materials. The team will consist of three artists. The requirements for each structure type are provided in the tables below. The table with material types indicates how many squares are required for each type of structure, and the table with the artists indicates how many of each structure type each artist is to create.

	Wood	Iron	Plastic
Sphere	10	5	12
Pyramid	5	14	10

	Sphere	Pyramid
Suzuki	5	5
Mona	5	15
Jamilica	10	5

How many 5-inch squares of wood does Jamilica need to create her structures?

    A.   150
    B.   125
    C.   52
    D.   39
    E.   29

18. Which of the following represents the least common multiple of 100, 60, and 20 ?

    F.   80
    G.   120
    H.   300
    J.   1,200
    K. 120,000

GO ON TO THE NEXT PAGE.

19. The right triangle below represents three stores—Teddy's, ValuTime, and Burger Burger—as its vertices. The distances given on the triangle represent the numbers of miles required to travel between the stores on a road. Two customers leave Teddy's to shop at ValuTime. If the first customer travels from Teddy's to ValuTime on Coles St., while the second customer travels from Teddy's to Burger Burger on Monmouth St. before taking Brunswick Ave. to ValuTime, how many miles shorter is the first customer's trip than the second's?

DO YOUR FIGURING HERE.

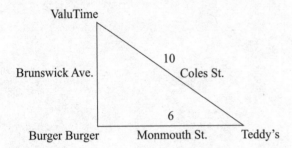

A.   2
B.   4
C.   6
D.   10
E.   14

20. Which of the following expressions is equivalent to $\left(y^6\right)^{12}$?

F. $72y$
G. $12y^6$
H. $6y^{12}$
J. y^{72}
K. y^{216}

21. Given the function $f(x) = 2x^3 + x^2$, which of the following represents the value of $f(-2)$?

A. -24
B. -20
C. -16
D. -13
E. -12

22. The Merry Mechanics Shop has just ended its discount program, raising the price of all repairs by 20%. Which of the following gives the price, in dollars, of any repair with price r ?

F. $0.2r$
G. $r + 0.2r$
H. $r - 0.2r$
J. $r + 0.2$
K. $r + 20r$

GO ON TO THE NEXT PAGE.

DO YOUR FIGURING HERE.

23. A local television advertisement offers 3 pairs of shoes for $30.97. Given the price of the shoes, how much would it cost to purchase 5 pairs of shoes?

   A. $10.32
   B. $10.33
   C. $20.65
   D. $51.61
   E. $51.62

24. Terra is opening a store. Her monthly earnings are calculated by subtracting her monthly expenses from the total amount she earns each day. If her monthly expenses are $500, and she earns $100 per day on a particular month, which of the following graphs represents her earnings as a function of the number of days of business.

F.

G.

H.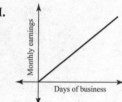

J.

K.

25. The positive integer $x!$ is defined as the product of all the positive integers less than or equal to x. For example, $4! = 1(2)(3)(4) = 24$. What is the value of the expression $\frac{6!4!}{5!}$?

   A. 1
   B. 2
   C. 4
   D. 72
   E. 144

GO ON TO THE NEXT PAGE.

26. Alfred spent $25 to purchase 65 stamps. If each stamp costs either $0.20 or $0.45, how many of the more expensive stamps did he purchase?

   F.   17
   G. 48
   H. 56
   J.   65
   K. 125

27. A square with a side length of 2 feet is circumscribed, as shown below.

What is the area of the shaded region, in square feet?

   A. π
   B. $\pi-4$
   C. $2\pi-1$
   D. $2\pi-2$
   E. $2\pi-4$

28. Two similar triangles have sides that are in the ratio 3:4. The length of one of the sides of the larger triangle is 12 feet long. What is the length, in feet, of the corresponding side of the smaller triangle?

   F.   6
   G. 7
   H. 9
   J. 11
   K. 16

29. For the polygon below points *V, Z,* and *Y* are collinear. Which of the following represents the length, in inches, of $\overline{VZ}$?

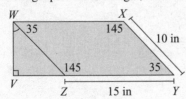

   A.   10

   B. $10\cos 35°$

   C. $\cos 35°$

   D. $\dfrac{15}{\cos 35°}$

   E. $\dfrac{10}{\cos 35°}$

DO YOUR FIGURING HERE.

GO ON TO THE NEXT PAGE.

30. The perimeter of a rectangle is 144 feet, and one side measures 32 feet. If it can be determined, what are the lengths, in feet, of the other three sides?

F. 32, 40, 40
G. 32, 32, 46
H. 32, 48, 48
J. 32, 66, 66
K. Cannot be determined from the given information

31. If $9 + 4x < 2x - 7$, which of the following represents the solution?

A. $x > -12$
B. $x > -8$
C. $x < -8$
D. $x < -2$
E. $x < 8$

32. The drama team wants to post a triangular advertisement for its next play. The base of the advertisement will be 2.25 feet, and the height will be 3.5 feet. Which of the following is closest to the area, in square feet, of the advertisement?

F. 3.0
G. 3.9
H. 6.0
J. 7.9
K. 9.0

33. $-8|-2-7| = ?$

A. -112
B. -92
C. -72
D. 40
E. 72

34. In a local deli, some sandwiches have only one kind of meat, and other sandwiches have more than one kind of meat. Using the information given in the table below about the kinds of meat in the sandwiches, how many sandwiches have roast beef only?

Number of sandwiches	Meat
8	at least roast beef
10	at least chicken
12	at least turkey
4	both chicken and turkey, but no roast beef
1	both roast beef and turkey, but no chicken
3	chicken only
2	roast beef, chicken, and turkey

F. 9
G. 7
H. 5
J. 4
K. 2

DO YOUR FIGURING HERE.

GO ON TO THE NEXT PAGE.

Use the following information to answer questions 35–37.

The 4-H club at Arlington High School cares for various animals in the school's stockyards. The members of the clubs sell the animals in order to raise funds for the club, and Marcus and Jae are taking inventory of the animals. The table below gives the numbers of groups of animals. For example, there are 5 groups of pigs with 1 pig per group, 20 groups of chickens with 5 chickens per group, and 20 groups of rabbits with 10 rabbits per group. All of the animal groups have been counted except for the 5-animal groups of rabbits.

Animals	Number of 1-animal groups	Number of 5-animal groups	Number of 10-animal groups
Chickens	0	20	30
Rabbits	5	?	20
Pigs	5	10	0
Goats	22	10	0

35. Marcus finishes the inventory and afterward tells Jae that the number of rabbits is equal to the number of chickens. How many 5-animal groups of rabbits are in the stockyards?

   A. 15
   B. 25
   C. 35
   D. 39
   E. 195

36. Mrs. Bradshaw purchased $\frac{1}{5}$ of the chickens for $1,200.00. What was the price of 1 chicken?

   F. $10.00
   G. $15.00
   H. $20.00
   J. $60.00
   K. $120.00

37. Bethany takes all of the goats in the 1-animal groups and combines them to create as many 5-animal groups as possible. How many complete 5-animal groups of goats can Bethany create?

   A. 22
   B. 14
   C. 10
   D. 5
   E. 4

GO ON TO THE NEXT PAGE.

Use the following information to answer questions 38–40.

Isosceles triangle *DEF* is shown in the standard (*x*,*y*) coordinate plane below. The coordinates for two of its vertices are *D*(0,0) and *E(c,d)*.

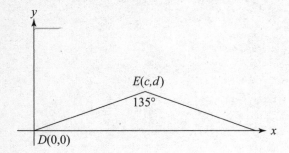

38. What are the coordinates of *F* ?

   F. (0,   2*d*)
   G. (2*c*,   0)
   H. (*c* + *d*, 0)
   J. (2*c*,   2*d*)
   K. (*c* + *d*,2*d*)

39. What is the measure of the angle formed by *DE* and the *y*-axis?

   A. 22.5°
   B. 30.0°
   C. 45.0°
   D. 60.0°
   E. 67.5°

40. Isosceles triangle *DEF* is rotated clockwise (↵) by 180° about the origin. At what ordered pair is the image of *E* located?

   F. (−*c*, *d*)
   G. (*c*,−*d*)
   H. (−*d*,−*c*)
   J. (−*c*,−*d*)
   K. (*d*, *c*)

GO ON TO THE NEXT PAGE.

41. A gallon is 231 cubic inches. Which of the following is closest to the area of the base, in square inches, of a pyramid shaped container, shown below, with height 15 inches and volume 2 gallons?

    (Note: The volume of a pyramid with base area b and height h is $\frac{1}{3}bh$.)

    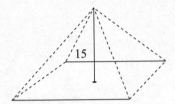

    A. 92
    B. 132
    C. 276
    D. 432
    E. 1,296

42. For law school, Nathan must read a book of legal cases in 6 months. He reads $\frac{1}{8}$ each of the first 2 months. For the remaining 4 months, what portion of the book, on average, must Nathan read per month?

    F. $\frac{3}{16}$

    G. $\frac{3}{32}$

    H. $\frac{1}{16}$

    J. $\frac{1}{32}$

    K. $\frac{1}{64}$

43. Which of the following equations indicates the correct application of the quadratic formula to the equation $2x^2 + 3x - 10 = 0$?

    A. $\dfrac{3 \pm \sqrt{9 - 4(2)(-10)}}{2(2)}$

    B. $\dfrac{3 \pm \sqrt{9 + 4(2)(-10)}}{2(2)}$

    C. $\dfrac{-3 \pm \sqrt{9 + 4(2)(-10)}}{2(2)}$

    D. $\dfrac{-3 \pm \sqrt{9 - 4(2)(-10)}}{2(2)}$

    E. $\dfrac{-3 \pm \sqrt{9 - 4(2)(10)}}{2(2)}$

GO ON TO THE NEXT PAGE.

44. In the standard (x,y) coordinate plane, the point $(-2,5)$ is the midpoint of the line segment with endpoints $(-7,3)$ and (c,d). What is (c,d) ?

 F. $(-19,8)$
 G. $(-12,1)$
 H. $(-12,7)$
 J. $(3,\ \ 1)$
 K. $(3,\ \ 7)$

DO YOUR FIGURING HERE.

45. A straight 4-meter-tall lamppost casts a shadow at an angle of 55°, as shown in the figure below. Which of the following expressions gives the length, in meters, of the shadow along the level ground?

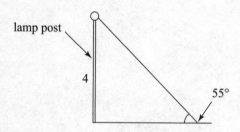

 lamp post 4 55°

 A. $\dfrac{4}{\tan 55°}$

 B. $\dfrac{4}{\cos 55°}$

 C. $\dfrac{4}{\sin 55°}$

 D. $4\tan 55°$

 E. $4\sin 55°$

GO ON TO THE NEXT PAGE.

46. One of the following equations is graphed in the standard (x,y) coordinate plane below. Which one?

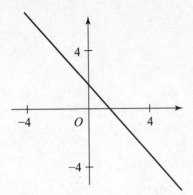

F.　$y = 2x + 2$

G.　$y = \dfrac{1}{2}x + 4$

H.　$y = -\dfrac{1}{2}x + 2$

J.　$y = -2x + 2$

K.　$y = -2x - 4$

47. The vertices of $ABCD$ have the (x,y) coordinates indicated in the figure below. What is the area, in square coordinate units, of $ABCD$?

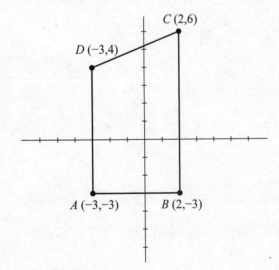

A.　25
B.　29
C.　40
D.　45
E.　81

GO ON TO THE NEXT PAGE.

48. Ms. Parker's economics class is reviewing slopes of lines. The class is tasked to graph the total expenditures, E, required for p products that cost 45¢ each. Ms. Parker instructs the class to characterize the slope between any 2 points (p, E) on the graph. Francine gives a correct answer that the slope between any 2 points on this graph must be:

   F. two.
   G. multiple positive values.
   H. multiple negative values.
   J. one positive value.
   K. one negative value.

DO YOUR FIGURING HERE.

49. If the first four terms of a geometric sequence are 10, 15, 22.5, and 33.75, what is the fifth term in the sequence?

   A. 35
   B. 50.625
   C. 56.25
   D. 70.625
   E. 75

50. The total surface area of a cube is 54 square inches. What is the volume, in cubic inches, of the cube?

   F.   9
   G. 18
   H. 27
   J. 81
   K. 729

51. In the figure below, a region of a circle with a radius of 5 is shown shaded. The area of the shaded region is 15π. What is the measure of the central angle of the shaded region?

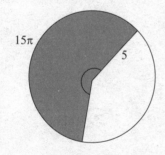

15π

5

   A.   72°
   B. 144°
   C. 215°
   D. 216°
   E. 315°

GO ON TO THE NEXT PAGE.

DO YOUR FIGURING HERE.

52. Which of the following equations represents the graph of a circle with center (2,–6) and radius 4 coordinate units in the standard (x,y) coordinate plane?

    F. $(x-2)^2+(y+6)^2=4$
    G. $(x+2)^2+(y-6)^2=4$
    H. $(x-2)^2+(y-6)^2=16$
    J. $(x-2)^2+(y+6)^2=16$
    K. $(x+2)^2+(y-6)^2=16$

53. In $\triangle XYZ$, the value of $\angle X$ is 53°, the value of $\angle Y$ is 88°, and the length of $\overline{YZ}$ is 11 inches. Which of the following is an expression for the length, in inches, of $\overline{XZ}$?

    (Note: The law of sines states that for any triangle, the ratios of the lengths of the sides to the sines of the angles opposite those sides are equal.)

    A. $\dfrac{(\sin 88°)(\sin 53°)}{11}$
    B. $\dfrac{\sin 88°}{11\sin 53°}$
    C. $\dfrac{\sin 53°}{11\sin 88°}$
    D. $\dfrac{11\sin 53°}{\sin 88°}$
    E. $\dfrac{11\sin 88°}{\sin 53°}$

54. The radius of a circle is p feet shorter than the radius of a second circle. How many feet shorter is the circumference of the first circle than the circumference of the second circle?

    F. $\sqrt{p}$
    G. p^2
    H. πp
    J. p
    K. $2\pi p$

55. If $y\le-3$, then $|y+3|=$?

    A. $y-3$
    B. $y+3$
    C. $-y-3$
    D. $-y+3$
    E. 0

GO ON TO THE NEXT PAGE.

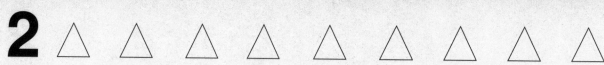

56. There are 18 countries in the trade union. Of these 18 countries, 7 have fewer than 20 cities, 7 have more than 21 cities, and 2 have more than 22 cities. What is the total number of countries in the trade union that have 20, 21, or 22 cities?

   F.   15
   G. 11
   H.   9
   J.   7
   K.   4

57. If $\sin x = -\dfrac{3}{4}$, what is the value of $\cos 2x$?

(Note: $(\sin x)^2 = \dfrac{1-\cos 2x}{2}$)

   A. $-\dfrac{3}{4}$

   B. $-\dfrac{1}{4}$

   C. $-\dfrac{1}{8}$

   D. $\dfrac{1}{8}$

   E. $\dfrac{13}{4}$

58. Let $f(x) = x^3$ and $g(x) = \dfrac{x}{2} - k$. In the standard (x,y) coordinate plane, $y = f\big(g(x)\big)$ passes through $(-2,8)$. What is the value of k?

   F.   2
   G.   1
   H. −3
   J. −8
   K. −9

59. A plane contains 7 vertical lines and 7 horizontal lines. These lines partition the plane into disjoint regions. How many of these disjoint regions have a finite, nonzero area?

   A. 12
   B. 14
   C. 25
   D. 36
   E. 49

60. Which of the following must be less than 0, if x, y, and z are real numbers and $x^3y^4z^6 < 0$?

   F. xy
   G. xy^2
   H. yz
   J. xyz
   K. $x^2y^2z^3$

DO YOUR FIGURING HERE.

END OF TEST.
STOP! DO NOT TURN THE PAGE UNTIL TOLD TO DO SO.

Chapter 13
Math Practice Test 2:
Answers and
Explanations

SCORE YOUR PRACTICE TEST

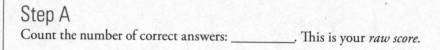

Step A

Count the number of correct answers: _____. This is your *raw score*.

Step B

Use the score conversion table below to look up your raw score. The number to the left is your *scale score*: _____.

Math Scale Conversion Table

Scale Score	Raw Score	Scale Score	Raw Score	Scale Score	Raw Score
36	60	27	45–47	18	24–25
35	59	26	42–44	17	21–23
34	58	25	40–41	16	17–20
33	56–57	24	37–39	15	14–16
32	55	23	35–36	14	11–13
31	54	22	33–34	13	9–10
30	52–53	21	31–32	12	7–8
29	50–51	20	29–30	11	6
28	48–49	19	26–28	10	5

MATH PRACTICE TEST 2 ANSWER KEY

1.	A		31.	C
2.	F		32.	G
3.	D		33.	C
4.	F		34.	H
5.	E		35.	D
6.	G		36.	G
7.	D		37.	E
8.	H		38.	G
9.	E		39.	E
10.	H		40.	J
11.	C		41.	A
12.	H		42.	F
13.	B		43.	D
14.	H		44.	K
15.	C		45.	A
16.	G		46.	J
17.	B		47.	C
18.	H		48.	J
19.	B		49.	B
20.	J		50.	H
21.	E		51.	D
22.	G		52.	J
23.	E		53.	E
24.	G		54.	K
25.	E		55.	C
26.	G		56.	H
27.	E		57.	C
28.	H		58.	H
29.	B		59.	D
30.	F		60.	G

MATH PRACTICE TEST 2 EXPLANATIONS

1. **A**   In a figure where two parallel lines are intersected by a third line, all small angles have the same measurement, and all large angles have the same measurement. In this figure, since lines C and D are parallel to each other, the same is true about the angles they make with lines A and B. Because the angle in question is a large angle, it has the same measurement as the marked large angle, 110°.

2. **F**   Begin by distributing the 5, $5x - 15 - 3x + 10$. Then combine the x terms, $2x - 15 + 10$. Finally, combine the −15 and 10 to get the correct answer, $2x - 5$.

3. **D**   To shift a point up four units, add 4 to the y-value: $-7 + 4 - 3$. To shift the point to the left 10 units, subtract 10 from the x-value: $4 - = 10 - 6$. The new coordinates of the point are $(-6, -3)$. Choice (E) incorrectly shifts the original point down 4 units and to the left 10 units.

4. **F**   Multiply the number of club members by the member price to get $13x$, and the number of non-members by the non-member price to get $15(30)$. Add the two together to get the total cost, $13x + 15(30)$.

5. **E**   The formula for percent change is as follows: % change $= \dfrac{\text{difference}}{\text{original}} \times 100\%$. Start by finding the difference between the old price and the new price: $\$650 - \$500 = 150$. To find the percent increase, divide the difference by the original price and multiply by 100%, $\dfrac{150}{500} \times 100\% = 30\%$. Be careful of (C); to get this answer, you'd be incorrectly dividing 150 by the new price, \$650.

6. **G**   A parallelogram has parallel sides, and its opposite angles are equivalent. Therefore, if $\angle W$ and $\angle Y$ are congruent, this must mean that $\angle X$ and $\angle Z$ are congruent, and $\angle Z = 112°$. Subtract the measures of $\angle X$ and $\angle Z$ from 360° for a difference of 136°. Then, because $\angle W$ and $\angle Y$ are congruent, $\angle Y$ must be half of this remainder, 68°.

7. **D**   Take the number of maroon marbles plus the number of tan marbles, $6 + 10 = 16$, and divide by the total number of marbles to get $\dfrac{16}{32} = \dfrac{1}{2}$. Choice (A) gives the probability of picking only a maroon marble. Choice (B) gives the probability of picking only a tan marble.

8. **H**   The distance formula is $d = r \times t$. Plug in the information you have to get $100 = r \times 1\frac{1}{3}$. Divide both sides by $1\frac{1}{3}$ to solve, $r = 75$. Choice (G) incorrectly multiplies 100 by $\frac{1}{3}$ only. Choice (K) incorrectly multiplies 100 by $1\frac{1}{3}$.

9. **E**   Begin by discarding the lowest performance review value, 22. Add the others, $26 + 35 + 43 + 23 + 31 = 158$, then divide by the number of values, 5, to get the average, $158 \div 5 = 31.6$. Choice (A) discards the highest value. Choice (B) averages all 6 performance review values without discarding any. Choice (C) is the median of the five remaining numbers, not the average. Choice (D) discards 23 instead of the lowest 22.

10. **H**   Multiply both sides of the equation by p to get $3x = pq$, then divide both sides by 3 to get $x = \dfrac{pq}{3}$.

11. **C**   Start by solving for x. Add 16 to both sides to get $3x = 21$, then divide both sides by 3 to get $x = 7$. Plug 7 in for x in the expression $5x$ to get $5 \times 7 = 35$. Choice (A) gives the value of x, but the problem asks for the value of $5x$.

12. **H**   The formula for the area of a square is $A = s^2$. Plug 25 in for A to get $25 = s^2$. Take the square root of each side to get $s = 5$. The perimeter of a square is $P = 4s$, so plug 5 in for s to get $4 \times 5 = 20$. Choice (F) is the length of one side. Choice (G) is $s \times 2$. Choice (J) is the area.

13. **B**   Start by expanding out the expression 3.22×10^4 to get 32,220. Since "of" means "times", multiply 32,220 by 11%, or .11, to find $.11 \times 32,220 = 3,542$. Choice (A) takes 322×10^4, leaving out the decimal point. Choice (C) multiplies 322 by .11.

14. **H**   To factor $x^2 + 3x - 18$, find two numbers that multiply to -18 and add to 3. Those numbers are 6 and -3. The factored expression is $(x + 6)(x - 3)$. If you chose (F) or (G), you may have reversed the negative signs.

15. **C**   In order to make this problem easier to handle, start by making all the inequalities "less than" signs. You have $v < w$, $x < y$, $y < v$, and $w < z$. Then order the expressions to get $x < y$, $y < v$, $v < w$, $w < z$, where x is the smallest, so (C) is the correct answer.

16. **G**   Plug the numbers given into the definition of the function, $w = 3$, $x = 2$, $y = 5$, and $z = 0$. $(3 \times 0 - 5 \times 2)(3 \times 2 + 5 \times 0) = (0 - 10)(6 + 0) = (-10)(6) = -60$. Choice (K) misses the negative sign. Choice (J) is the value of the second set of parentheses only. Note: This problem may seem intimidating if you don't know what the ♣ sign means, but remember, the problem gives you its definition!

17. **B** Start with the bottom chart to find that Jamilica is making 10 spheres and 5 pyramids. Each sphere requires 10 wood squares, and each pyramid requires 5 wood squares. Multiply the number of spheres by 10 and the number of pyramids by 5. Then add them together to get the total: $10 \times 10 + 5 \times 5 = 125$. Choice (A) incorrectly accounts for 10 wood squares for both pyramids and spheres. Choice (E) adds the number of squares of each material required to make one pyramid.

18. **H** Try each answer choice, starting with the smallest one since the question asks for the least common multiple. Choice (F) is a multiple of 20 but not of 100 or 60. Choice (G) is a multiple of 60 and 20 but not of 100. Choice (H) is a multiple of 100, 60, and 20, so it is the correct answer. Even if (J) and (K) give multiples of the three numbers, this problem is asking for the *least* common multiple.

19. **B** Begin by finding the distance between ValuTime and Burger Burger along Brunswick Ave. The side lengths given fit the Pythagorean triplet ratio of 3:4:5, multiplied by 2 to create a 6:8:10, so the missing side length is 8. The distance the first customer travels is 10, while the distance the second customer travels is 6 + 8 = 14. The difference between the two trips is 14 − 10 = 4. If you chose (D) or (E), you haven't found the *difference* between the two trips.

20. **J** When raising an exponent to a power, multiply the exponents: $(y^6)^{12} = y^{6 \times 12} = y^{72}$.

21. **E** Plug In −2 in for x in the $f(x)$ expression: $f(-2) = 2(-2)^3 + (-2)^2 = 2(-8) + 4 = -16 + 4 = -12$.

22. **G** Plug in $100 for the original price of a repair, r. To increase the price 20%, multiply $100 by 1.2, $100 \times 1.2 = \$120$. Plug $r = \$100$ into the answer choices and find the one that equals $120. Choice (F) gives 20% of $100 only. Choice (H) subtracts the 20% instead of adding it. Choice (J) adds .2 to $100 instead of adding $.2 \times 100$. Choice (K) multiplies $100 by 20 instead of by .2.

23. **E** If 3 pairs cost $30.97, divide that price by 3 to find the price of one pair: $\$30.97 \div 3 = \$10.32\overline{3}$. Then multiply the single pair price by 5: $\$10.32\overline{3} \times 5 = \$51.61\overline{6}$. Round the decimal up to get the correct answer, $51.62. Choice (D) incorrectly rounds the decimal down. Choices (A) and (B) are possible prices for one pair of shoes, and (C) is the price of two pairs of shoes.

24. **G** Plug in a number of days to find a point on the graph. If Terra's store is open on no days, she earns no money. Subtracting her expenses then gives $0 - (500) = -500$. Choice (G) is the only one that has the point $(0, -500)$ on it.

25. **E** Expand out the 6! and the 5! in the original expression to get $\dfrac{6 \times 5 \times 4 \times 3 \times 2 \times 1 \times 4!}{5 \times 4 \times 3 \times 2 \times 1}$. Cancel out all the numbers in the denominator, and you're left with $6 \times 4!$. Since the problem tells you that $4! = 24$, multiply 6 by 24: $6 \times 24 = 144$.

26. **G**   Try PITA for this one. Since they're in order, start with (H). If Alfred buys 56 stamps for $0.45 each, he spends $56 \times \$0.45 = \$25.20$ on the more expensive stamps. Since the total he spends on all stamps is $25, (H) is too large, and you can also eliminate (J) and (K). Try (G): if Alfred buys 48 stamps for $0.45 each, he spends $48 \times \$0.45 = \$21.60$ on the more expensive stamps. Because he bought 65 stamps total, subtract the number of $0.45 stamps to find the number of $0.20 stamps: $65 - 48 = 17$. Multiply 17 by $0.20 to find the amount Alfred spent on the less expensive stamps: $17 \times \$0.20 = \$3.40$. Add the amount he spend on the more expensive stamps to the amount he spent on the less expensive stamps: $\$21.60 + \$3.40 = \$25$. This total matches what you're given in the problem, so (G) is correct.

27. **E**   To find the area of the shaded region, find the area of the larger figure and subtract the area of the smaller figure. If the square has a side of length 2, its area is $A = s^2 = 2^2 = 4$. To find the area of the circle, draw a diagonal in the square, which is also the diameter of the circle. Dividing the square in half diagonally gives you two 45-45-90 triangles. Since the ratio of sides of a 45-45-90 triangle is $x:x:x\sqrt{2}$ and here $x = 2$, the length of the diagonal is $2\sqrt{2}$. The radius of the circle is half the diameter, so divide the length of the diagonal by 2 to find the radius: $2\sqrt{2} \div 2 = \sqrt{2}$. The area of the circle is $A = \pi r^2 = \pi(\sqrt{2})^2 = 2\pi$. Subtract the area of the square from the area of the circle to find the area of the shaded region, $2\pi - 4$.

28. **H**   Set up a proportion using the ratio given for the triangles, and the one side length given, $\dfrac{3}{4} = \dfrac{x}{12}$, then solve for x. Cross multiply to get $36 = 4x$, then divide both sides by 4 to get $x = 9$. Choice (K) sets up the proportion as $\dfrac{3}{4} = \dfrac{12}{x}$, which incorrectly matches the length of 12 to the smaller triangle in the proportion.

29. **B**   Start by finding the measure of $\angle VZW$. Since $\angle WZY$ and $\angle VZW$ make a straight line, $\angle VZW = 180° - 145° = 35°$. As figure $WXYZ$ is a parallelogram, you know the measure of $\overline{WZ}$ is equal to 10, the length of $\overline{XY}$. You can now solve for $\overline{VZ}$. Use this information to find out that $\cos 35° = \dfrac{\text{adjacent side}}{\text{hypotenuse}}$, and so $\cos 35° = \dfrac{\overline{VZ}}{10}$. Multiply both sides by 10 to find that $\overline{VZ} = 10 \cos 35°$. You may notice that (D) incorrectly uses the measure of side $\overline{ZY}$; (C) ignores the side of the triangle adjacent to $\angle VZW$; and (A) incorrectly assumes that $\overline{VZ}$ has the same measure as $\overline{WZ}$. If the measure of $\angle VZW$ is 35°, the measure of $\angle WVZ$ must be 55°, so the measures of the opposite sides cannot be equivalent.

30. **F**   Try PITA. Since a rectangle must have 2 sides of one length and 2 sides of another length, (G) is incorrect. All four sides added together, the 32 given in the problem plus the 3 sides in the answer choice, should add up to 144. For (F), 32 + 32 + 40 + 40 = 144, the correct answer. Choice (H) adds up to 160, and (J) adds up to 196.

31. **C**   Start by subtracting 9 from both sides of the inequality, $4x < 2x - 16$. Next, subtract $2x$ from both sides: $2x < -16$. Finally, divide both sides by 2: $x < -8$. If you chose (B), you may have flipped the inequality unnecessarily.

32. **G**   The formula for the area of a triangle is $A = \dfrac{bh}{2}$. Fill in the dimensions you're given: $A = \dfrac{(2.25)(3.5)}{2} \approx 3.9$. Choice (J) is $(2.25)(3.5)$ without dividing by 2.

33. **C**   Begin with the expression inside the absolute value: $|-2 - 7| = |-9| = 9$. Then multiply by -8: $-8(9) = -72$. Choice (E) misses the negative sign. Choice (A) incorrectly multiplies the 7 and 2 inside the absolute value. Choice (D) incorrectly adds +2 to −7 inside the absolute value.

34. **H**   Start with the number of sandwiches that have at least roast beef, which is 8. Eliminate (F) because only 8 sandwiches have roast beef. One sandwich has both roast beef and turkey, but no chicken, so subtract that from 8: 8 − 1 = 7. Two sandwiches have roast beef, chicken, and turkey, so subtract that from 7: 7 − 2 = 5, to get the number of sandwiches with roast beef only. This eliminates (G), and because there is no indication that any of the remaining sandwiches contain roast beef with any other meet, the answer must be (H).

35. **D**   Find the total number of chickens by multiplying the number of groups of each kind by the number of animals in the group and adding them together: (0)(1) + (20)(5) + (30)(10) = 400. The counted rabbits include 5 1-animal groups and 20 10-animal groups for a total of (5)(1) + (20)(10) = 205. To find the number of uncounted rabbits, subtract the counted number from the total: 400 − 205 = 195. To find the number of 5-animal groups, divide the uncounted rabbits by 5: 195 ÷ 5 = 39. Choice (E) gives the number of uncounted rabbits instead of the number of 5-animal groups. Choice (C) incorrectly counts the 5 1-animal groups as 5-animal groups. Choice (B) makes the number of groups of rabbits equal to the number of groups of chickens, but yields different total numbers of each animal. Choice (A) subtracts the number of 1-animal groups from the number of 10-animal groups of rabbits.

36. **G**   Find the total number of chickens by multiplying the number of groups of each kind by the number of animals in the group and adding them together: (0)(1) + (20)(5) + (30)(10) = 400. Find $\dfrac{1}{5}$ of the

total: $\frac{1}{5}(400) = 80$. To find the price per chicken, divide the total price by the number of chickens purchased: $1,200 ÷ 80 = $15.

37. **E**   There are 22 goats in 1-animal groups. To find the number of 5-animal groups that could be created, divide 22 by 5: $22 ÷ 5 = 4.4$, or 4 with a remainder of 2, so 4 complete groups can be created. Choice (D) incorrectly rounds 4.4 up to 5. Choice (B) adds the correct answer, 4, to the existing number of 5-animal groups of goats, 10. Choice (A) gives the number of goats.

38. **G**   Since point F is on the x-axis, the y-coordinate must be 0, which means that (F), (J), and (K) can be eliminated. You know triangle DEF is isoceles, so DE must be equal to EF since $\angle DEF$ is obtuse. Point E then comes halfway between points D and F, meaning the x-coordinate of point F is twice the x-coordinate of point E, or $2c$.

39. **E** $\angle EDF$ and $\angle EFD$ add up to $180° - 135° = 45°$. Since triangle DEF is isoceles, each angle is $45° ÷ 2 = 22.5$. To find the measure of the angle formed by DE and the y-axis, subtract $\angle EDF$ from $90°$: $90° - 22.5° = 67.5°$. Choice (A) gives the measure of DE and the x-axis. Choice (C) gives the measure of $\angle EDF$ and $\angle EFD$ together.

40. **J**   When the triangle is rotated 180°, point E will lie in Quadrant III. In Quadrant III, both coordinates will be negative, which means (F), (G), and (K) can be eliminated. Point E will be the same distance from the origin on both the x- and y-axes, but in the opposite direction, so both coordinates should be the opposite of the original values, or $(-c, -d)$ as in (J).

41. **A**   The total volume of the pyramid is 2 gallons, or $2 × 231 = 462$ in^3. Plug the values you know into the given equation to get $462 = \frac{1}{3}b(15)$. To solve for b, multiply both sides by 3, $1,386 = b(15)$, then divide both sides by 15, $b = 92.4$. Round down to get (A).

42. **F**   Nathan read $2\left(\frac{1}{8}\right) = \frac{1}{4}$ of his book in the first month. That leaves him $\frac{3}{4}$ to read in the remaining 4 months. To find how much he must read in each of the remaining 4 months, divide the amount left by the number of months, $\frac{3}{4} ÷ 4 = \frac{3}{4} × \frac{1}{4} = \frac{3}{16}$.

43. **D**   The quadratic equation is $x = \frac{-b \pm \sqrt{b^2 - 4ac}}{2a}$. In this equation, $a = 2$, $b = 3$, and $c = -10$. Start by looking at the $-b$. Since $b = 3$, (A) and (B) can be eliminated. Choice (E) can be eliminated because it incorrectly suggests that $c = 10$. Of the remaining choices, only (D) correctly puts a subtraction sign in the middle of the radical.

44. **K** The midpoint formula is $\left(\dfrac{x_1 + x_2}{2}, \dfrac{y_1 + y_2}{2}\right)$. Start with the x-coordinate, $-2 = \dfrac{-7 + x_2}{2}$, and solve for x_2. Multiply both sides by 2: $-4 = -7 + x_2$, then add -7 to both sides to get $x_2 = 3$. Eliminate (F), (G), and (H), all of which have the incorrect x-coordinate. Do the same with the y-coordinate: $5 = \dfrac{3 + y_2}{2}$. Multiply by 2, $10 = 3 + y_2$, then subtract 3, $y_2 = 7$. Choice (K), (3,7) is correct.

45. **A** Since the unknown side is adjacent to the 55° angle, and the height of the lamppost is known, use $\tan 55° = \dfrac{\text{opposite side}}{\text{adjacent side}}$ to get $\tan 55° = \dfrac{4}{x}$. Multiply both sides by x, $x \tan 55° = 4$, then divide both sides by $\tan 55°$, $x = \dfrac{4}{\tan 55°}$.

46. **J** Because the line shown crosses the y-axis above the origin, the y-intercept, or b in the slope-intercept equation $y = mx + b$ must be positive. Choice (K) can be eliminated because it gives a negative value for b. Because the line shown slopes down, the slope, or m, must be negative. Choices (F) and (G) can be eliminated because they have positive values for m. Because $m = \dfrac{y_2 - y_1}{x_2 - x_1}$ and the line crosses the x-axis at about 1, a slope of -2 is appropriate, and (J) is correct.

47. **C** Divide the quadrilateral into a rectangle and a triangle by drawing a horizontal line from point D across to the point (2,4). To find the dimensions of the rectangle, count the number of units from point A to point B, which is 5, and the number of units from point A to point D, which is 7. The area of the rectangle is $A = l \times w = 5 \times 7 = 35$. Add to that the area of the triangle on top, $A = \dfrac{bh}{2} = \dfrac{(5)(2)}{2} = 5$ for a total area of $35 + 5 = 40$.

48. **J** An increased number of products will mean increased expenditures, so the slope of the line will be positive, and (H) and (K) can be eliminated. Choice (F) can be eliminated because you don't have any information about what the expenditure per product is, so you can't assign a specific value to it. A line passing between two points can't have more than one slope, so (J) is correct.

49. **B** A geometric sequence has a constant ratio between terms. To figure out what the ratio in this sequence is, divide the second term by the first term: $15 \div 10 = 1.5$. To find the fifth term, multiply the fourth term by the ratio of 1.5: $33.75 \times 1.5 = 50.625$.

50. **H** The surface area of a cube is $SA = 6(s^2)$. Plug in the given surface area, and solve for the length of a side, s, $54 = 6(s^2)$. Divide both sides by 6, $9 = s^2$, then take the square root of both sides, $s = 3$. The volume of a cube is $V = s^3$, so $V = 3^3 = 27$. Choice (F) gives the area of one face of the cube. Choice (G) multiples the area of one face of the cube by 2 instead of by 3. Choice (J) squares the area of one face of the cube. Choice (K) uses 9, the area of one face, instead of 3 for s. Note: If you can't remember the formula for surface area, draw a figure.

51. **D** The area of the shaded region has the same proportion to the area of the entire circle that the central angle of the shaded region has to 360°. Begin by finding the area of the entire circle: $A = \pi r^2 = \pi(5)^2 = 25\pi$. Then set up the proportion, and solve for x: $\dfrac{15\pi}{25\pi} = \dfrac{x}{360°}$. Cancel the π on the left side, and then multiply both sides by 360°: $\dfrac{(15)(360°)}{25} = x$, or $x = 216°$. Choice (B) gives the central angle of the unshaded region.

52. **J** The circle formula is $(x - h)^2 + (y - k)^2 = r^2$, where (h,k) is the center of the circle, and r is the radius. Use Process of Elimination. Choices (F) and (G) can be eliminated because they do not square the radius. Choice (K) can also be eliminated because the x-coordinate of the center is $+2$, so the first part of the equation should be $(x - 2)^2$, not $(x + 2)^2$. Choice (H) can be eliminated because the y-coordinate is -6, so the second part should be $(y + 6)^2$ not $(y - 6)^2$. Only (J) remains.

53. **E** $\overline{YZ}$ is the side opposite $\angle X$, and $\overline{XZ}$ is opposite $\angle Y$. Set up a proportion according to the law of sines given in the note, $\dfrac{\sin 53°}{11} = \dfrac{\sin 88°}{\overline{XZ}}$, then solve for $\overline{XZ}$. Cross-multiply first, $(\overline{XZ}) \sin 53° = 11 \sin 88°$, then divide by $\sin 53°$: $\overline{XZ} = \dfrac{11 \sin 88°}{\sin 53°}$.

54. **K** Plug in a value for the radius of the circle, $r_1 = 3$, then pick a value for p: $p = 2$. Since the radius of the first circle is p feet shorter than the radius of the second circle, $r_2 = 3 + 2 = 5$. The circumference of the first circle is $C_1 = 2\pi r = 2\pi(3) = 6\pi$, and the circumference of the second circle is $C_2 = 2\pi r = 2\pi(5) = 10\pi$. To find the difference in circumference, subtract C_1 from C_2: $10\pi - 6\pi = 4\pi$. Plug $p = 2$ into the answer choices to find the one that gives you the correct difference of 4π, which is (K).

55. **C** Plug in some values for y to solve this problem. If $y = -4$, then $|y + 3| = |-4 + 3| = 1$. Plug $y = -4$ into the answer choices to see which ones match. Choice (A) can be eliminated because it gives you $-4 - 3 = -7$. When you plug in for (B), you get $-4 + 3 = -1$; eliminate this choice. Plugging in for (C), you find that $-(-4) - 3 = 1$; keep this choice. Choice (D) can be eliminated because $-(-4) + 3 = 7$. Eliminate (E) because 0 does not match the target. Therefore, the correct answer is (C).

56. **H** The first piece of information given is the countries that have fewer than 20 cities. Since these cities do not have 20, 21, or 22 cities, subtract them from the total: $18 - 7 = 11$. The next piece of information, the countries that have more than 21 cities, doesn't affect the total because some of those will have 22 cities. The third piece of information, countries that have more than 22 cities, does need to be subtracted from the new total, $11 - 2 = 9$, which gives the number of countries with 20, 21, or 22 cities.

57. **C** Plug the information given into the identity given in the note: $\left(-\dfrac{3}{4}\right)^2 = \dfrac{1 - \cos 2x}{2}$. Apply the exponent to get $\dfrac{9}{16} = \dfrac{1 - \cos 2x}{2}$, then multiply both sides by 2 to get $\dfrac{9}{8} = 1 - \cos 2x$. Subtract 1 from both sides, $\dfrac{9}{8} - 1 = \dfrac{1}{8} = -\cos 2x$, then divide both sides by -1 to get $-\dfrac{1}{8} = \cos 2x$.

58. **H** The point $(-2, 8)$ gives the x and y values for the functions given, so that $8 - f(g(-2))$. Substitute x^3 for $f(x)$ to get $f(g(-2)) = [g(-2)]^3 = 8$. Solve for $g(-2)$ by taking the cube root of both sides: $g(-2) = 2$. Then substitute $\dfrac{x}{2} - k$ for $g(x)$ and -2 for x to get $g(-2) = \dfrac{-2}{2} - k = 2$, or $-1 - k = 2$. Add 1 to both sides, $-k = 3$, then divide both sides by -1 to get $k = -3$. Choice (K) solves for k using only $g(x)$.

59. **D** Disjoint regions are non-overlapping regions. 7 vertical lines and 7 horizontal lines overlapping each other create a grid with a 6×6 section of enclosed rectangles, which each have a finite, nonzero area. There are also 2- or 3-sided areas around the outside that are open on 1 or 2 sides, which would have an infinite area. So the number of disjoint regions is $6 \times 6 = 36$. Choice (E) incorrectly counts 7×7 disjoint regions, and (C) incorrectly counts 5×5 disjoint regions.

60. **G** Because any number raised to an even power will always be positive, in order for $x^3y^4z^6 < 0$ to be true, x^3 must be less than 0, which means that x must be less than 0. Since y and z can be either positive or negative, start by plugging in negative numbers for all three. Plug $x = -2$, $y = -3$, and $z = -4$, into the answer choices. Choice (F) is incorrect because $(-2)(-3) = 6$. Choice (H) is incorrect because $(-3)(-4) = 12$. Next try changing the y value to positive, so that $x = -2$, $y = 3$, and $z = -4$. Choice (J) is incorrect because $(-2)(3)(-4) = 24$. Then change the z value to positive also, so that $x = -2$, $y = 3$, and $z = 4$. Choice (K) is incorrect because $(-2)^2(3)^2(4)^3 = (4)(9)(64) = 2{,}304$. Only (G) is less than 0 with any combination of values.

NOTES